For Marianne – Partner Extraordinaire.
Wing to Wing and Oar to Oar.

Jonathan Klein

BACK TO THE TREES AND CAVES

A Wilderness Journey

AUSTIN MACAULEY PUBLISHERS™

LONDON * CAMBRIDGE * NEW YORK * SHARJAH

Ordering Information
Quantity sales: Special discounts are available on quantity purchases by corporations, associations, and others. For details, contact the publisher at the address below.

Publisher's Cataloging-in-Publication data
Klein, Jonathan
Back to the Trees and Caves

ISBN 9798889109440 (Paperback)
ISBN 9798889109457 (Hardback)
ISBN 9798889109464 (ePub e-book)

Library of Congress Control Number: 2023921363

www.austinmacauley.com/us

First Published 2024
Austin Macauley Publishers LLC
40 Wall Street, 33rd Floor, Suite 3302
New York, NY 10005
USA

mail-usa@austinmacauley.com
+1 (646) 5125767

Writing isn't easy and I am grateful to the many who provided ideas and support as I struggled to scribble and scribe. Above all thanks to my wife, Marianne, who dropped whatever she was doing to patiently listen to every passage as it was written, rewritten, and rewritten anew.

Table of Contents

Author's Note

I was on a hike not long ago, in the desert southwest. Sandstone cliffs, these colossal walls of red, towered above me, and scrub oak and cottonwood, in autumnal glow, lined the benches along the banks of the shallow stream I splashed through. It was sublimely beautiful and I was in the moment, high on nature, and possibly something else, until a dull thud intruded upon this peaceful scene.

A helicopter! Soon the thing appeared, clattering above the canyon's rim, a blot in the otherwise unblemished sky. It was a sightseeing flight with tourists onboard who paid good money to see the country it would take me five days to hike through in a fifteen-minute fly-by. The intrusion pissed me off. Is no place sacred? No place free from motors? No place off limits to the limitless exploitations of man?

Suddenly, I had the urge to shoot that motherfucking machine out of the sky, not that I had the means to, or would if I did, but the thought of it mortally wounded, falling and spinning against the red walls until crashing to the ground and bursting to flame, was a delicious one. From this happy thought, soon emerged another as I recalled an incident I had read about years before involving a helicopter similarly invading wild space with someone on the ground threatening to shoot it down, in this instance, a man with a bow and arrow no less.

This happened over a small island in the Indian Ocean, part of the Andaman archipelago consisting of more than 500 islands scattered between India and Indonesia. Most are uninhabited, but a few have people, friendly natives for the most part save one; North Sentinel, where the natives are anything but. This island is home to a Stone Age society who have occupied it in isolation for the past 50,000 years, employing survival strategies basically unchanged over the span of that time.

The North Sentinelese, understanding that contact with the outside world will doom their way of life, do not take kindly to strangers. Go there and most likely, in fact almost certainly, you will be killed.

I first learned of this place after reading about a young American missionary who ventured to it in 2018 intent on saving the heathen soul. The undertaking was ill-advised. Not only is accessing North Sentinel strictly forbidden under international law, but doing so usually proves fatal to anyone foolish enough to try.

Yet, despite legalities to the contrary and myriad warnings not to go, the would-be soul-saver, compelled by a higher calling, paddled to the island in a small boat and, clutching his Bible, waded ashore where he was promptly dispatched, the old-fashioned way, and buried in sand.

Not to seem callous, but to me this story has a happy ending; clearly not for the hapless young man who died, but for the North Sentinelese. Keeping the outside world out is the only way they can endure. Through the ages these people, living on a speck of land surrounded by sea, have been amply provided with all that's required and care naught for our baubles, comforts, or gods, and ask only to be left alone.

Intrigued that Paleolithic people persist to this day, I Googled North Sentinel and up popped a photograph that struck me. Taken from an Indian Coast Guard helicopter flying over the island in the wake of the 2004 Indian Ocean tsunami, the grainy image shows a near-naked man standing alone on a broad expanse of beach.

In his hands, he holds a bow and arrow pointed up at the machine, clearly telling it to go away or else. I suppose that when the helicopter did fly off, the islander figured he had scared it and probably felt pretty badass about it. No way could he have known just how puny his arrow was.

The pages that follow are an arrow of another sort but also brandished in defense of wilderness. The difference between my *arrow* and that of the brave North Sentinelese is this: I realize just how puny mine is, but what we both seem to understand is that one does have to try.

Ennis, Montana
January, 2023

Introduction

I retired the year I turned sixty and decided to take advantage of my new-found freedom with an adventure, one of a kind I had long contemplated, an expedition really, through country wild as the day it was made. The plan was to go by canoe from Saskatchewan to Hudson Bay, eight-hundred miles across half a continent of wilderness, and to do it alone.

I was clear eyed about the hazards, drowning being foremost among them in the many rapids I would encounter and enormous lakes that had to be crossed. Or a medical emergency might befall me—something as simple as an infected cut or burst appendix, from which there would be little hope of rescue. A violent storm might topple a tree and squish me or blow away my little boat, leaving me stranded without food or shelter. And there were animals to consider, those that sneak up and pounce. Particularly worrisome were the polar bears I was sure to see as I closed in on the bay.

I calculated the chances of survival at ninety percent, computed not by any methodology but from a gut feeling. Ninety percent is pretty good odds all told, and about right for an honest to goodness adventure, for what is adventure without at least a modicum of risk?

The word *adventure* is commonly misapplied with what passes for it often nothing more than run-of-the-mill experience. A cross-country journey by passenger train does not constitute adventure, any more than would a Princess cruise up the inside passage. Adventure of a similar ilk would involve hopping a freight or sea kayaking amidst floating ice and orcas.

One can't realize adventure from the vista dome of a train or deck chair of a luxury liner because adventure isn't a spectator sport, it's participatory— being in the scene, hauling yourself through it, not passively watching it passing by.

Adventure is something you do, requiring effort, probably pain, maybe even blood, and things may not go the way you plan because such undertakings are a gamble, a roll of the dice with an outcome less than certain. But for those choosing to venture thus, the rewards are commensurate to the risks and far exceed those mere experience can provide. It's a harder the battle, sweeter the victory sort of thing.

In addition to the sweetness of victory, should I survive to enjoy it, the trip would serve as a bridge between my old life and new. I'd had a job since fourteen and now, without one, no idea what to do next. We are commonly defined by the work we do, so I would have to come to grips with a new iteration of myself.

I am a restless person by nature, with a low tolerance for routine. Golf, making widgets in a woodshop, taking up landscape painting or puttering with petunias: none of that appealed to me. But long days in the canoe would provide immediate purpose and perhaps help sort things out for the future.

I had actually envisioned a trip like this since college—really since boyhood. For reasons that remain unclear, wilderness has always beckoned. Why a city kid should be so lured is a mystery, but hemmed in by all that concrete and the cookie-cutter geometry of urban blocks caused a craving for a life less restrained, away from crowded sidewalks and horn-honking commotion.

And so, the free days of my youth were spent in wandering the *terra incognita* of San Francisco's wilder haunts—of which surprisingly there are some—and wilderness became, as Wallace Stegner put it, part of the 'geography of my soul'.

When I came of age, I had not outgrown this penchant and eventually surrendered to it, moving to Montana to ultimately manage Wilderness for the USDA Forest Service.

Over the course of that thirty-four-year career, it grew clear that what passes for wilderness today, at least in the lower forty-eight, isn't truly wild but something akin to wilderness theater where managers act as stagehands, manipulating props and backdrops that lend an illusion of wild. The fact is that the continental U.S. just doesn't have the space for real wilderness.

Consider that the furthest one can get from a road is twenty-two miles. That's it. A piddling distance many could walk in a day. And, the farthest a crow need flap for a Big Mac within these same confines is only 104 miles. Hence, what we refer to as *wilderness* would more fittingly be termed 'erness' because the wild is gone. Sadly, that's the best we can do.

Don't get me wrong. What America has managed to protect is a remarkable achievement, especially considering our capacity for rapacity: more than 111 million acres, five percent of the total U.S. landmass secured as part of the National Wilderness Preservation System.

Clearly, I should be more sanguine, see my Sierra Club cup as five percent full rather than ninety-five percent empty, but instead, I felt gypped and decided to do something about it. Real wilderness may not exist in the lower forty-eight, but there are places it does. I would find one and go there. It would be a retirement gift to myself.

When my father caught wind of the plan, he flipped.

"Why, in God's name," he demanded to know, "do you want to do that?" He was ninety-two and not long for this world. Worried that I wasn't long for this world either, he tried to talk me out of it.

"Please, Jonathan," he said, "if you have to go, at least, don't go alone. It isn't safe." He had already tried his colonel's voice and was now practically pleading, looking up from a La-Z-Boy with a pained expression on his old man face.

Of course, he was right, as he most always was, but what he didn't get and couldn't understand was that not being safe was a big reason to go. The world is overly safe already, overly comfortable and predictable too. My life, and the lives of most everyone I know, reeks of excess and ease, and is fraught with trivialities about the size of TVs and what wine pairs with which cheese.

I needed to step away from that for something elemental and real: an adventure involving challenge, struggle, and risk by which to gauge my mettle, to see whether I was strong or weak, brave or chicken-shit, competent or inept. And there was no time to spare. Not only are the wilds rapidly falling before the press of humanity, but at sixty, I could ill afford to wait. It wouldn't be long before I'd be like my father, dismantled by age, caring mostly about a good BM and a cookie. So, I would go, and soon.

"Dad, I don't know how to explain it to you, but this is something I need to do."

"Jonathan," my father said, exasperated now, "mankind has spent the last two million years climbing down from the trees and crawling out of the caves and you just want to climb back up and crawl back in!"

What could I say? As usual, he was right.

Chapter 1
Around the Bend

Day 1. Missinipe, Saskatchewan. June 21, 2012.

The hamlet of Missinipe is canoe central and has been since the days of the fur trade. Canoes are everywhere—atop cars, under porches, and racked in tiers on specialized trailers. More lie beside the river, the Churchill, scattered along its bank in multispectral display. They come in all sizes, from big expedition boats with space for eight, to small playboats, built for one, and are wrought from a variety of materials—aluminum, wood, plastic, fiberglass, and Kevlar—but despite these differences, their shapes unite them, leaving no doubt as to their pedigree. They are canoes. *Ka-nu.* The word rolls off the tongue like a poem and leaves the lips in the shape of a kiss.

We're staying at Churchill River Canoe Outfitters, a canoe rental and guide business owned by Ric Driediger. Ric is a paddler of repute and looks it, all beard and torso up top, with arms like thighs and legs on the spindly side, as if these parts were mistakenly switched during assembly. If you want to know anything about canoeing the Canadian north, Ric is your guy. He's also the guy who got me into this, for it was he who suggested the trip on which I am about to embark.

The suggestion came eight years earlier when Marianne, my wife, and I visited Missinipe the first time. In casual conversation with Ric, I mentioned an ambition that had simmered in my brain since college: the undertaking of a grand adventure through country wild as the day it was made. Ric retrieved a scrolled map from a corner of the room, unfurled it atop a table, and began tracing a route with his finger from Missinipe to Hudson Bay.

"First down the Churchill to here," he said, tapping the map to indicate a tributary flowing in from the north. "Then up this, the Barrington River," *tap,* "and over this divide and down to the Seal," *tap, tap*, "and from there on to the bay."

Eight-hundred miles of boreal forest, taiga, and tundra through some of the purest wilderness left on earth, and, as far as Ric knew, only accomplished solo once before.

Now, quite suddenly, I am on the cusp of this undertaking. How in the world did June 21st get here so soon? When I selected it as D-Day nearly a year before, the date seemed an impossibly long way off, as if to never arrive, but suddenly it appeared, springing from the calendar with evil glee and shouting, "Surprise!"

Until late yesterday, the thought of actually going through with this didn't seem real, but over the course of a sleepless night in one of Ric's cabins, the magnitude of what I am about to do dawns on me with the day, and I find myself nearly paralyzed by fear. My heart thumps so hard it feels like some crazed critter banging against my ribcage, trying to break free.

Breaths come fast and shallow, as if drawn through a straw. Too feeble to carry a sufficiency of oxygen to the brain, I find it hard to think, to speak, to act. My hands tremble, my mouth is dry, and butterflies flock through my stomach in successive waves. Worse is a persistent urge to pee that no amount of peeing can allay.

Marianne knows how scared I am. She's scared too.

"You don't have to go," she intones. But I do. I've blabbed and bragged about this trip to everyone, brushing off concerns of safety with clench-jawed bravado, so now, the humiliation of not going would kill me more surely than the river might.

Nervously, I go through my stuff for the umpteenth time, concerned I've got too much, worried I don't have enough. It amounts to three hundred pounds. Before leaving Montana, I packed it all into the canoe to make sure everything fit, and it did, barely. The boat is a seventeen-foot Mad River Explorer with a Kevlar hull the color of eggplant. Although weighing just fifty-five pounds, the craft can hold twenty times that, more than I need or want. I have to be careful with weight. According to Ric, there are two dozen portages, give or take, where I'll have to haul everything around rapids and falls, making several trips back and forth each time. When Ric saw the immensity of gear I intended to take, he blanched and hinted I pare it down some. So, I pare a pair of pants and next consider my father's army jacket from the Korean War.

After my mother passed, I found it stashed in a footlocker while cleaning out her apartment. My father had died just three months before, still convinced I shouldn't take this trip. He was a good father, a good friend and a great guy. I wanted to bring along something of his, but then, I *am* something of his, so I refold the jacket and add it to the little pile atop the jilted pants.

The hardest thing to part with is the bug shelter. Ric thinks I can manage without it, but I don't feel good about leaving it. On previous trips to taiga and tundra, I've experienced the terror of bugs that even Stephen King couldn't conjure up in his wildest imaginings. However, the shelter is heavy. It weighs eleven pounds, which accrues to 220 pounds when hauled across twenty portages.

Assuming Ric knows what he's talking about, I heed his advice and leave it, although with marked reluctance. I also ditch the camp chair. From decades of sitting on saddles, stumps, hard ground, and rocks, my derriere craves the comfort of a chair. This is one of those cheap folding jobs with beer can holders in the armrests, but since there will be no beer to hold, and since I didn't come here for comfort, I purge it as well, shedding two more unnecessary pounds.

Reorganized, we leave Missinipe, heading south on Saskatchewan Highway 102, a slender gravel road that divides the forest like a part through hair. There are three of us. My friend Gene came along to assist with the driving and see me off. We all sit up front, Marianne in the middle, pressed hard against me.

The mood is somber as we proceed, bouncing and slewing over washboards and potholes, the tires spitting pebbles and flinging up contrails of dust. Stanley Mission, a Cree village and the point of embarkation, is fifty miles away. Then forty-nine. Then forty-eight. I watch the odometer rolling over, tracking the distance a tenth of a mile at a time, feeling like a man condemned to an ineludible fate.

The Cree name for Stanley Mission is *Amuchewaspimewin*, which is probably why it isn't called that anymore. The community is perched on a high bench above the river. We pull off onto a grassy bluff and start schlepping gear down to the beach and across an expanse of sand to the water's edge. Across the road from where we parked, a First Nations woman begins rhythmically sweeping the porch of a small house. Puffs of dust rise and brighten in sunshine with each swish of the broom.

Glancing up to notice us, she stops, pauses a beat, and then shouts a warning, "Don't leave your truck there or nothing will be left of it when you get back," she says before returning to her task.

We make quick work of emptying the truck and filling the canoe. Seeing the loaded boat ends all misgivings about not having enough stuff. It's jammed stem to stern, mostly with food. I'd anticipated the trip taking six to seven weeks but packed provisions for eight weeks just in case, having read too many stories about starving explorers. The food is divvied up between a blue plastic barrel, a big yellow dry bag, and a large army surplus medical box. I agonized over whether or not to bring the box.

Made of heavy gauge aluminum, the thing weighs twenty-two pounds before putting a nut in it, but being watertight, bear resistant, and easily stowed beneath the center thwart, I ultimately decided to take it. With ten latches, the box is virtually impregnable when closed. Critters might chew into the dry bag, or breach the barrel, but they won't get into that box. I have enough trouble getting into it myself.

Another item agonized over was the shotgun. I didn't want to bring something I had no intention of using, and beyond swatting bugs and catching a few fish, had no designs on killing. The gun is a Remington 870 12-gauge, the Mariner model, cast in stainless steel so it won't rust. I've carried it on northern trips ever since an incident with a barren ground grizzly years before.

In that encounter, the bear approached camp and was disinclined to leave. I had the bear spray out, safety off, thumb on the trigger, ready to deploy. The little can was all I had, and although knowing intellectually that pepper spray is more effective than lead in deterring a bear, it seemed a puny defense. Hence, I purchased the shotgun for subsequent trips, mostly as a piece for inner peace. It's loaded to give any animal the benefit of the doubt with the first four rounds out all non-lethal; a cracker shell, then two rubber bullets, and finally pepper spray deployed directly from the barrel.

After those are expended, the ammo does get serious, but the last thing I'd want to do is shoot a bear. Sometimes I even muse that it would be better to be killed than to kill in a confrontation with a wild critter but realize that would not likely be my final answer if so confronted. Still, I would hate myself forever were I to shoot a bear. Venturing into wilderness is already a violation of sorts, like entering private property uninvited. To trespass so and end up killing an animal trying to survive in one of the last places it can would be, for me, unforgivable.

Bears are the only animal of real concern. Wolves don't attack people and although moose are occasionally dangerous, getting stomped by one is hardly likely. So, it's bears. There is no cause to worry about grizzly bears because there aren't any, not according to the habitat map I Googled. The boreal forest is no place for them. Black bears abound, but they don't scare me. I've run into black bears on countless occasions, and they invariably flee at, "Boo!"

However, there is another ursine species with a well-earned reputation for ferocity: *Ursus maritimus.* Polar bears are the largest land carnivore on the planet, up to ten feet long from nose to tail and weighing as much as 1,500 pounds, they are bigger than a horse, and while other bear species have the good sense to balance diets with healthy portions of vegetables, polar bears are pure carnivores, and I, being pure *carne*, have good reason to fear them. That I will encounter *Ursus maritimus* is a foregone conclusion.

Every party on the Seal sees them. It isn't called the Seal River for nothing, and bears congregate in large numbers along its delta with the bay each summer waiting for ice, waiting for seals, and looking for something else to eat in the interim. At least I won't have to sweat it anytime soon. Hudson Bay is six to eight weeks away, so I sheath the gun into a dry bag and stow it beneath the rest of the load.

Once ready, one can delay only so long. There's an inevitability to departures that stalling only makes increasingly awkward. Marianne seldom worries about me, but she's worried now. Tears track her cheeks. This is serious. She almost never cries. I tell her I'll be fine but know I don't sound very convincing, not sure I believe it myself.

It's hard to disengage from the last embrace, aware it could really be that. I hold her, trying to press the feel of her into me as if I'm made of memory foam. I hug Gene too. We pat each other on the back, as men do to make the gesture somehow less intimate. Then there is nothing left to do but go.

I push off and float free: free of land, free from work, free of the predictable and mundane. Let the adventure begin! Forgetting to zip up my life jacket, I lay the paddle atop the canoe, but it teeters off a gunwale and falls into the river.

Gene and Marianne yell, "Paddle! Paddle!" with alarm, as if some major calamity has already befallen me.

After zipping up the PFD, I retrieve the paddle, grip it and take a stroke to back away from the beach. The canoe glides out onto green water, catches current, and starts down.

On the opposite shore stands a church, the Holy Trinity Anglican Church, slender, spired, and gleaming white. It's the mission part of Stanley Mission, the oldest surviving building in Saskatchewan, built in 1860 to teach the Cree about Jesus and make good Christian fur trappers out of them. If I were a God-fearing man, I'd paddle over to pray for deliverance, but I'm not.

Instead, I head down toward a bend where the river turns away from civilization and flows to wilderness, my church, the water flashing bright and moving briskly. Glancing back, the big white truck atop the bluff looks like a Tonka toy. Two small dark figures stand against it, waving madly with arms held high.

I raise the paddle to wave back an instant before the current sweeps me around the bend. The town, the truck, the church, Marianne, and Gene, all disappear behind a wall of green. For me now, everything lies ahead.

Chapter 2
Nuts (To Put It Nicely)

In the boat and moving, I immediately relax. Waiting is the worst—pre-game jitters. Now underway, I'm occupied, putting that nervous energy to work. I fall into the familiar pattern of paddling, the comfortable rhythm of dipping and pulling. The T-grip fits well against the palm of one hand, the varnished shaft just right in the other. This paddle is an old pal. The weather is friendly with sun, the river tranquil, lovely forest all around, no people, no buildings.

The boat, though heavy, handles well. I've turned it around for solo paddling, sitting backward on what would normally be the forward seat. This positions me closer amidships, thus reducing the boat's tendency to veer away from the side paddled on. Even so, I employ a J-stroke, a quick flick out with the paddle at the end of nearly every stroke to keep the canoe tracking true. Without the 'J', the scenery would soon start looking very familiar.

Around noon I hear rapids. Rapids are invariably heard before they are seen and even the runts sound intimidating. Having spent fifteen years whitewater kayaking, I am no stranger to this sound, yet it never fails to garner my full attention. These are Stanley Rapids, the first of many I will face. Scanning down to pinpoint the source of the hostile hissing, I can't at first locate it, so stand for a better look. There! Flashes of white splash up in a line across the river two hundred yards below.

A surge of adrenaline releases to my bloodstream, making me feel instantly anxious despite seeing nothing to warrant the reaction. From what I can tell, Stanley is easy. There is an obvious tongue, a V of smooth water, flowing between boulders, with ample room to maneuver. I'm confident I can run it no problem, so sit back down and get ready. But wait! I see people on shore portaging the rapid.

Why? Did I miss something? I stand again for another look and carefully inspect the rapid from top to bottom and bottom to top. It still seems clean. I'm running it. I've drifted too far down to do anything else, anyway.

The river steepens and picks up speed while the scuff of water grows louder. I try lowering my center of gravity by kneeling on the floor but can't fit my feet beneath the seat with all the stuff crammed under it so scramble back up just before reaching the drop.

The canoe tops a swell and rolls down the other side toward shards of white breaking against rock. I angle away from this obstacle with strong sweeps, punch a hole, and drift to calm water below. The boaters who portaged paddle out to talk.

"Boy," says one, "you sure made that look easy, eh?"

I don't want to tell him it looked easy because it was.

"Thanks," I humbly acknowledge the compliment, careful not to let it go to my head, having learned the hard way, more than once, how River Gods delight in chastening the proud.

Below Stanley, the Churchill becomes Nistowiak Lake. For the next five-hundred miles, this river is less river and more of a series of lakes, big lakes ten to a hundred miles long, and separated one from the next by rapids or falls. When I digitally flew the route on Google Earth before leaving home, I was unnerved by the immensity of water shown, a confusing profusion of water stretching out in every direction to shores beyond which more water lay.

Getting lost in this aquatic maze of lakes, islands, bays, and backwaters seemed more likely than staying found, and sure enough, I quickly lose my way on Nistowiak and have to resort to the GPS to see just where it is I am amidst this enormity of water.

By late afternoon, after wayward wanderings that add several miles to the day, I blunder upon the end of the lake and the beginning of Potter Rapids, the first portage. The portage trail passes through the yard of an upscale fishing resort of genteel rusticity. Two flags, the Stars and Stripes and Maple Leaf, flutter side by side above a dock where I take out.

At first, the place seems deserted, but then I see movement ghosting behind large picture windows of the main lodge. Somebody's there, so I knock on the door. It's opened by a bone-thin woman, about fifty, with reddish-orange hair shorn short and spiky. She has a whiskey voice and nicotine-stained teeth.

Across a non-existent ass, large pink letters sewn onto the seat of her pants read, 'I'm Hot'.

The woman gives her name, Roxanne, and shakes my hand. She's the cook. Roxanne asks if I'd like something to drink. I'm hoping for beer, but she hands me a cold can of ice tea instead, then lights a cig and smokes while we chat.

"A couple of girls tried to run Potter two days ago," she tells me, "but they didn't make it." Looking at the rapid, I'm not surprised. "They had to be rescued by the guides. And get this. They're going ALL THE WAY to Hudson Bay, if you can believe that."

"That's where I'm going," I tell her, matter of fact.

Roxanne stares at me slack-jawed. Even the wisps of smoke coiling from her nostrils seem to freeze in surprise.

"Alone!" she blurts. "You're a crazy motherfucker!"

The resort has a wheelbarrow that Roxanne lets me use to shuttle my stuff, which makes the portage a snap. Once repacked, I wheel it back to the lodge and thank her for the hospitality. She looks at me with some perplexity before again calling my sanity into question in the same manner as before.

"Good luck," she says. "You're going to need it."

Drinking Water Lake is next. Narrow and intimate, it's beautiful, especially in the soft tones of evening. I glide past lush forests of competing greens and float beneath towering cliffs that rise steeply from shore. The canoe tracks easily across the lake's unblemished surface, water gently burbling against the hull, silver chevrons fanning out behind.

Halfway down, I find a good spot to stop and settle in for the first night out. After setting up and eating, I lounge upon a ledge of smooth shield, sipping rum and taking in the scene. Several beaver ply the still water but shatter the silence with sharp slaps of their tails when sensing my presence.

Fluty undulations of loons reverberate up and down, while fish leap from concentric rings of shimmering light. High above, eagles soar languidly upon their giant wings.

Then the sound of a motor inserts itself and a small skiff appears and pulls up beneath my perch. There are three Cree aboard, a man and two women, friendly and glowing with drink.

"Where you heading?" the man asks. His name is Miles.

"Hudson Bay," I say.

A pause while this sinks in.

Then, "Long way," one of the women says.

"Two girls went through here two days ago, going to Churchill in a canoe," Miles informs, "but you probably won't catch them. They look strong."

Cackles all around.

"Maybe you can give me one of your women," I joke. "You have two."

More cackles. All three live in Stanley Mission and have their entire lives. We chat about the roads, disliking them, but for different reasons.

"They are too rough," Miles complains.

He wants the province to pave them. I nod, but my sympathy is disingenuous. Build a good road and before long you'll have a Dairy Queen, miniature golf, and a real estate office hyping 'Lots for Sale'.

Miles tells me about a rock painting of a buffalo not far from here and takes my map, scrunches his face over it, and makes a mark.

"Right there!" he exclaims, handing the map back.

He takes a pull on his beer, passes the can to one of the women, and pulls again, this time on the outboard's starter cord. The engine whirrs to life and Miles pops it into reverse and begins backing away.

"Good luck," they wish me.

I thank them for the visit. They were nice. Soon it is quiet again. I go back to my rum, thinking about how the Cree once depended entirely on the canoe but no more, thinking about two girls somewhere ahead, trying to figure out what bison were doing in this boreal jungle, and wondering how far Marianne and Gene made it toward home today.

Then I start considering what Roxanne said—about me being crazy. Was it crazy to paddle to Hudson Bay through 800 miles of mostly uninhabited, untouched country and to do it alone? I didn't know anyone who would embark on such a journey, or even consider a lesser one without a companion, yet here I was.

Certainly, going alone is risky, but for me it was essential. Intimacy with the wilds demanded it. A partner could only detract from that. There would be fart jokes and prosaic discussions on politics and the plight of the planet, plus decisions to be made and mutually agreed to about where to camp and what to eat, and idle chitchat employed only to dispel silence.

Well, I did not want silence dispelled or any other disturbance to keep me from the essence of what I sought. Consequently, it was necessary to go alone.

After more contemplative sipping, I pronounce myself sane and conclude that the crazy thing would be not doing this. I was retired. I was healthy and fit. To squander the opportunity to do something I had long dreamed of doing—now that would be crazy.

Before turning in, I check the map to see how many miles I managed today and figure it at fifteen, not counting getting lost and un-lost on Nistowiak Lake. Not bad for the first day. Fifteen miles is what I hoped to make as a daily average. I'm right on schedule. Only 785 left to go.

Chapter 3
Ferality: A Brief Aside

The great debate over which has the bigger influence over a person's character, nature or nurture, is settled. It's nature, and I'm the proof, having been born with an innate ferality that was not the product of any nurturing. Nature was in my nature. Had Anna Lou, my mother, had her way, it would not have been so.

She nurtured me, her only child, to be an urbane urbanite, refined in taste and manners. From an early age, I was dragged to museums, plays, the symphony, and even obliged, at thirteen, to take ballroom dancing lessons, replete with coat, tie, and silly white gloves, but none of it took, despite her efforts.

Anna Lou loved city life, the buzz of humanity living in close proximity, with cultural outlets galore, social stimulation, good food and drink. She would have been a bona fide bon vivant if able to afford it, but hopes of that were dashed when she and my father divorced. So, instead of high society, she ended up in a high school teaching English to support us. English instruction was not confined to her day job for as soon as she got home I was her constant pupil.

Me and I, lay and lie, speech, grammar, syntax, and spelling were lessons dispensed at every opportunity, and I resided in what seemed a red-lined world of correction. It was all very tedious for a boy who just wanted to be outside, but for my mother, proficiency in language mattered so she made me suffer through.

How one spoke mattered, as did how one dressed. So too did using the proper utensil when dining, avoiding the faux pas of confusing the salad fork for the dinner fork for example. Such comportments were important in a civilized world and, indeed, fundamental to maintaining one.

My worldly parents were keen on civilization, both as students of history, where they learned that its rises were far more pleasant than its falls, but more so from having borne witness to the horrors of World War II—my mother as a Red Cross volunteer in Germany immediately after its surrender and my father as an army officer during the war.

They saw great cities rendered to ruin and legions of displaced persons struggling to survive. Civilization was not the natural state of mankind according to my father, who frequently warned of its fragility and need for constant tending.

"It will fall away the minute men stop wearing coat and tie to luncheon," was his common refrain.

I was expected to do my part in upholding civilization by wearing my *good* clothes a lot. Just before he left us for his dazzling German secretary when I was six, my father bought me a suit woven of wool so scratchy the Spanish Inquisitors could have used it to good effect in compelling heretics to confess their sins. The short pants caused agonizing itching every time I wore them, which was generally on Sundays for church.

One isn't supposed to suffer in the Unitarian Church, that being the purview of Catholics, but suffer I did as my little legs sweated and stuck to the leather lined pews while the rough weave assailed my tender thighs like a cilice.

Anna Lou, embarrassed by my non-stop squirming, would pinch me and hiss, "Sit still!" which was more than I could do.

Those pants ruined any chance that religious dogma of any ilk would ever establish a beachhead in my brain, and by seven, I adamantly refused to go to church and instead spent that day, as I did most others when not otherwise occupied, outside, increasingly becoming a feral child, albeit an occasionally well-dressed one.

We lived in San Francisco in a small rented flat on city's western edge. From my bedroom window, when no fog obscured the view, I could gaze out across several blocks of flat-roofed cityscape upon a broad expanse of ocean. On especially clear days, the Farallon Islands appeared as a tiny blip along the arc of an otherwise unmarred horizon, one that perfectly divided the blues of sea and sky. In bed at night, I would hear the moan of foghorns, bray of sea lions, and crash of waves breaking against the coast.

Where we lived was ideal habitat for a feral child. Golden Gate Park and Ocean Beach were only six blocks from our apartment, and a magnificently wild place called Lands End just a ten-minute trot from my front door. Lands End is an unruly patch of federal land perched on bluffs above the entrance to the Golden Gate. Mankind had tried to claim it, building the Great Highway through it, and before that a trolley line, but those 'enhancements' were tumbled by quake, slide, and slump.

And, so defeated, Lands End was left to Mother Nature, who dictated that snarls of verdure reclaim and occupy those parlous soils and that all works of man be erased. I spent countless hours exploring its secrets; bunkers and gun emplacements abandoned since the war, beaches and sea caves exposed only when tides were low, and wind-blown promontories where gnarled cypress stood against the infinite sea.

On a bench above Lands End, in air redolent with eucalyptus, can be found the remains of a Chinese cemetery dating from the late 1800s. The graves were removed early last century to make room for the expansion of Lincoln Park Golf Course, but several monuments endure, pillars of granite inscribed with graceful Chinese symbols.

These rise from the ground canted and weathered, evoking the trunkless legs of stone from Shelly's epic poem, *Ozymandias*. I knew the poem. It was one of Anna Lou's favorites. She could recite it from memory and used it in an attempt to excite me to poetry.

"What does the poem say to you?" she asked, in her didactic way.

I told her it meant that nature would eventually overtake civilization and vanquish it.

"Not exactly," she rejoined.

"Ozymandias' civilization is gone, not civilization per se. It's a metaphor about comeuppance, a mockery of conceit, about one person's insignificance and the transience of power."

"Same difference," I countered.

The poem, like Lands End, like grass poking through cracks in concrete, was for me, the feral child, a sign of great hope.

Chapter 4
Paddling in a Parallel Universe

Day 2

For the first time in a long time, I enjoy a good night's sleep, free from stress and worry. Over the previous months, between wrapping up my career and preparing for this trip, I was too wound up to let Morpheus do his thing, my mind awhirl with details and loose ends needing attention while the clock's green glowing digits advanced hardly at all toward dawn. But since launching, those burdens were left upstream and life is now decluttered and simple. I need only eat, sleep, and paddle.

It has been my habit to rise early, mostly because I hate to hurry, especially in the morning. Thus, I've made it a practice to get up in plenty of time to begin each day with an hour of doing nothing. I call it *humanizing hour*. Humanizing hour entails sipping coffee in quiet repose. Essentially, it's meditation with caffeine. So, this morning I'm up at 5:30, humanizing on a rock above the lake. From the nearby woods, I hear the pitched call of a goshawk, *ki-ki-ki*, and catch sight of it blurring through the trees.

Goshawks can be very aggressive, dangerously so, especially around a nest. I heard tell of someone who lost an eye when attacked by a bird of this breed, so when it's time to squat over a hole, I walk to the woods with sunglasses on, my hat pulled low, and a forearm held up to my brow in a classic woe-is-me pose, just in case.

It is not a peaceful poop, with the agitated eye-gouger screeching and flapping noisily above. I finish and retreat in haste, hoping the bird imagines that it scared the shit out of me. The animal kingdom deserves a victory over humankind, at least the sense of one, every now and then.

Once underway, I only manage a mile before a small runabout, skippered by a Cree fishing guide with three clients onboard, glides up alongside the canoe. The guide's name is Cameron and he bears a striking resemblance to Miles—same round head, good looks and affable manner. As it turns out, the men are cousins.

After the preliminaries about where I'm from and where I'm going, and the predictable wide-eyed response upon learning my destination, Cameron shares the news that there are two girls ahead of me in a canoe.

"You don't say," I say.

I'm interested in hearing the particulars, their age and what they look like, but the clients are anxious to fish, so we go our separate ways before any details are divulged, Cameron and crew to a secret spot teeming with pike and me in the wake of the mysterious girls.

Plugging in the iPod, I paddle the remainder of Drinking Water Lake to the dulcet sounds of Mark Knopfler and Emmy Lou Harris. As a rule, I don't approve of music in the backcountry, but it can sometimes help one push through periods of adversity and suffering in the way of convicts singing in a chain gang. I don't listen long, feeling a bit impure, but when the music stops, static still fills the earbuds. I take them out, but the sound persists. Then I realize it isn't static: there are rapids ahead.

According to Miles, there are two options in getting from Drinking Water to Keg Lake, the next lake down. One is keeping to the main channel and portaging a rapid and the other by way of a narrow passage that splits off to the left. The buffalo art Miles marked on the map is on this latter route, so I take it.

Immediately, I am whisked through a mature forest of dark spruce and silver-barked birch, tall trees that arc across the river as if to shield it from threats above. Shafts of light stab down through this canopy in oblique angles and bounce along the forest floor in frenzy amidst clumps of blooming fireweed. Several mounds of large gnawed logs rise high above the river's surface, the homes of fat-cat beavers.

Keeping an eye out for the buffalo, I spot it on a rock wall overhanging the river. Miles had it mapped just right. Clearly a bison, it's drawn in red ochre, a pigment processed from iron oxide common to pictographs worldwide, including the most celebrated, discovered in a cave near Lascaux, France and said to be 17,000 years old.

There is nothing close to that age here because ice, up to two miles thick, covered this land for centuries until retreating 10,000 years ago, so, relatively speaking, this buffalo is *art nouveau*. Miles said it was 1,500 years old.

It dawns on me that 1,500 years ago is about when Rome was sacked by Vandals, a Germanic tribe with scant regard for civilization. Strange to think that this bison was painted here, amidst this timber, while a world away, on the Tiber, a great city blazed. These events, separated not by time but by space so unbridgeable, may as well have occurred on different planets. The course of human history—invasion, invention, reigning, and waning—played out more or less in isolation, in a universe completely cut off from this one.

While Vikings raided and Normans conquered, and Saladin clashed with Crusaders; while Mongols savaged and the Black Plague ravaged; while Guttenberg printed his Bible, this bison has stood, unaffected and unchanged, a silent sentinel in this land apart.

For all that time, the ancestors to Miles and Cameron lived here, fished and trapped, hunted and moved through this land in boats, existing as their grandparents did and as their grandchildren would, until the end was presaged when a lost Italian bumbled onto the Bahamas. After that, it was just a matter of time until these universes would be parallel no more, destined by the accident of discovery to converge and collide.

Setting off below the buffalo, I come to a small rapid, really only a swift, and pass it easily, but soon encounter a rapid worthy of the name. Although marginally runnable, I opt for caution and portage around.

Reassembled on Keg Lake, I start out in regal sunshine with a tailwind's benevolent nudge, but clouds soon swirl the sky. What felt friendly in sunshine becomes menacing in gloom. Rain begins to fall and visibility degrades to a fuzzy cast. I can't make out any landmarks to find my way so just keep paddling in a direction that feels right. The forest closes in. Trees moan and sway.

Long skeins of moss flutter eerily from their branches, lending the land an illusion of movement. The lake's surface turns rough and waves rap against the hull. I paddle harder to quell a rising panic, making great time, but as it turns out, in the wrong direction. Soon I find myself in the boater's equivalent of rim rocked. I've paddled into a cul-de-sac cove. Checking the map provides no help. The maps are small-scale: 1:250,000, meaning one inch on the map represents four miles on the ground.

Unless I constantly monitor progress against the maps, it will be difficult to stay oriented, especially in conditions such as these. Once again, I am forced to turn on the GPS, something I am loathe to do for purity's sake, but clearly without this device I'd be in trouble. Plotting my location, I discover I've gone a mile the wrong way, so head back, against the wind this time, in penance for my navigational sins.

With rain falling harder, I stop to put on the dry suit, and then, hermetically sealed, continue, keeping track on the map and GPS to ensure that all progress is actually that.

At Keg's outlet, the river braids into several channels and somewhere below an unseen rapid grinds. I have no idea which channel to take, so choose one because one must be chosen. The scrape of water grows louder as I proceed, but I can't see much in the gloaming until, rounding an island, glimpse whitewater below. Standing for a quick look, I find a line just off the right bank and mark it, using a tree for reference.

Opposite the tree, I drop to my knees, this time forcing my feet beneath the seat to create space for them amidst all the jammed in gear. My focus is to the immediate front, eyes darting back and forth, scanning for danger and creases of safe passage. The paddle never leaves the water. It pushes, pulls, pries, and braces, making the boat do what I want.

I start feeling like a hot shit with a perfect run until, almost done, I top a swell to confront a reef of rock dead ahead. It's unavoidable and the boat slams down upon it and scrapes across with a sickening sound, the nautical equivalent of fingernails on a blackboard, before coming off and floating free. Thinking I may have holed the hull, I hurry to shore and find, with the boat turned over, the gelcoat rasped to the Kevlar core in several places and the rear strike plate shattered.

Big chunks of fiberglass are missing or sticking out like snaggled and broken teeth. Without the plate, added to armor the bottom against this very eventuality, I would have likely broken the boat. I probe and press the impacted areas with my fingers, looking for cracks and soft spots and happily discover everything seemingly sound. Perhaps it will be okay, as long as all future crashes are confined to other parts of the underside.

Back on the water, tired and traumatized, I look for a place to stop. It's been a long day, and I'm cold, wet, and woozy. Finding one, I set up the tent, get into dry clothes, and eat. I made fourteen miles today, not counting an extra two getting lost and found. Looking around, I am pleased with the view. There is only forest, water, sky, and no sign of my kind.

Elsewhere babies are born, ground broken, deals sealed, caskets closed, goals scored, horns honked, triggers pulled, but none of that matters here, in this world apart; a world watched over by a 1,500-year-old bison. I pray this land remains as is, pure and wild, but fear Vandals are already gathering at its gates.

Chapter 5
Hommes Du Nord

Day 3

I awake in the dead of night and slowly become aware of a faint rustling that hadn't registered earlier. My ears are rested and acute. It is so quiet I can almost hear the thrum of planets as they spin and chime of stars as they twinkle. The Bushmen of the Kalahari claim that stars do in fact make noise, a soft *pssst pssst*, like the sound used by hunters to alert their dogs to prey.

I listen intently but don't hear it, much as I'd like to. Still, the rustling is real. It must be Keg Rapids, the rapids above that nearly broke the boat, so I go back to sleep, unconcerned.

Up at dawn and more alert after coffee, it becomes clear that what I hear is sourced ahead and not behind. With the binoculars, I peer across a wide expanse of river and catch splashes of white blinking in sunshine. I get the map, edge line it with the view, and realize that what I hear and see is the top of Grand Rapids, a waterfall that entails the first major portage.

In preparing for this trip, I did almost no research about what I was getting into. I never read a guidebook or blog, examined trip reports, watched YouTube videos, or spoke to anyone who had come this way before, other than Ric. My maps, lacking detail, were of scant help. Thus, I had no clue about the rapids, their number, location, or severity; or that there were so many large lakes and long portages.

In part this was by design. I wanted to experience the river as early explorers had, with little foreknowledge of what lay ahead. But such romantic notions aside, I didn't take the time to delve into these details because I didn't have it, being preoccupied with other things, mostly work, and freaked out about retiring.

Retirement is a huge transition and the notion of no longer being who I was, coupled with the uncertainty of who I would become, left me feeling discombobulated and lost. Plus, I was busy, trying to wrap things up at the Forest Service before walking out of the building I had occupied twenty-four years for the last time. I couldn't be bothered researching this trip beyond a few preliminaries.

When I got to Missinipe and Ric saw how clueless I was, he took pity on me and printed up a trip report written by a party who had traveled the first 200 miles, from Missinipe to the village of Pukatawagan, some years before, and gave it to me. (I found out later that Ric was convinced I would never make it out alive, and if I managed to reach Hudson Bay at all, it would be floating face down.)

According to the trip report, the carry around Grand Rapids is 630 meters. I convert that to feet to learn that it's a little more than a third of a mile, which doesn't sound like much. So, as I head toward the trip's first big portage, I'm ignorant enough to actually be looking forward to it.

Arriving at the take out above the falls, I grab a load and start down, reminding myself not to hurry.

"You're sixty," I caution.

A twist, tweak, sprain, or strain could have serious consequences. The first trip takes twenty-five minutes, fifteen down and ten back. It's no big deal. Nor are the next three trips big deals, but the last two are. Trip five is the food box. It weighs a hundred pounds and just getting it into carrying position is almost more than I can do.

First, I lash the box to a pack frame, brought just for this purpose, and then lift it to rest on a thigh while fishing one arm through a pack strap before swinging the burden onto my back. Next, I wiggle my free arm through the other shoulder strap, then fasten the hip belt and tug it tight until my waist cinches in like an ant's thorax.

Then I start, with tentative steps, lumbering down the trail like a drunken Quasimodo. My knees are not pleased. They grind and grate in constant protest.

The last load is the canoe. Although not particularly heavy at seventy pounds with spray deck attached, it's cumbersome. Experienced voyageurs can lift a canoe into portage position with the ease of donning a hat. I attempt to emulate this technique but bounce a gunwale off my brow, misjudge the balance point, and can't prevent the bow from crashing to the ground. On the next try, it's the stern's turn to bang down. I'm proving a failure as a fulcrum, but eventually teeter and totter to tenuous equilibrium and begin, moving slowly, step by step.

I can't see to the front of me because my head is buried deep inside the hull; plus, a flap of spray deck hangs over my face like a niqāb, only without the eye holes cut in. The only way to navigate is by looking directly down to follow the little bit of trail exposed at my feet. At every turn, the canoe bonks into trees, causing me to stumble a few steps back and reposition the boat in line with the trail. My hands, committed to the gunwales, allow the bugs to bite with impunity.

Unable to swat, I can only shake my head, horse like, and blow at them from the corners of my mouth. It's a poor defense. The omission of portage pads, I realize within the first few steps, was a colossal mistake as the thwart digs painfully into the base of my neck and shoulders. Clearly, portaging is going to be misery and much tougher than anticipated. Of course, I've portaged on previous trips, but always had others along to help.

It takes three hours and five-and-a-half laps to get everything around, turning that measly one-third-mile trail into a four-mile trial.

After refreshing with a swim, I start down Trade Lake. Winds are brisk and abeam, raising waves, but nothing to worry about, I think, until spotting a capsized sixteen-foot skiff on shore, battered and broken—a clear indication that worry is sometimes warranted here.

I keep at it until 6:00, then stop on the upstream end of an island big enough to have a name: Archibald Island. After setting up, I lay on the ground and close my eyes to rest. When I open them again, I see something glinting in the uppermost branches of a tree. It's a bottle suspended by a strand of monofilament. I climb up to retrieve it.

Weathered like frosted glass, the bottle once held Captain Morgan, but now, instead of rum, it holds a tightly rolled scroll. A message in a bottle. How quaint! I brighten at the prospect it might be from the two girls who can't be too far ahead.

"To whom it may concern. Hi. We are a couple of lonely young women hoping to meet a man to…"

I extract the note and read it. It is not from the girls, but rather from a bunch of boys, students at Saint John's School in Alberta who became *Hommes du*

Nord (Men of the North) by portaging a 'height of land' on June 21, 2005, seven years before, almost to the day.

Although it doesn't specify, I surmise that the height of land referenced is Frog Portage, a place of great significance during the fur trade, and not far below this island. The note includes the following oath which the newly minted Hommes du Nord had to recite and swear to:

I promise (it starts)…

1) To remain loyal to the company;
2) To never kiss another voyageur's wife without her permission;
3) To repeat the ceremony of initiation whenever bringing a new voyageur across a height of land.

Signatures occupy the rest of the note, twenty from the initiates and three more bearing witness. Twenty-three people in total. I'd hate to be here with that kind of crowd. All those voices intruding on bird songs and river music. *Hommes du Noise* is more like it.

I roll up the note, return it to the bottle, and the bottle to the bough from which it hung. Then I fetch a bottle of my own, one that does have rum in it, Bacardi 151, the strong stuff. After several sips, my mood turns reflective. It was a good day, one of work and satisfaction derived from making sixteen miles, not counting four more back-and-forth around Grand Rapids.

Twenty miles accomplished with muscle power alone. I gaze at the river, watching it roll smoothly by, as it has forever rolled through this timeless space, moving from the past toward the future with nothing to differentiate the two. Wilderness. Unchanged. Unchained. I tip the bottle.

A generous slug of amber fluid glugs into the cup. I take a swig, and then another, and it occurs to me: *I'm the goddamn Homme du Nord around here!*

Hell yeah! I really am.

Chapter 6
Encounter with a Scary Critter

Day 4

It's foggy when I awake, not outside, but inside, inside my head that is. I'm not sure where I am until hearing river noise intrude above the buzz in my brain and then remember—Archibald Island. It's a Sunday worthy of the name as I discover upon crawling out of the tent into blinding light.

Ow! My head hurts. Too much rum. One-fifty-one is potent stuff. I learned it was the quaff of choice for river runners from a pair of long-toothed paddlers Marianne and I met years before on a river in northern Nunavut. Invited to their camp for cocktails, we found the bar limited exclusively to 151.

When asked, "Why just 151?" they responded in unison, "Why pack water?"

Made sense, so ever since, 151 is what I bring. The problem is I haven't learned to recalibrate the allocation to account for the augmented strength and sometimes overdo it.

Despite the hangover, I'm on the water early, bound for Frog Portage, a place of enormous geopolitical significance during the fur trade because it connected two major river systems, the Churchill and Saskatchewan, over a low divide that was easily passed. Although the upper Churchill can be safely navigated, the lower river has several daunting rapids that imperiled cargo and crew. Thus, leaving the Churchill for the Saskatchewan via Frog Portage was the prudent thing to do.

Although First Nations people no doubt traversed the route since time immemorial, no one knows who the first European was to use it, but likely it was a Hudson Bay Company (HBC) man named Louis Primeau.

In 1766, Primeau was sent out from York Factory, HBC's operation center on Hudson Bay, with orders to seek out furring grounds in the upper Churchill and beyond it, over the continental divide to waters that flowed west to the Pacific and north to the Arctic. He almost certainly crossed Frog Portage that year and, before long, this height of land became a bustling boulevard of commerce.

In 1774, Samuel Hearne, an intrepid Englishman also employed by HBC, built a trading post on the Saskatchewan 150 miles below Frog Portage. He named it Cumberland House and it was the company's first inland trading depot.

Prior to Cumberland House, trappers and traders had to journey to one of HBC's seaport forts, entailing months of hard travel, but when competitors from a rival fur company based in Montreal began building trading posts in the interior, where furs could be exchanged for goods without having to cross half of North America, HBC was forced to follow suit. Cumberland House proved an immediate success.

To tap into this lucrative trade, the opportunistic Primeau, having since left HBC to throw in with the Montrealers', built a small trading post right at Frog Portage just months after Cumberland House became operational. The business model was simple; intercept fur-laden canoes before they reached the HBC post and entice the trappers to trade with them instead, often using watered-down rum as an inducement. It proved an effective strategy in the cutthroat world of the fur trade.

The story goes that Frog Portage got its name from a snub directed by the Cree toward the Chipewyan, or Dene people, whom the former derided for the perceived inability of the latter to hunt beaver or properly prepare their skins. The Cree left a frog skin stretched and hanging along the trail as a sign of their sartorial contempt.

I reach the portage after an hour's easy paddle and go ashore to walk its length to stretch my legs and clear my head. A wooden track, similar in design and function to a railroad track, extends across the portage upon which boats can be easily transported using a wheeled cart. Thick brush, growing tight against the track, obliges me to walk along one of the rails.

Although not exactly a tightrope, my equilibrium, being no equal to the rum still coursing my system, is off, so I proceed unsteadily, arms out and flapping for balance. Ahead, something anomalous lies atop the rail I'm walking on. It looks furry, like a pelt, about the size of a small dog. I figure it to be a dead something, because only a dead something would remain so exposed in this predatory neighborhood. When quite close, I recognize it as a hoary marmot, on the XL side.

The poor thing is obviously dead and, wondering what killed it, I lean in close, looking for signs of trauma. With my face just inches above the inert form, its eyelids suddenly snap open and the thing jolts to life, gaining its feet in a flash and gnashing long, fearsome, yellow teeth at me in a rapid staccato that is pure menace.

I shriek and recoil, flailing at the air to keep from falling onto jumbled rock below. Concerned that the rat is about to attack, I chance a leap to the opposite rail, three feet over, and somehow stick the landing. The marmot stands its ground, gnashing away and eyeing me with malevolence as I edge past, giving it as wide a berth as the limited space allows.

I am still hyperventilating upon reaching the Saskatchewan side of the portage. My heart may have stopped momentarily when the creature sprang so unexpectantly to life, but it is more than making up for it now. Generally, it's never good when something you presume dead turns out not to be.

I stall awhile before daring to head back, both to calm down and to allow the pint-sized terror time to decamp. Granted, real men should not fear rodents, but I'd wager that even Mr. T would have peed his pants if confronted by this one. Fortunately, when I pass back through, the little chicken-shit is gone.

Departing Frog Portage, I enter Uskik Lake. Progress is slow. I'm tired, still hungover, and shaken from my meeting with the marmot. A headwind kicks in, adding to these burdens, so at 4:30 I take out to camp.

There is a marvelous rock set against the river that has been water-sculpted into the shape of a throne. My sleeping pad converts it to a comfy chair. On it, I spend the evening in tranquil repose, surveying my domain. Wind swishes pleasantly through the birch boughs and teals fly over, their wings generating a faint whistle. The river flows and coos.

My brain goes into neutral. It doesn't have to conjure up thoughts or solve any problems. I find myself in the moment and realize, to my surprise, that I am actually *being here now*. A rarity. Seldom do I reside in the present, instead reflecting on things done or those yet to do.

But now is now. I stay in the moment for a surprisingly long time, maybe even minutes, until images of yellow teeth impose on my awareness to break the Zen-like state. Still, I have an epiphany; being here now is infinitely better than being here gnawed.

Chapter 7
Wisdom

Growing up, I never figured to leave California, unaware that other options even existed. However, I did know that San Francisco was not for me. A big city isn't fit habitat for a feral kid. Instead, I set my sights on Santa Barbara, 300 miles to the south, where I envisioned a life of sun and sand. Santa Barbara is my ancestral home, if you don't go back too many ancestors, being the place where my mother was raised.

We summered there, she and I, once freed from our respective schools, staying with my grandfather. Santa Barbara had a great feel to it—laid back with a hint of old Mexico, everyone in shorts and sandals, the air heavy with the scent of citrus and magnolia.

I ended up going to college at UC Santa Barbara, majoring in hedonism initially until an inspiring professor named Rod Nash sparked an interest in environmental studies. Dr. Nash was a historian and authority on the environmental movement, and known for a book he had written entitled *Wilderness and the American Mind*, a seminal work that explored American attitudes toward wilderness and how they evolved, from howling waste to sacred space, over three hundred years of European occupation.

Through his lectures, I was introduced to a pantheon of luminaries who championed wilderness preservation, men such as John Muir, Aldo Leopold, Howard Zahniser, and Bob Marshall, and although I didn't know it then, Dr. Nash had sown the seeds to my future.

After graduating, I hung around Santa Barbara, working as a busboy at Joe's Cafe, playing frisbee golf, smoking too much pot, and getting too much sun. It was a life without substance or purpose, and I realized it shouldn't, couldn't last. I gave it a year and then decided to seek more meaningful existence elsewhere.

It rained the day I broke free of Santa Barbara's strong gravitational pull, a hard rain from a tropical storm that washed the streets in sheets. I was soaked by the time my old International Scout was packed with what little I had—skateboard, guitar and camping gear mostly.

I didn't have much of a plan, other than to head north. For some reason, north seemed like the way to go. Sensing the weight of fate, I inserted the key into the ignition and turned it. I didn't know where I was going, but I was on my way.

By mid-June I was in Montana, having spent the previous two months backpacking in deserts, canyons, and mountains as I zigged and zagged up the map. Snow still capped the peaks of the mountains surrounding the Big Hole Valley when I pulled into the tiny town of Wisdom, population one hundred.

I planned only a quick stop to call my father, hoping to ease his worried mind about his wayward, homeless, unemployed son. He wanted me to get settled, find a career, and make something of myself. I was reluctant to talk with him since I didn't have any news he'd care to hear.

As I exited the car and walked to a pay phone, swarms of mosquitoes, for which the Big Hole is famous, descended on me in biblical profusion. Fifty vied for position on the hand trying to drop a dime into the phone's coin slot while hundreds more, frantic to feed, buzzed throughout the booth. Hanging up before connecting, I beat a hasty retreat for a bar across the street, passing a cowboy going the same way. "You got any blood left?" I asked.

"Yeah. I think so. It's flying around here somewhere," he quipped.

We burst through the door of the Antler Saloon and ordered beers. It was the first and last beer I had to buy. The place was rocking, crowded with ranch hands, booted ranch feet, and cowboy-hatted ranch heads. A bell rang frequently above the twang, signifying that someone had bought a round for the house, and each time that bell chimed, another frosty cold can was placed before me on the bar.

Soon several were arrayed like soldiers on parade awaiting my command. The jukebox blared, pool balls clacked, conversation and laughter ebbed and flowed. A long-haired Indian kid jumped up on a table and danced, dropped his pants and mooned us. There were girls too, plump, giggly gals stuffed pleasingly into tight jeans. Wisdom, Montana. Heck. I could live here a while.

"Is there any work around?" I shouted above the din to the guy whose blood was flying around outside.

"What?" he said.

I asked again, louder this time.

"Hell yeah! *Youcancumnwerkwifus.*"

And just like that, because mosquitoes chased me into a bar, the trajectory of my life was forever changed. That day, I became a hay hand for the Huntley Ranch, a big, sprawling outfit halfway up the Big Hole Valley toward Jackson. I became a Montanan that day too, and a cowboy, sort of.

Won't Dad be pleased, I thought, popping the top of another cold can.

When I got to the ranch, it seemed I'd landed in a Steinbeck novel. There were twenty-eight of us on the hay crew: misfits, dimwits, drifters, drunks, broke-down cowpokes, a pair of college kids and me. Several of us shared the bunkhouse, a long clapboard building with two bunk-lined rooms separated by a communal bathroom which featured a fissured mirror that made the face looking back from it appear the subject of a Picasso painting from his Cubist years.

The mirror was set above a rind-encrusted sink where the porcelain darkened concentrically in proximity to the drain, residue of tractor oil, Brylcreem, and Big Hole dirt washed off by generations of ranch hands who had come before. Each sleeping room had a double-barreled stove, jerry-rigged contraptions fashioned from two fifty-five-gallon drums, one perched above the other and conjoined with stovepipe.

The bottom barrel held the fire while the top helped hold the heat. The Big Hole is a high valley and even in summer many nights were cool enough to warrant a fire. Pine bolts snapped and popped, and yellow light, emanating from the stove's slotted vent, played a cross-hatched glow upon the dull green walls as we slept, or tried to, amidst the snoring, farting, and dream talk.

By late August, with the hay up and mounded across the valley like so many giant loaves of bread, most of the crew had gone—back to school, the next dead-end job, or the bars of Butte. I stayed on and had the bunkhouse all to myself.

September in Montana is when winter makes its initial appearance, bringing fresh snow to the upper elevations. I worked the wooded hills above the ranch, felling lodgepole pines for firewood and fencing. The trees swayed against a pallid sky as the saw cut through, then toppled to land quietly, muffled by snow.

Later, we rode the summer ranges, pushing cattle through dark stands of timber to gather them up. They emerged from the trees in small bunches and came together like water, converging from drops to rivulets to rivers that flowed down from the frosty heights to tawny fields below.

One blustery Sunday afternoon, on a rare day off, I was back in the Antler, sitting at the bar making desultory conversation with a hand from another ranch and trying to decide whether to try a pickled turkey gizzard from a bell jar on the backbar that looked more science experiment than food. I wasn't fully engaged in the idle chitchat coming my way until I heard him say something about the Forest Service and jobs.

"What's that?" I asked, swiveling around to face him.

"All the college kids quit to go back to school," he repeated. "They're looking to hire, but you gotta have a college degree."

"I have one," I said.

"You got to be shitting me!" he bellowed in unfeigned surprise.

I just smiled and bought myself a turkey gizzard.

The Forest Service hired me to conduct something called *stand exams* which entailed walking through the woods to locate a predetermined plot where a coworker and I would count and measure all of the trees within a prescribed area and record our findings onto a form. The information would be used to determine whether or when a stand could be logged. When finished with one plot, we'd trudge off to the next to count, measure, and record anew.

Lodgepole pines are propagated in dense stands of even-aged trees that sacrifice girth for growth as they race each other toward sunlight. Walking through a forest of these arrow-straight trees makes one feel like an ant in grass, and the light, flickering down in crazy angles, lends the scene the choppy look of a silent film. Chattering squirrels and ruby-crowned kinglets call from canopies a hundred feet up while you measure, count and record the information that could render all this splendor to two-by-fours.

I remember the moment of epiphany well, when a small grain of inspiration appeared from out of the blue on a gray December day. It wasn't anything tangible, just an idea that popped into my head from nowhere. I was part of a crew working in the mountains west of Wisdom, cleaning up debris left over from a timber sale, stacking it into windrows so it could be burned and disposed of. I liked the work—mindless and hard. We slogged through snow, our noses red and runny, earflaps deployed and breath expelled like cartoon dialogue balloons.

The grain came while I was dragging a cat-faced trunk segment cored with rot. It orbited my head like a teensy satellite, spinning ever faster until suddenly it careened, out of control like an epileptic fly, and smacked me behind an ear. Penetrating the temporal lobe, the grain continued into my brain, plowing up a furrow of gray matter before finally coming to rest deep within the cerebral cortex. Then it let its purpose be known.

"You," said the grain, "should be a wilderness ranger!"

Dr. Nash's seed had taken root. *A wilderness ranger, hmm?* That sounded good to me.

Chapter 8
Fools and Drunks

Day 5

I face a dilemma today. A fat section of Uskik Lake is coming up that has to be gotten around, one way or another. There are two options. One is beelining across a mile-and-a-half of open water. The other is detouring around the lake, hugging shore, and crossing where it narrows. The choice is between short or safe. The safe way will add three miles to the day's paddle, while the riskier route will take me far from land.

My initial inclination is to beeline it. I am not particularly risk adverse, probably since no consequence greater than humiliation has ever resulted from the myriad dumb things I've done. I don't consider myself particularly brave but have come to trust in luck which has led to poor decisions that generally turned out okay, like hopping freights, riding in a rodeo, and bullfighting in Portugal.

With these and other harebrained exploits, providence has always proved benevolent. Still, one must be circumspect when factoring luck into fateful decisions as relying on it too much could prove unlucky.

Reaching the jumping-off point where Uskik turns fat, where the choice must be made, I find myself unsure. What concerns me most is fetch, the amount of open water to windward. There is two miles of it here. Wind sweeping over that much water, unimpeded by land, can generate waves capable of turning Uskik from millpond to maelstrom faster than I could say, "Mayday," and Uskik is no millpond now; small whitecaps already dot its surface and heavy, dark clouds roil the sky above.

If the seas get even a little bigger, they could swamp the boat, loaded as it is without much freeboard. Then again, I do have a spray deck across the top, designed to keep water coming over from getting inside, but some always gets in anyhow, through gaps and seams. Ric Driediger is no fan of spray decks, reasoning they feed a false sense of security that tempt one to try what they ought not, such as crossing Uskik in conditions like these.

"You'll be safer without it," he cautioned. But Ric's a traditionalist. To my way of thinking, the deck cannot help but help.

I bob and stall a while, trying to make up my mind, until indecision becomes a burden too great to bear, so utter the words used by many a stalwart adventurer when determining a course of action after long deliberation, "Fuck it!" I choose the beeline and head straight out.

That this was ill-considered is immediately made clear. The wind intensifies and bears on abeam, bringing in swells that grow bigger as they near. The canoe rocks heavily from side to side as the waves pass under and I remind myself to stay loose, with hips gimbaled to the seat and swiveling with the motion, and to lean downwind to cant up the craft's windward edge to better deflect the surging seas.

Even so, water comes alarmingly close to topping the gunwales and an occasional breaker smacks the hull and washes over. After a few of these, I feel liquid pooling at my feet. To remain broadside in these conditions is untenable, so I fall off to put wind and wave quartered astern.

I am not sure how the boat will handle this new attitude. Generally, I don't like following seas—not when they run high—because you can't easily see what's bearing down on you and instead have to rely on sensing the motions of the boat and reacting to them. Essentially, it's boating by braille. As each wave reaches the hull and begins to overtake it, the stern rises and the bow drops.

Sometimes, with steeper swells, the boat will actually surf the wave's face until driven into the wave ahead, which then brings all forward motion to a full stop. With no momentum, a small boat handles like a barely moving bicycle, becoming alarmingly tippy until speed and stability can be regained.

Fortunately, conditions on Uskik are only bad, not disastrous, and I scud across, more or less in control, and soon make the safety of shore. Beaching the boat, I sponge out about ten gallons of lake water that found its way in, and then carry on, into the wind this time to gain Uskik's outlet. Luck has once again favored me, but the crossing is a sobering reminder that poor decisions could prove deadly and I vow to be more careful next time.

Back on moving water, I check the map to see that Kettle Falls is coming up. Kettle Falls is a mandatory portage.

The trip report stresses that 'MISSING THE EDDY ABOVE THE FALLS MAY PROVE FATAL!' and warns of fast, tricky currents that make reaching the take-out difficult. This has me on full alert, but for naught. As is often the case with guidebook descriptions, catastrophe is seldom as advertised and I land without issue.

Happily, there's a log skid running the length of the portage on which to slide the canoe, so I need carry only two loads and can sled the rest left in the boat.

The falls seen from below validates the warning about fatal consequences should one miss the take-out. The guide wasn't hyperbolic about that. The entire river, a quarter-mile wide, plunges twenty feet straight down in an unbroken curtain of white and explodes at the bottom in spectacular mayhem; jets of water blasting from the turbulent flow, shooting out in all directions.

Just beyond this impact zone, several pelicans float insouciantly upon the rowdy waves. They are fishing. I've seldom seen this breed feed. White pelicans are common in Montana, but whenever I've observed them they are either floating, flying, or flocked on rocks. But now they're on the hunt, paddling through rollicking surf and peering intently into the depths. When something is spotted, the great beak stabs downward and the entire body follows, save for a tuft of tail.

It looks as though the birds are bobbing for apples. Before long, the odd-looking animal corks back up to reveal a throat pouch distended to bursting. A pelican's pouch can hold three gallons of water, and with luck, a fish. If indeed the bird has secured prey, it will point its bill skyward and gulp it down. I am left to wonder whether a pelican can feel the meal squiggling from pouch to paunch? That would creep me out but for a pelican I suppose the sensation is pleasing.

Leaving the birds to their movable feast, I paddle on to the confluence of the Churchill and Reindeer Rivers. The Reindeer is a major tributary, nearly doubling the Churchill's volume. Ric warned me to stay sharp here because powerful currents form as the river adjusts to its new flow, and sure enough, like a page from Jules Verne, a whirlpool materializes directly beneath me, spinning the canoe around and acting to suck it down. I brace with the paddle as the craft whirls and tips, yelping in fright at every near flip.

Beyond the confluence with the Reindeer, there are three rapids to contend with. Although late in the day, I want to get past them before stopping. Camping above a rapid and anticipating a run first thing the next morning is not conducive to a good night's sleep.

The guide recommends portaging these rapids, but, from what I can tell scouting from the boat, they don't look bad enough for that. The first two go as planned, but I run aground on the third and have to drag the canoe a hundred yards over rocks to regain deep water. Purple streaks of gelcoat mark my passage across the shoal like a dotted line upon a map.

Finally, I can stop. Tired and still shaken from the crossing at Uskik, I decide a drink or two might be in order. After all, if God truly does protect fools and drunks, doesn't it make sense to be both?

Chapter 9
Giddy Up: A Brief Aside

I got my first wilderness ranger job in 1980, in the Seven Devils Mountains near Riggins, Idaho. The guy initially hired for the position discovered he wasn't keen on camping and quit. He returned to California to play French horn.

"Do you play French horn?" That was the first question posed in the phone interview for the opening.

I was in Helena, Montana, talking with a selection panel in Lewiston, Idaho. There were three of them doing the asking. I had waited a long time for the chance to be a wilderness ranger. My only other employment possibility was with the CIA as a drudge in a dark room interpreting satellite images. My father encouraged me to join. He'd been with the agency after his army career, and I applied to get him off my back, but figured the CIA probably wouldn't want me after poking into my checkered past.

I didn't want them either. I wasn't designed for inside work or city living. Besides, I had loftier goals in mind, lofty as in mountains, but wilderness ranger jobs were few and competition for them fierce. Getting this one depended on how I did in the interview.

I wasn't sure where I came up with the answers to all the questions asked, but knew I was doing well, despite not really knowing what I was saying as I said it. My mouth moved and words came out, and I heard them, as if fresh to my ears, and waited while they coalesced to meaning. When they did, it sounded good. I would have hired me on the spot. They did.

A week later, I was enroute to Riggins in an ancient VW bus, replete with an Indian tapestry, bequeathed from the previous owner, adorning the headliner. All my worldly possessions were on board, not much more than when I had left Santa Barbara three years before, save for cold-weather clothing.

The Seven Devils are part of the Hells Canyon Wilderness Area: 84,000 mostly vertical acres. Eight-thousand feet separate the peaks from the Snake River, slithering through its canyon below. The job involved multi-day patrols through this perpendicular terrain on horseback.

Except for riding a few times on the Huntley Ranch, I had only ridden the kinds of steeds found in merry-go-rounds, so it was with some trepidation that I assumed responsibility for the three equines my boss delivered one day.

"This is a horse," she said, leading the first down the ramp of a stock truck to the corral.

We spent that day and part of the next expanding on that theme. I learned how to catch and halter, lead, tie and hold, brush, bridle and saddle; how to lift a leg to check the shoes, making sure they were tight; and how to clean their feet with a delicate little instrument called a hoof pic. I was shown the proper way to apply bug dope, sprayed from a large squirt bottle and wiped in using a puffy, red mitt.

I also learned that, since horses are a prey species and easily spooked, especially when confronted by anything new, *slow* and *easy* are the operative words when working around them. Always let them know where you are and what you're up to. Talk to them constantly when close, murmuring endearments, soft and sweet, like pillow talk.

After going over the rudiments of riding, we moved on to the packing part of equine arts. A packhorse can carry twenty percent of its body weight, or about 200 pounds for the average animal. Cargo is hauled in panniers (French for *bag*), attached to a pack saddle composed of trees, bows, half-breeds, D-rings, breast collars, breechings, spiders, latigos, and a bunch of other horsey sounding things.

It's important that the opposing panniers weigh exactly the same or the loads won't balance, but scales to determine weight weren't allowed. That was cheating, said the boss. Instead weight had to be gauged by hefting onc bag and then the other, and then the first again, and then the second again, maybe moving an ax or a boot from one to the other, and lifting some more.

Once satisfied that they balanced, the panniers could be placed on the horse, but…check the cinch first! Horses are sneaky. They'll bloat when first saddled to make you think the cinch is tight when it's actually looser than a pair of prison pants. With the bags on, it's time for the top load—the light bulky stuff, like sleeping bag and pad. Arrange these items on the horse's back between the panniers and spank them down to compress them.

Now get the mantie, that big square of canvas, and hold it up for the horse to see and smell so he knows it is nothing to fear, and then, moving in slow motion, fling it over the load.

"Easy, fella."

Tuck the corners under the bags so it looks neat and pretty. Good! Now all that remains is to lash it down with a diamond hitch. Put that end of the rope here. Throw the other end there, hook it under the belly and snug it up. Then, weave this part through that part and pull. Hmmm…maybe more zirconium than diamond, but not bad.

The next morning, the boss now gone, and after taking several hours fumbling around to put into practice what I had been taught, I mounted up and headed out on my first wilderness patrol, a ten-day hitch to clear trails, clean camps, and learn the country. I was riding to a place called Horse Heaven, astride one steed and leading the other two.

The glorious wild country was spread out before me like a diorama, the river a narrow band of glinting green beneath a line of jagged peaks that poked up into the clear blue sky. I was a wilderness ranger.

"Giddy up, Lucky! Let's go, Chance! C'mon, Cupcake! Hup, Hup!" I tentatively urged my ponies forward, hoping that they would comply.

Chapter 10
A Ballbuster for the Ages

Day 6

Not even a week since I embarked on this adventure and I'm hagged, about as tired as I've ever been, and now there's Wapumon Gorge to deal with. Wapumon is a terror to behold, an un-runnable class VI where the entire river hurtles through a narrow slot of dark rock in an apocalypse of white. Miss the take-out and you're done for—you and your pretty little boat, too.

The guide I got from Ric includes the coordinates for the portage trail around the gorge, which I had earlier entered into the GPS to ensure I wouldn't miss it. However, when I reach the spot where the instrument shows X and Y converging, where the trail is supposed to be, there is no trail—nothing I can see. Below, the river disappears into fury. No way am I poking any further down until locating the trail, so I beach the boat and head inland to find it. It can't be far.

I strike out with map, GPS, and compass, but despite these navigational aids, strikeout is what I do. Both map and GPS show a linear feature indicating what can only be the portage track, but when the blinking cursor, representing me on the GPS, merges with this feature, there is no trail, only jungle all around. The only explanation that makes sense is that I haven't yet gone far enough in, so I push on into a perplexity of green.

Having not anticipated a long walk, I foolishly set off clad only in a bathing suit and t-shirt with sandals for shoes. Fallen logs, leaning trees, and clumps of prickly plants force me over, under, or around. My legs are assaulted by thorny stems, poked, abraded, and bloodied by branches and bark. The air turns hot and muggy, bringing out black flies first, then mosquitoes, buzzing and biting.

The forest closes in, blotting out the sun. Wielding a heavy stick like a machete, I bash a path through thickets of branches and vines. My hair is snagged and my shirt torn as a rising panic competes with reason for authority of action. I try to quell it with deep breaths and positive thoughts. *Everything is fine*, I tell myself. *The trail has to be here somewhere.*

The sound of water booming through the gorge is a constant, unnerving, but strangely comforting too. With it, I know more or less where I am. I can't get lost; could navigate with ears alone.

Slashing through another green wall, I step out of the woods onto a shore that shouldn't be there. Somehow, I've gotten below Wapumon without crossing the trail. How can that be? Either I crossed without noticing, started out on the wrong side to begin with, or there is no trail. This is beginning to feel like an episode of *The Twilight Zone.*

Following the shore, I start back upstream, keeping to land where possible and wading through waist-deep water when impelled to the river by terrain features or fallen trees. In the water, my legs sink into cloying muck, and I must pull up forcefully to free them. Occasionally a sandal is sucked off a foot, and to retrieve it I shove an arm shoulder-deep into the ooze and grope for it like a blind predator seeking prey.

Finally, I strike a faint track. It looks more like a seldom-used game trail than the portage, but the portage it must be. I follow it up a rise and back into the woods away from the river, which doesn't seem right until it brings me to the bank of a cove. This is the take-out. Set well off the main current and concealed by willows, I couldn't see it from above.

To mark it, so as not to miss it when returning with the boat, I tie a bandanna as high as I can reach onto the branch of a tree. Then, circling the cove and wading an inlet, I gain a forested knob and arrive back at the river two hundred yards below the canoe. Seeing the boat brings a huge sense of relief; my imagination having tormented me with visions of it drifting away or wrecked by a marauding animal. That little vessel holds my life.

The ordeal to find the trail took almost two hours and, now that I've found it, I have to use it. The portage is three-quarters-of-a-mile long and hasn't been cleared in years. Several trees lie fallen across, blocking it. I chop out those I can't go over or under, save for two giant spruce too big to mess with. These compel a detour off-trail through heavy brush and deadfall.

It takes another four hours and seven miles of walking, back and forth, to get everything around. Gear not needed for camping is piled at the put-in, such as it is, with camp a hundred yards away on the only flat ground I can find; a site so littered with jack-strawed trees that I spend an hour chopping out a spot big enough for the tent.

At 7:00 p.m., too tired to eat and too buggy to remain outside, I crawl into the shelter hot, sticky, muddy, bloody, and itchy. My legs are aflame from myriad bites, cuts, scrapes, and scratches. The roar of the gorge is like a jet engine revving for take-off, but what has me completely unnerved is the put-in, or more accurately, the lack thereof.

There is no good place to get the canoe back on the river because the flow below the gorge surges in and out like an ocean tidepool, two feet up and down in fifteen-second cycles. Water gushes in to fill a small basin just beyond the reach of speeding current, and then rushes out to expose sharp, pointy rocks at the only possible spot to launch.

Attempting to reload here will continually bash the boat onto these rocks with every outgoing tide and potentially hull it. I don't have a clue what to do, and I'm too exhausted to think on it now. I'll come up with something. There is no choice but to think of something, necessity being the mother of invention, but right now, I just want my mother.

Chapter 11
Ramping It Up

Day 7

Wapumon Gorge is beyond noisy. Despite my utter exhaustion, the booming and crashing of the rapid, combined with worries about how to relaunch, denied all possibility of sleep. At 04:30, too stressed to even pretend to rest, I get up and start the stove for coffee. Normally, the pressurized fuel system generates a loud hiss, which now can't be heard above Wapumon's roar.

I am not humanizing today, being too nervous for that, so instead, once the coffee is ready, pour a cup and take it with me to the put-in to ponder the problem at hand. Watching the surge as it heaves and flows through the little basin makes my stomach churn. It is so violent. With a partner, launching would be easy.

One of us would simply stand thigh-deep in water, holding the canoe against current beyond the problematic rocks, while the other waded back and forth to load it. But how to do it alone? I sit, sip, think, and it occurs to me that maybe I could build a ramp.

Returning to the campsite, I ruminate on the ramp idea while folding, stuffing, and packing. The trick will be supporting the canoe above the rocks and upper limit of the surge for the several minutes needed to load it.

Back at the put-in, I pile everything on the bank, organized for quick placement into the boat. Then, taking the ax, I head to the woods and chop several rounds from small-diameter logs lying on the ground and drag them back, one by one. Each log is eight feet long, the length necessary to bridge the gap between the nearly vertical shore and the now-you-see-em, now-you-don't rocks.

I wedge the first piece into place and weight it with the partially loaded canoe so it can't be lifted and washed away when the water comes up. Then, one by one, add the rest, continually sliding the canoe down onto them until it is fully supported above the rocks. It's a precarious perch. With every incoming tide, water laps at the logs and wiggles them a bit. Clearly, the ramp won't last long.

I throw stuff in as fast as I can, but the structure is engulfed and destroyed before I finish. The canoe starts floating away amidst the jumble of logs. Fortunately, as a precaution, I had the painter looped around my wrist and pull the craft back in, but now, with no ramp, it falls hard onto the rocks with every outgoing flow, banging and grinding upon them.

In desperation, I fling in the last remaining items and then shove the boat out to deeper water while hanging off the stern. After hoisting myself aboard and drifting free below Wapumon, I feel the euphoria of a prisoner having effected a daring escape.

Before long I reach Wintego Rapids, a set of three in quick succession. The first, according to the guide, is a class III, the second a II, and the third a dangerous VI that must be portaged or else. Wintego I is a snap, but the second rapid presents no clear line. The guide recommends a right run, but left looks better at a glance, so I swing around and paddle hard for that side, find a chute, and drop below Wintego II without a bump.

Only then do I look up to see the river, all of it, tumbling into a ginormous hole a quarter-mile below. It's way bigger than anything on the Grand Canyon and would easily flip a raft and probably turn my canoe into kindling. Had I more thoroughly read the guide, I would have realized that a right run was necessary on Wintego II to reach the portage around this hole. Now I'm stuck on the wrong side of the river with no good way to get back over.

Shit!

What if I can't work my way down from here? I'll have to carry a mile back up and rerun Wintego II to get to where I should have been in the first place. But that option is almost beyond consideration. Even if managed in five trips, it would take eleven miles of back-breaking back-and-forth to complete. There has to be a better way. Beaching the boat, I start down, hoping to find one.

Hallelujah!

There is a way, not an easy one but easier than the alternative. I'll have to line and drag the canoe through a quarter-mile of shallows to gain a point of land jutting out from the left bank that terminates just above the hole. From there, a two-hundred-yard carry across the point will bring me to a sluice of current I can ride to skirt the hole and get below it. The mission now clear, I get cracking.

I live in dread of losing the GPS. At first, I wasn't even going to bring one, the use of electronic devices in wilderness being less than pure. However, the first white explorers didn't navigate on their own. They had something better than GPS: native guides to show the way. Lacking this advantage, I brought the GPS, planning to use it only in extremis, but extremis is a fairly common occurrence in this befuddling water world.

Without the GPS, the success of the expedition and safety of its member would be in constant and certain peril. Thus, I take great pains to keep it safe and secure, but now have a lapse.

While repacking the canoe after portaging the point, my attention is momentarily diverted by a flock of terns flying over. These elegant avians enthrall me, and I stop to watch them soar gracefully through the air, even after hearing something plop into the water at my feet. *What could that be*, I wonder, letting a beat or two pass before looking down to see.

The bailing bucket, into which I had placed the GPS for safekeeping, is half-sunk and floating away in fast current. I splash after it and snatch the bucket from the river by its bail. Fortunately, the GPS, which does not float, is still inside, but completely submerged. I know it's supposed to be waterproof, but what if it isn't?

What if I didn't have it properly sealed the last time I changed batteries? I open the back to inspect. The innards appear dry, but I lay it out anyway, exposed to sun and wind, and leave it for an hour to be on the safe side.

While waiting, I walk out to the end of the point where I can peer into the hole and chance to see three otters, a mother with two half-grown pups, waddling around it on the other side, using the portage trail. The locals always know the way to go.

The kits frolic behind, playing tag, their long bodies stretching and contracting like inchworms, but when Mom barks an order, they dutifully follow her into the river, and all three disappear beneath its surface.

Otters must have it good here, I think, with no people to worry about and plenty of fish to eat. No doubt, just the way they like it.

I could have caught a fish myself today. While lining the canoe through shallows, I spooked a walleye, about eighteen inches long. The fish tried to secret itself under some rocks but managed only to hide its head, leaving the rest of the body fully exposed.

I reached down and stroked it, thought about nabbing it for dinner, but decided to let it be. Everything deserves a bit of luck sometime. Maybe what goes around comes around. Maybe the walleye will pay it forward.

When time to test the GPS, I close the cover with trembling hands, utter an uncharacteristic prayer and press the power button. The thing blinks to life and I give thanks to every deity that comes to mind.

Chapter 12
Daydreams of Dying

Day 8

Prisoners are commonly banished to islands: Elba, Devil's, Robben, and Alcatraz, to name a few. Although my island has no name, I am a prisoner just the same.

Late last night I made it to a dot of rock in the middle of Pita Lake and camped. The wind howled all night, wracking the tent and making sleep all but impossible. By the time I get up, the weather shows no sign of let up. Looking at the lake through the open tent flaps reveals angry water too dangerous to tempt.

Oh, I might chance it if I really felt the urge to move, but I don't. Fatigue has dampened ambition. If ever I've been this tired, I'm too tired to remember when. Bone weary and sore, I can barely roll over in bed. Doing so requires little flop hops that turn me a few degrees at a time. But rolling over is easy compared to getting up from the ground.

That requires the use of some object, one I can crawl to, a boulder or the food barrel, upon which to hoist myself. Although just gaining one's feet is not generally an achievement worthy of fanfare, it seems so now.

Ric did explain that expedition solo paddling was like running a daily marathon. I didn't believe him. Even now, after a week of such marathons, I still don't think it quite equates, but neither is it far off the mark. I've met the goal of averaging fifteen miles a day, almost all on lakes with no current to help, and more often than not into headwinds, but it's been a struggle.

I don't lily-poke when I paddle but go at it hard, yet despite these efforts have averaged only two-and-a-half miles per hour on flat water. So far, I've traveled a hundred miles, not a blistering pace perhaps but respectable under the circumstances. If able to maintain it, I'll make Hudson Bay in seven more weeks.

The tent shudders in blasts of wind. Needing to better secure it, I crawl out to pound in more stakes and guy the tent to them, then crawl back in, tired from the effort. Gravity presses on me like an X-ray apron. I rest, a tranquilized sloth in torpor, in stupor, in trance.

Around noon I get up and resume a horizontal position outside. The wind has only intensified. Out on the lake, powerful gusts rip the froth from whitecaps and send them flying. It doesn't bode well for getting off the island today. *Good!* I'll use the weather as an excuse to rest.

I lay lump-like on my pad until guilt overcomes inaction and atone by washing clothes, hanging them on a length of parachute cord to dry. While the clothes snap and flag in wind, I go through the food box, taking inventory of its contents.

It's a pleasant diversion, organizing everything by taxonomic classification: the dried fruit group to one side, the meat phylum to another, pasta consolidated with grains—it all gets neatly arranged. I find handling the food comforting. Starvation seems the least of my worries.

Next, I bring my journal up to date. I'm keeping one with the thought of writing a book about this trip, should I survive it, or, as a record of events preceding my demise if it comes to that.

Realizing the journal really could chronicle my last days has me striving for profundities and lyrical prose I hope will compare favorably with the likes of Robert Falcon Scott or Everett Ruess, explorers bold who ventured forth into wild country but not back, leaving journals to lend clues as to the circumstances that befell them.

A daydream reels through my brain, flickering like frames from a silent film. *Action!* The camera pans across bleak tundra, a light snow falling. Into this scene, in mid-distance, an object appears—indeterminate, out of focus. The camera moves past it, then stops, swings back, and zooms in to reveal a tent, faded, tattered, and torn.

Drawing in, we hear footsteps crunching snow and sounds of labored breathing. Directly above the tent now, the interior is glimpsed through rents in fabric. Something is inside, lumpy and perfectly still. A hand, blue with frost, is stretched out as if reaching for a sheaf of papers that flutter in eddies of breeze as an unseen narrator begins to read.

Words, poignant, lovely, and achingly sad weave a tale of hope and struggle, but with no hint of regret. Snowflakes tic upon the pages, dissolving the ink where they land into runnels of blue that course down the sheets like tears. The camera pulls back, the tent becoming smaller and smaller until it vanishes into vastness. The wind wails, accompanied by the sound of someone, somewhere, softly crying. *Fade to black…and cut!*

Chapter 13
The Absence of Suffering

Day 9

Yesterday's rest did me good—mind, body, and soul. This morning I even get to my feet without need of rock or barrel. However, in truth, the triumph is only managed with the liberal application of *geezer noises*—groans and moans uttered in protest of motion.

Eager to get back on the water and make up for lost time, I truncate humanizing and launch early. Today is much nicer than yesterday, with high cirrus filtering the sun and a warm breeze puffing.

The better, or bitter news—depending on your point of view—is that there are no portages today; better for making progress, but bitter since the rapids and falls that once graced this reach of river were inundated in 1930 with the completion of Island Falls Dam. One of the falls had a sixty-foot drop, but a mine needed electricity, so it thunders no more.

The forests around Pita Lake, from its shoreline to distant hills, were burned in a stand-replacing fire some years back, so instead of dark spruce, the land is colored in the soft hues of seral green, alder and birch, species that return first after fire.

There is nary a conifer in sight, save for the blackened spears of once-towering trees poking up through the monochromatic canopy here and there. Certainly, tiny spruce seedlings gather on the forest floor beneath their leafy cousins in time to reclaim dominion, until their turn to burn, subject as are all things to the vagaries of some terrestrial tide.

The next lake is Pikoo. The fire that torched Pita didn't make it here, and the land is a mottled mosaic of manifold greens, a climax forest pleasing to behold. The boat moves swiftly through this sylvan splendor, pushed by wind, aided by current, and abetted with robust strokes of my paddle.

I am closing in on the village of Sandy Bay, as evidenced by the presence of motorboats. Most are only heard and unseen, but a few show as mere motes, flitting across the horizon like floaters in your eye, and a couple come within a few hundred yards, close enough that I can make out the orbs of heads clustered within.

Apparently, no one spots me for, surely, they would stop. The boats recede and fade away, but their droning lingers, an irritant that hangs in the air long after they have vanished from view.

I opt to stop early to maintain some distance from humanity for one more day and start seeking a campsite by mid-afternoon. Three hours later, I still haven't found one, every possibility proving too buggy, swampy, brushy, or steep. Finally, at 7:00, I settle for a spot that is merely buggy and brushy.

Before retiring, I scan the skies, trying to intuit the weather. Deciding there is no threat of rain, I forego attaching the fly since it is cooler and more pleasant without it. That weather prognostication is not my forte is made evident in the middle of the night by a gentle tapping atop the tent that soon becomes an insistent rapping as rain pours down.

I am out in an instant to get the fly on before everything is soaked inside. The mosquitoes, lying in wait, could not be more pleased. They love naked people. I swat and shake, buckle and stake, and then dive back under cover, bitten and wet. About thirty of the insects get in with me.

These must be hunted down and dispatched before a return to sleep is possible, but just when you think you've got them all, one more is sure to make her presence known with an irritating whine dopplering around your head. Finally, I surrender to the laws of diminishing returns and leave an arm out to sate and quiet the last of them. A few more bites won't make a bit of difference.

Overall, the bugs haven't been bad thus far, and I don't regret leaving the bug shelter behind, loathe as I was to do it, having suffered terrors untold from winged bloodsuckers the first time I ventured this far north.

That trip was to the barren lands of Nunavut on a river called the Thelon. Marianne and I picked the Thelon because it flows through a wildlife sanctuary occupied by several species of Arctic megafauna. Indeed, we saw bears, wolves, foxes, muskox, caribou, and even a wolverine.

However, the Thelon also has a reputation for another animal, one you don't want to see: a tiny fly known as *white sox*. Tales of their depredations are the stuff of legend.

After the plane dropped us off and flew away, we stood huddled together, girded in bug clothes like beekeepers, anxiously awaiting the insect onslaught. But, to our happy surprise, none showed, not one. After a time, I disrobed and giddily ran around without a stitch, flaunting my flesh to taunt them, fully convinced that the horrific accounts relayed to us about white sox were just another northern myth, a tale embellished to scare tourists.

That first week on the river remained bugless. We didn't attribute this good fortune to the strong winds that were a constant during that time. Bugs weren't the curse, wind was, and we hoped every day that it would cease. On the day it did, we were portaging a two-mile section of whitewater. I carried the boat on my shoulders and Marianne followed, lugging a dry bag.

The canoe was hard to control in the strong gusts that spun it like a weathervane, so when the wind suddenly stopped, I was thankful, but only for an instant because in that same instant, white sox began emerging from the ground. First, they came in pairs, then in gangs, and ultimately in clouds that engulfed us.

Marianne, in the midst of them, appeared to be out of focus, fuzzy, and furred at the edges, and my exposed neck soon took on the look of raw burger. The bugs were in our eyes, ears, mouths, and noses. There was no orifice sacred. They crawled through our hair and got into our clothes through any opening, no matter how small—cuffs, collars, even buttonholes—and commenced tearing off tiny chunks of flesh with their razor-sharp mouth parts.

We dropped the loads and ran, sprinting for camp, a mile back, where we had left the bug hats and jackets. After putting them on, we hosed each other down with DEET, but to no avail. I started a smudge fire with wet wood, which also failed to blunt the attack.

With no other means of escape, we set up the tent and got in. In the few seconds the doors were unzipped for us to enter, hundreds of white sox got in too and hundreds more emerged from our clothes as we disrobed. Peeled down to my briefs, I was shocked to see blood stippling them in the worst of all possible places. Afraid to look, but having no choice, I slipped the underwear off and watched in horror as squadrons of flies flew up from my nether lands.

For the next hour, Marianne and I squished them one by one, gleefully rolling each between a finger and the tent wall until they made a satisfying little pop, each murder marked by a tiny smear of blood left streaked upon the fabric; their blood comingled with ours. Afterward, we cowered in shock and fear while the bugs pounded on the tent like rain, desperately seeking a way in.

The assault continued unabated for the next ten days, a time when we viewed the world only through a veil of mesh. Our bug clothes were to us as space suits to astronauts: a tear sure to result in agonizing death. We learned to love the smell of DEET. We learned to poop no later than 3:00 a.m. when the white sox were least active.

I peed while turning in circles and gallantly flapped a towel for Marianne when she had to go. It got so bad that even I, a devout non-believer, resorted to prayer, praying with fervor unfeigned to any deity willing to help, beseeching Him, Her, or It to send a wind that would force the bugs to ground.

Day after day, my prayers went unanswered, and I was beginning to doubt their efficacy, until the blessed day came when they actually worked, bringing back the wind to deliver us from bug hell.

The experience taught me a valuable lesson, one that has served me well ever since. Sometime all that it takes to be perfectly content is the absence of suffering. That's it. One needs nothing more.

Chapter 14
Sandy Bay

Day 10

Mosquitoes and rain conspire to create a disincentive to action. Instead of springing up to ready for departure, I listen to the buzz and drop, cocooned in the tent, lingering and malingering well past my usual rise-and-shine time. There is no cause to hurry. I am only going to Sandy Bay, and Sandy Bay is just ten miles away. I can cover that in four hours of easy paddling. Once there, I plan to indulge myself, get a meal at the best eatery in town and maybe even splurge on a night in a hotel. Although I've only been gone ten days, it's been hard traveling and I can use a bit of pampering.

It's a breeze paddling without one, and I cruise easily along Sokatisewin's mirrored surface. A light drizzle starts to fall, so to keep my shirt dry, I take it off and paddle bare chested, feeling strong and manly, enjoying the slight shock of cool drops against my skin.

Soon, signs of human occupancy appear, a few cabins here and there, a cell tower in the distance, then power lines and a low, linear feature spanning this river-lake that can only be Island Falls Dam.

The write-up gives a location for the portage around the dam as beginning from a small cove just to its north. I arrive at the spot, beach the boat, and go ashore, but there is no obvious sign of a trail. Evidently the portage isn't used much. I grid back and forth through the low vegetation until I find it.

Once everything is carried around, I take a dip to make myself presentable for the big city—but only after first peering into the depths looking for leeches. After a recent swim, I discovered a wet leaf stuck on a toe that wasn't a leaf but a leech. That was a new bloodsucking experience for me, and one I hope not to repeat.

For some reason, I've been imagining Sandy Bay as an upscale resort community catering to wealthy sport fishermen, but my first glimpse of the place disabuses me of that. It is immediately clear that Sandy Bay is no resort, upscale or otherwise, but a worn and run-down rez town. At the marina, several derelict docks jut haphazardly into the river, canted and barely afloat.

Fuel drums and coils of rusting cable lay abandoned along mudflats littered with plastic and chunks of Styrofoam. Three guys in a boat hunkered around an outboard engine glance up at me as I pass. Their expressions are not friendly, but four handsome kids, a girl and three boys, none older than ten, make a fine welcoming committee. They are playing on the dock where I stop and crowd around after I step out of the boat, elbowing for position.

"Where you going?" they eagerly ask.

"What's that?" one wants to know, pointing to the compass around my neck.

"And that?" asks another, indicating the binoculars, before I can answer the first.

They know binoculars are something for looking through, but don't know the name and have never tried a pair.

"Here, take a look," I say, handing them over.

"Oh!" they are amazed. "How big they make everything look!"

Next, I demonstrate the compass.

"Do you know what this does?" I ask, pointing to the arrow. "Watch. When I turn the compass in a circle, the arrow always points the same way. Do you know what direction that is?"

One does.

"Snorth!" he says.

These charmers offer to watch the canoe while I go to town, so I leave it in their charge and enter Sandy Bay.

First stop, the Northern Store to replenish supplies of cheese, peanut butter, and fresh fruit, and to buy some beer. From outside, the building looks more like a prison than a business. Iron bars cover the doors and every window. Inside the store is small and not particularly well stocked. Still, I find everything I'm looking for, except the beer.

When the clerk rings me up, a small block of cheese, one orange, two apples, and a quart of orange juice comes to $17. I hand her a U.S. $20. She looks at it puzzled.

"We can't accept this," she says.

"It's not German," I tell her, but she's unconvinced so takes it back to the boss, who knows about greenbacks and tells her it's okay.

An earnest young man bags my groceries, and I ask him if I can buy beer or liquor somewhere.

"Not legally," he says, giving me a conspiratorial grin.

It didn't occur to me that Sandy Bay is a dry town, and one would never have guessed it by walking through. Many residents appear drunk, and it is scarcely past noon. The locals are not overly friendly, but some wave shyly or call out greetings from perches on porches of the government pre-fabs lining the street. One young man, perhaps twenty, whose ambulation is seriously compromised, careens down a flight of stairs from an elevated deck.

Puppet-like with limbs akimbo, he slides to an unsteady stop just inches from me. His face is so close to mine it is indistinct and his eyes morph into one. The kid sports a do-rag and blue jeans low on his hips, nothing more. A skein of spittle burbles from one corner of his mouth that elongates into a frothy wattle as we talk. "HELLO," he says, aggressively friendly, shouting the word.

"Hello," I say, backing up a bit until he's no longer a cyclops. The young man sways like seaweed in tidewater.

"Whereyagon?" he asks.

"Hudson Bay," I say.

"Wanna drink?"

"No, thanks. I don't drink," I lie. I hate drinking with drunks. "Do you know you're foaming at the mouth?" I waggle a finger at my own chin to indicate the spot.

"Ice cream," he says, as if that explains anything. "Iz my birfday," he says. "Iz evybuddy's birfday." I telegraph incomprehension. "CANADA DAY!" he exclaims. "Tomorrow is Canada Day!"

I'm not entirely clear on Canada Day, but know it's their Fourth of July, just three days sooner. I wish him a happy birthday and retreat, looking to find the hotel.

The roads of Sandy Bay are unpaved. Noisy pick-ups—rusty, dented heaps—ply the streets, churning up clouds of dust as they go. Scrawny dogs are everywhere, either running loose or chained on anemic lawns littered with pee stains and shit. The canines bark, snarl, or whine, either ferocious or furtive, as I pass.

When I do find the hotel, it turns out to be a B&B in a doublewide trailer with tires on the roof and a weather-worn porch added on that looks like it was eyeballed by a blind carpenter. Visions of pampering vanish. I keep walking, this time looking for the office of the Royal Canadian Mounted Police.

The reason for seeking the RCMP is to check in. If I do disappear, the Mounties will know I at least made it this far. When I find their station, it looks like a miniature fort with small windows recessed into thick concrete walls. The doors are locked, but I can see someone inside, a First Nations woman in civvies.

She shakes her head, indicating I can't come in, and backs away. I assume she keeps an eye on the place when the Dudleys are on their appointed rounds, with strict orders not to let anyone in. Stymied, I start back for the boat, hoping the kids haven't stripped it. Near the marina, I meet a friendly gentleman named Robert. He's sober, curious, polite, and pleasant.

Robert tells me about an island not far below that would make a good place to camp for the night, adding, "A couple of girls stayed there four nights ago. Pretty good looking, too."

When I get back to the boat, the kids are still on duty and everything is just as I left it. Great kids! In a fit of largess, I decide to reward them and hand the little girl a *toonie*, a Canadian two-dollar coin. "Here," I say, "go buy yourselves some ice cream." They all look down at the coin in her hand, then up at me, crestfallen.

"How many ice creams will this buy?" one asks.

"That should be enough for all of you," I respond cheerily, without really considering the question, and they walk off toward the Northern Store with heads hung low.

My egregious parsimony did not occur to me until later that evening when camped on Robert's island. *What was I thinking?* Two dollars doesn't buy squat up here. I should have given them a ten or twenty at least. The little darlings would be lucky to procure one ice cream from my benefaction, and realizing it makes me feel mean and ashamed.

I imagine those sweet children lined up, one ice cream between them, each taking a little lick and passing it on. I am generous by nature, and don't cotton to cheap people, which only increases my sense of mortification. I can only conclude that I'm too tired for rational thought.

I stay up late. There are no bugs and a sunset too glorious to abandon. Streaks of pink and orange shoot across the sky in every direction, as if exploded from a tropical fruit. Clearly, I am getting pampered after all.

Chapter 15
Can't-A-Da Day

Day 11

Well, it may be Canada Day for some, but for me it's more like Can't-a-da Day.

I am not in a good mood. After a restive night, I awake with a crisis of confidence, worried I've taken on too much, wondering if I can complete this trip as planned. My body is so thrashed, fatigue manifest in every moment and movement.

My battery is run down, my spring has sprung, and I am numbed with an abiding lassitude that takes great force of will to overcome. Sometimes, while holding a cup of coffee, I find it hard to muster the energy to lift it to my lips. My vocalizations are pretty much confined to "ugh," or other geezer utterance emitted in protest of motion.

The days are a daze, blurred and indistinct, one from another, and marked by hours of dogged, zombie-like paddling. Often, in evenings, I nod off before making it to the tent, an unread book splayed open on my lap.

This morning, with nearly 700 miles and God knows how many more portages ahead, I am left to seriously wonder whether I can see this through and so begin to consider options. I can:

1) Paddle to Pukatawagan, the next town down, about four days away, and call it quits. There are no roads in or out of Pukatawagan, but there is a weekly train I could ride to Winnipeg.

2) Proceed another 150 miles past Pukatawagan to Leaf Rapids, a village connected by road to Thompson, Manitoba, where again I could catch a train for Winnipeg. I'd probably have to abandon the canoe in order

to hitchhike the 130 miles from Leaf to Thompson, but by then I'd likely be glad to be rid of it.

3) Continue to Hudson Bay but keep to the Churchill River instead of portaging to the Seal.

4) Hire a floatplane in Leaf Rapids to fly me over the divide to the Seal River.

5) Suck it up and stay the course.

I spend the day pondering these possibilities while paddling. The first two options I dismiss out of hand. I'm not going to quit. Once you start quitting there could be no end to it, so it's Hudson Bay or bust.

Option three, keeping to the Churchill, is worth a hard look. It would shorten the trip by a hundred miles and negate the mother of all portages. The distance between the Churchill and Seal Rivers, judging from the maps, is eighteen miles.

I'd have to track up the Barrington River, then up small tributaries; portage, paddle, and pole through thickets, ponds, and mosquito-infested swamps to gain the divide; and then do more of the same down the other side. The longest single carry looks to be two miles. If managed in six trips, a two-mile portage becomes twenty-two miles. Twenty-two miles!

When a three-hundred-yard carry leaves me pooled like melted butter, what might a two-miler do? And how long would it take to complete? A week? More? If sticking to the Seal, I need to reach Hudson Bay by August 15th or Jack Batstone, the guy I've arranged with to pick me up in his small boat and transport me to Churchill, won't come. After that date, autumnal storms typically make the bay too treacherous for travel.

Option five, the floatplane alternative, would be cheating, so I drop it from further consideration, leaving number six: the original plan. I keep this as an option because I hate deviating from original plans.

So, my choices are condensed from five to two, either staying the course or staying on the Churchill. One problem with the latter is that I don't have maps for the lower river or know anything about it. I don't know how many rapids there are, their location, or difficulty. Ditto for portages.

I don't know if the lower Churchill is mostly river or lake. No idea. I do know that the two young women ahead of me are going that way, so it must be doable. Hopefully, if I decide on the Churchill, I'll be able get maps and find out what I need to know in Leaf Rapids.

Distracted by these musings, I make sixteen miles today, hardly realizing it. No matter how tired I am, once I get in the boat, strength and energy return. It occurs to me that I am like a seal, clumsy on land but nimble afloat.

I also had the advantage of a bit of moving water today, and no portages, which really helps. Tomorrow will be business as usual with another gigantic lake to deal with, Loon Lake this time. On it, I'll cross from Saskatchewan into Manitoba.

Chapter 16
Wilderness-Ish

The life of a wilderness ranger is fabulous, providing one can manage without plumbing, be continually outside in all kinds of weather, work like a beast, smell like a horse, and tolerate long periods of being alone. That's me in a nutshell. I liked the job so much that I often went backpacking on my days off, a busman's holiday.

However, the calling does have its drawbacks. Chief among them is that it does not constitute a career. There is no wilderness ranger retirement, health care, or future other than a gimpy and impoverished old age. After five seasons, these hard truths became evident and it dawned on me that I could not do this kind of work forever.

Here I was, thirty-three, with no permanent job, few prospects for finding one, and a single-minded ambition for a career managing wilderness. It seemed a pipe dream, but I decided to pursue it anyway, this time in Montana. Montana had been my state of mind ever since Wisdom, and not a day passed in the intervening years that I didn't yearn to return.

Whether by chance or portent, my homecoming coincided with April Fool's Day. The calendar alleged it was spring, but it didn't seem so with all the snow still blanketing the streets of Bozeman. Although delighting Otter, my Siberian husky, the cold and snow left me feeling lost, alone, and vulnerable. I parked my truck on the campus of Montana State University, secreted behind the football stadium, and slept in the back, under a shell, cozied up to Otter for warmth and emotional support.

The next morning, I paid a visit to the Gallatin Forest Supervisor's Office, a five-story building that passes for a skyscraper in downtown Bozeman. I was hoping for a lead on a job. With only $200 to my name, I needed to find one fast. The forest's recreation officer was wonderfully helpful.

"There are a couple of possibilities," she said.

One was with the Montana Department of Fish, Wildlife, and Parks (FWP) as a seasonal ranger on a river in west-central Montana, the Smith, and the other with the Bureau of Land Management (BLM), as river/wilderness ranger for the agency's first designated Wilderness Area, Bear Trap Canyon, in the southwestern part of the state.

The news about the BLM job had me over the moon. I'd been trying for years to land a permanent position doing the only thing I wanted to do, but there were few openings for these jobs in the best of times and now, with Ronald Reagan downsizing government, there were essentially none. But suddenly, here was a chance. I was eminently qualified too, except for the river ranger part, but that was remedied when FWP hired me for the Smith.

The next two months, while patrolling the Smith River by canoe and raft, I fretted over the Bear Trap job, anxious for news. BLM was apparently in no hurry to fill it. I made a pest of myself, continually checking in to ask when the hire would be made and chatting up the official who would make it.

When the call finally came offering me the position, I had to be scraped off the ceiling. After a decade of itinerance, I could finally settle down. No more couch surfing, bunking in cabins, truck beds, tepees, and tents. I could unpack my books and knick-knacks from cardboard boxes and put them on shelves, eat off crockery instead of aluminum, build Otter a doghouse, and maybe even get a cat. I would have a home.

The Bear Trap suited me. The office had a ceiling open to sky, granite walls, and plenty of running water—class III and IV. Once or twice a week I floated the nine-mile stretch of canyon in the government raft.

Otter always came along, sometimes in the boat, but usually preferring to follow from shore, Siberians not being a water breed. It was a happy time, and I figured to do it 'til doomsday, but three years later, when a recreation position opened with the Forest Service in Ennis, offering a promotion and greater responsibility, I traded in BLM's neoprene for Forest Service green.

For the next twenty-four years, until the day I retired, I managed Recreation and Wilderness for the Madison Ranger District of the Beaverhead-Deerlodge National Forest. An administrator now, I spent more time in the office than I cared to, doing things managers do, like budgeting, personnel, and planning.

As to planning, the Forest Service does an inordinate amount. Although I never planned to be a planner, it seems everyone in the agency is eventually sucked into it.

I was not a fan, seeing much of the planning we were required to do as a waste of time, and worse, taking time from more important things, like being in the field clearing trails, spraying weeds, patrolling, and otherwise assisting the public in ways that mattered.

Of course, some level of planning is necessary, but the Forest Service has gone overboard, diverting vast sums from fieldwork to paperwork until funding fell like virga rain, evaporating before ever hitting the ground. Instead it was used for vision statements, mission statements, white papers, and lists of goals and objectives that filled bulging binders soon marooned on backroom bookshelves and forgotten.

Much of the planning involved the Lee Metcalf Wilderness, 250,000 acres administered between two National Forests and the BLM. Working with a team of specialists, we drew lines on maps like urban planners, dividing the area into zones—pristine, backcountry, and transitional—and established standards and objectives for each.

We inventoried, monitored, measured, quantified, and yammered on in never-ending meetings about threats and issues that had no solution, at least none practical, affordable, or palatable. The academic nature of these discussions convinced me that a single wilderness ranger in the field was a far better investment for the U.S. taxpayer than a room full of well-paid planners.

Wilderness planning has limits. You can plan for a high level of air quality, but how do you prevent polluted air from drifting over? And acid rain won't be stopped by a standard. Social impacts are likewise difficult to address. Wilderness is ideally managed to provide *opportunities for solitude,* but what does that mean?

How many people can enjoy solitude together, and how many are too many? Social scientists may provide a number, but what does management do once that number is exceeded? The only tool that comes to mind is a permit system to restrict the number of people allowed within wilderness at any one time, but permit systems are prohibitively expensive, to say nothing of unpopular, and will never be implemented for an area like the Lee Metcalf when budgets aren't even adequate to maintain trails.

People are the problem. There are simply too many of us, and the pressures we exert on wildlands constantly diminish them. Wilderness planning can mitigate impacts to some extent, but only family planning will solve them. Take Bear Trap Canyon, for instance. This unit of the Lee Metcalf is a measly 6,000 acres, just nine miles long and only a mile-and-a-half wide where it narrows.

The trailhead is a scant thirty-minute drive from Bozeman, now the fastest growing community of its size in the country and bursting with Patagonia-clad outdoor enthusiasts. The first three miles up the trail follows an old Jeep road, and as you walk it, you'll pass plenty of fishermen angling for trout native to Europe and smile pleasantly at the multi-colored multitudes hiking with their hounds.

You'll wave to boaters floating in rafts and bright plastic kayaks on a river released from an upstream dam. And, if you know what you're looking at, that pretty purple flower is knapweed, a nasty invader from the steppes of Russia, and like the tsars, intent on empire.

Cross Bear Trap Creek, if you dare, atop a slippery log, to gain the next rise, and you will be rewarded with a magnificent view of the inner canyon, the river flowing beneath swarded hills and dark gray cliffs; but looking up you'll see something else: cell phone towers piked to the sky along a distant ridge. Check your phone. Service is guaranteed.

The Forest Service portions of the Lee Metcalf are similarly compromised. Established in three non-contiguous sections to allow for a snowmobile trail from West Yellowstone to Big Sky and to reserve the most productive timber lands for logging, the area is ringed by highways, bordered by clearcuts, and riven with resorts, golf courses, and million-dollar mansions.

From the summit of Cedar Mountain, in the heart of the area, Ennis can be seen in one direction and, in the other, linear striations of ski runs cut through the forest of an exclusive gated community for the ultra-rich. On calm summer nights, the strains of rock and roll can be heard wafting up from Scissorbill's Saloon, the happening spot in Big Sky.

And, in winter, supercharged snowmobiles roar up improbably steep slopes right to the wilderness boundary, and sometimes, if the lure of powder proves too great, beyond it. Several times each day, jets ply the wilderness skies coming and going from Bozeman's Gallatin Field, and in summer other aircraft may pass over, perhaps with firefighters who jump from planes to douse the flames of wildfires essential for ecosystem health but which can't be allowed to burn due to the proximity of human development.

Or helicopters, landing to rescue someone fallen from a horse, to monitor wolves, or dump non-native fish into high mountain lakes so anglers have something to catch. Meanwhile, back on the ground, the masses from the ever-expanding metropolis of Boz-Angeles troop in from every portal, seeking solace and solitude, the elusive wilderness experience, only to meet others, like themselves, coming the other way, seeking same.

Managers will struggle on, planning and doing what can be done in the attempt to keep wilderness wild, but sadly, wilderness-ish is about the best they can do.

Chapter 17
Death and Progress

Day 12

Rain comes at 3:57 a.m., the drops hitting my face, waking me. Once again, I hadn't bothered with the fly so must hurry out to attach it. It's a silly game I play, foregoing the fly unless rain is falling or imminent by the time I retire.

For some reason, the wager amuses me. There's a thrill to it. If I win, that is, if no rain falls, I feel smug in correctly intuiting the weather. If I lose, I get a chuckle at my folly. Simple pleasures for simple minds.

At 4:03, the fly now on, I reenter the tent, cold and wet, and snuggle into the folds of my sleeping bag as the storm continues to build. Cozy in these confines, I luxuriate for an hour until the squall has passed and then crawl out to begin the day. It starts with the need to negotiate another big lake, Loon Lake, the largest so far.

I do not feel comfortable paddling the waters of these gigantic lakes. Their immensity gives me a sense of my own insignificance and I feel myself in fate's crosshairs, a tenuous flame that could be easily and instantly snuffed. Nothing here cares what befalls me.

Fortunately, it's a nice day and the colors are vibrant; the lake mirroring sky and the surrounding land jammed with trees pulsing green. I start early, to take advantage of the calm, but keep the pedal to the paddle and stay close to land where I can in case the wind does come up, as it is wont to do. An hour after starting, something incongruous atop the high point of an island catches my eye: something tall and white.

When close enough, I see that it's a cross, the religious variety, constructed of dimensional lumber and painted white. I get out to investigate. The base is supported by a substantial stone cairn, the soils here being too shallow to otherwise hold it up. A canoe paddle is attached to the cross by wire.

Obviously, this is a monument erected to someone who died nearby, evidently someone in a canoe, or more accurately, someone who was in a canoe, but then wasn't. Faded and forlorn, it's a sad little shrine. I look for a name, but if there ever was one, it has weathered to obscurity.

Red petals, fallen from plastic roses, litter the ground below. I return to my canoe, sad about the unnamed paddler and wondering what happened. If there's a moral to the story, it is this: big lake boaters beware.

As if another such reminder was needed, I come upon a second shrine two miles further on. This one is a mural painted on plywood about the size of a trailhead bulletin board. The artwork is pretty good. It depicts Jesus hovering above a rapid with arms outstretched, palms up in that benevolent way of His, and eyes that express great sorrow.

Across the bottom of the board, written in a neat hand, the mural reads, 'In memory of Ovide Bear and Marcel Daniels who drowned in Sisipuk Rapids, August 16, 1964.'

From the birthdates, I calculate that Mr. Bear was twenty-six and Mr. Daniels thirty-six at the time of their demise. This was the year I turned twelve. Even more notable, 1964 was the year the Beatles first came to America.

Forty-eight years had passed, during which my life had been a magical mystery tour, full of adventure, meaning, joy, love and fun, all the while Messrs. Bear and Daniels had no life at all, having drowned in a rapid I would soon run.

Several offerings lay on the ground around the mural: coins, drawstring pouches of tobacco, advent candles, and sprays of plastic flowers. I feel compelled to leave something too, as a token of respect, but also to curry favor with the fates.

I'll run Sisipuk tomorrow and don't want a monument put up to me. I rifle my pockets, looking for something appropriate, and settle on a Bic lighter. It seems a practical gift. Marcel and Ovide have candles, cigarettes, and incense, but nothing to light them with.

Departing this shrine and its spirits, I paddle on, overcome by a sense of melancholia from the encounters with the three ill-fated boaters, but also imbued with appreciation to be still among the living, thankful for everything I see and feel, thankful even for my aches.

Somehow, despite a commitment to observation, I pass from Saskatchewan to Manitoba without noticing. Supposedly a swath of clearcut marks the boundary, but if there is one, I don't see it and only know I'm in Manitoba from the GPS, the blinking cursor showing my location now on that side of the line. Manitoba doesn't look any different from Saskatchewan.

Still, it is gratifying to know I've passed from one province into another. Crossing borders means something; it means progress.

Chapter 18
A Dull Boy

Day 13

Something outside, moving just beyond the ripstop, pokes at my subconscious, willing me to wake—an animal of some sort. I resist acknowledging it until a loud screech brings me fully alert with a start. Something really is out there.

BEAR! That's always the first thing one thinks of, but this isn't a bear. It is some kind of scampery critter, and bears don't scamper. Bears don't screech either, so the next screech is alarming and calming both. *But, what can it be?* I wonder.

Again, I hadn't bothered with the fly and so am able to see out through the tent's mesh door flaps. Two opaque shapes, about the size of cats, dart in and out of shadow. I unzip the door and poke my head out to see…rabbits? Maybe, judging by how they spring straight into the air, but there are no telltale ears. They're engaged in a spirited game of grab-ass, pursuing and pouncing, rolling and bouncing in crazy antics.

Love or war, it's hard to say. Otters? They have long, slinky bodies that twist and turn as they roll and wrestle, but these don't seem fat enough in the middle. As my eyes adjust to the low light, one disengages from the other and jumps from a rock into the river and swims away, looking very much at home.

Then it dawns on me. They are mink! It seems too late in the year for mating, so it must be either a territorial brawl or young ones at play. Whatever, its first-rate entertainment and well worth being woken up to see.

When I awake for real a few hours later, the day is already oppressive with heat. There is no wind and the lake's surface reflects a gleaming sun—two suns really: one ascending into sky and the other falling into forest. So perfectly are these worlds reproduced upon the water that, once launched, I float as if suspended between them.

It is starkly silent, the only sound being the cadenced dip of paddle and hiss of water passing beneath the hull. I begin to really dig in, reveling in the work, feeling the boat surge ahead with every laid-on stroke. My breaths come fast and full, rhythmic as a metronome keeping time to the tempo of propulsion.

Small waves peel back from the bow and a silver wake vees out behind as the canoe slips between converging shores toward Loon Lake's end. Then a new sound inserts itself—the crash of water falling onto rock. Sisipuk!

The guide directs that this rapid be portaged and I fully intend to comply, especially considering the fates of Messrs. Daniels and Bear, but when Sisipuk comes into view, I see no reason not to run it. The line looks easy. Still, to be on the safe side, I beach the boat and walk down to scout. Studying the rapid from shore, it's hard to understand why anyone would drown here or why this is a mandatory portage. The setup isn't complex, and only one move is required to avoid trouble.

Still, when back in the canoe, readying to go, I'm nervous. People died here. I take several deep breaths for calm and courage and then exit the eddy on an upstream ferry, stroking hard against strong current. In mid-channel, still well above the drop, I stop paddling and allow the boat to spin around until it points directly down.

A sizable haystack, caused from water rolling over what must be a substantial boulder on the bottom, marks the start of the run. This is both landmark and target. The plan is to smack it sideways and bounce off onto current that will carry me clear of rocks below. It's a kayak move I've used countless times, and in this instance, it works with the canoe too. Apparently, leaving the Bic for Ovide and Marcel did the trick.

In 2019, I was able to track down Marcel Daniels' widow, who was pregnant with their child at the time of his death. She was also Ovide Bear's cousin. Nineteen hundred and sixty-four, she told me, was an exceptionally high-water year.

The two men were enroute to Pukatawagan from Sandy Bay, traveling in a small motor launch to attend a ceremonial rite. They never made it and were later found drowned below Sisipuk Rapid. Their boat had capsized. Nothing more is known as to the circumstances that befell them.

Beyond the rapid, the river turns back to lake, this one speckled with myriad small islands. Paddling through this archipelago feels safe, as I am never far from land. Enjoying the sense of security and relieved to have the rapid behind, I proceed in peace until a motor intrudes—the *bata-bata* of an approaching helicopter.

After a hard look, I see it, a dark speck growing bigger as it nears. The machine is vectoring toward a column of smoke rising from the forest a half-mile away that I just now notice. Through gaps between islands, I watch as a tree bursts to flame, tongues of fire rapidly scaling its branches. The helicopter has dropped from view, but I hear it hovering and then see three small yellow-clad figures rushing toward the tree.

Soon another sound inserts itself, one I am familiar with from my firefighting days, the cavitating whine of a Mark III pump. Almost immediately, jets of spray arc high onto the burning boughs, turning black smoke to white steam in an instant. Water is all you need to fight fire, and there is plenty of that in this country.

Soon, the pump sputters to a stop, and shortly thereafter the helicopter powers up and flies away, leaving me alone in a silence that now feels absurd.

Mid-afternoon, I opt to stop early. Initially, my plan was to treat each day as a workday and paddle eight hours, at least, but after attempting this for the better part of two weeks, I've given up. My body demands less work and more rest, and I have little choice but to obey. The new plan is: once I get in fifteen miles, I can call it a day if I want and today, I want.

After organizing camp, I go for a swim. The swimming has been sublime, with the water surprisingly warm—*warmer than Hawaii's ocean,* I think—heated as it is from long days of summer sun. Floating on my back, I watch the sky. The weather is changing. It is always changing and sometimes does so very quickly. The just-clear sky is now a mess of clouds.

I retreat to the tent just as the first drops of rain appear. A real blow follows. I hear water thrown hard against shore and realize I should go out to check the canoe and retrieve the ditch kit from within it, but I am stultified, held captive by inertia.

My limbs are heavy and I cannot will them to move. The ditch kit has the satellite phone and other essential survival gear. Were I to lose the boat and the ditch kit, I could die as a consequence. I am well aware of this yet remain in the tent as if paralyzed.

I am startled awake by a ferocious pounding—water and something else thumping against the shore. It dawns on me with horrific clarity that the thumping is the canoe. *HOLY MOTHER OF GOD!* I tear out of the tent and race to the boat to find it awash in surf and rolling from side to side.

The only thing keeping it from floating away, since I hadn't bothered to tie it, is the food box weighting it down, along with many gallons of water sloshing around inside. I tip the bulk of the water out before dragging the canoe well up the beach, then secure it to a stout tree, using many more knots than needed.

Back in the tent, this time with the ditch kit, I feel a stupendous dolt. To be so careless is indefensible, a dereliction of duty, like falling asleep on guard duty in enemy territory. If I do die here, I'd rather it not be from stupidity.

"Keep your head in the game," I admonish myself, saying it out loud for emphasis.

Perhaps talking to oneself is not a good sign, but clearly warranted in this case. It's obvious I need a good talking to. I know I need to stay sharp, but that seems a tall order after becoming so thoroughly dulled.

Chapter 19
An Act of Contrition

Nineteen sixty-four may not have been good for Ovide Bear and Marcel Daniels, but it was for wilderness because on September 3 of that year, President Johnson signed Public Law 88-577, better known as the Wilderness Act. With the stroke of a pen, something was done that had never been done before in the course of human history: wilderness was protected by law.

It took a long time for this achievement to be realized, you could say more than three-hundred years, since for most of the period between Jamestown to Johnson, Americans had little interest in protecting wilderness. Much to the contrary, we were bent on its destruction. Wilderness held no allure for those who stepped off the Mayflower onto Plymouth Rock to confront an entire continent of the stuff.

It was not a muse to inspire song or poetry, nor an idyllic Eden in which to frolic and commune. Rather, to the early settlers, wilderness was a godless waste, harboring devils, and wild beasts, and savage men. For them, survival demanded it be razed and replaced with cultivated fields, towns, and churches, and populated with *civilized, God-fearing* folk.

And so, by dint of axe and plough, wheel and cow, rail, rifle, and sermon, a campaign to eradicate the continent's wildlands was commenced and prosecuted with religious zeal.

That such efforts could erase all wildness from the American landscape was unthinkable. America was too big and its wilderness too vast to ever be totally expunged, or so it was thought. Thus, it came as a shock when, in 1890, Robert Percival Porter, the superintendent of the United States Census Bureau, made the surprising pronouncement that the frontier was no more.

Americans, he said, had spread across the continent from coast to coast and were rapidly filling up the spaces in-between.

It was bound to happen sooner or later. From the beginning of European occupation, a western migration was on, but it picked up in the wake of Lewis and Clark and grew from trickle to flood with the Louisiana Purchase, the California Gold Rush, Oregon Trail, trans-continental railroad, and Homestead Act, which gave land away for free.

Free land! What an inducement to settlement. One-hundred-and-sixty acres gratis to anyone willing to kick the Indians off it, graze it, farm it, fence it, mine it, log it, or otherwise strip the wild from it.

By 1890, there were already sixty-six million Americans, according to Mr. Porter's census (almost sixty million more than only ninety years before), and many, heeding Horace Greeley's exhortation to, 'Go West', did just that.

At the same time, another demographic shift was underway as people moved from rural America to urban hubs, enticed with the prospect of jobs created by the Industrial Revolution. Cities swelled into giant metropolises; overcrowded, squalid places, belching smoke and clanging with industry. For those living under such conditions, as well as those confronting a vanishing frontier, wilderness, became, quite suddenly, a place not to escape from, but to.

The famed naturalist John Muir helped inspire this attitudinal shift and turn it into a movement, writing in 1901:

"Thousands of tired, nerve-shaken, over-civilized people are beginning to find out that going to the mountains is going home; that wilderness is a necessity; and that mountain parks and reservations are useful not only as fountains of timber and irrigating rivers, but as fountains of life."

Thanks to Muir and his eloquent writings, this sentiment, by the turn of twentieth century, had coalesced into a crusade to save what little wilderness remained, a crusade first led by Muir, but later taken up by others who championed the cause, men such as Bob Marshall, Aldo Leopold, Olaus Murie, and other like-minded notables who banded together in 1935 to found the Wilderness Society, an organization dedicated to seeing wilderness protected by law.

For more than twenty years, the Wilderness Society labored toward this end, trying to get a bill before Congress, but without initial success. Most legislators of the time thought it unwise to 'lock' land away so it couldn't be profitably used.

Their battle cry was, "Not one cent for scenery!"

Undeterred, the Wilderness Society pressed on until finally, in 1956, they succeeded in advancing a bill before the House of Representatives. It was a short-lived victory. The proposal had no chance. Special interests for logging, mining, grazing, and commercial outfitting saw to that.

Even the Forest Service was opposed, resistant to a meddling Congress dictating management to its cadre of professional tree farmers. But, encouraged by growing public support, the Wilderness Society kept at it, introducing a new bill year after year, each slightly tweaked to mollify opposition.

Perhaps the biggest obstacle to the effort came from a Colorado congressman named Wayne Aspinall. Mining is big business in Colorado and Aspinall, as chairman of the House Interior and Insular Affairs Committee, had the power to keep the pending legislation from a floor vote until it was watered down sufficiently to allow digging and drilling.

Thus, it seemed, with all the opposition arrayed against it, the only wilderness bill with any chance of passage would have to permit mining, logging, grazing, motorized transport, and commercial guiding.

In the end, after nine years of disappointment and struggle, the sixty-sixth version of the bill came before Congress. This one featured several compromises to allow so-called *non-conforming uses* within areas designated. Non-conforming uses included grazing, commercial outfitting, and the utilization of motorized equipment to maintain dams and ditches.

Motors were also grandfathered in for motorboats in parts of the Boundary Waters Canoe Area and for airplanes at some backcountry landing strips beloved by bush pilots. As for mining, Aspinall got most of what he wanted. Established mines inside Wilderness could continue operations and exploration for new discoveries was authorized for twenty years following enactment.

The final vote was seventy-three ayes to twelve nays in the Senate and an astounding 373-to-one in the House, a show of bi-partisanship that is unimaginable today. The lone *no* in the House was cast by Joe Pool, representative from the Lone Star State.

The story goes that Joe, upon realizing his was the only dissenting vote, turned to a colleague and asked, "How am I going to explain this to the public and the press?"

"You can only tell them one thing, Joe," he was advised. "You had to vote *no* because the bill didn't go far enough in protecting wilderness."

In truth, the Act did not go far in protecting wilderness. It designated fifty-four areas and a paltry nine-million acres, but it was a start, and every president since has added to the system. Today there are 803 Wilderness Areas totaling 111 million acres, a hundred million more than originally established.

However, as gargantuan as those numbers may seem, they represent only five percent of the total U.S. landmass, and, because half of all Wilderness is in Alaska, only two-and-a-half percent of the lower forty-eight is protected under the law.

The Wilderness Act has been called an act of contrition, where Americans express regret for our near annihilation of the continent's once wondrous wilds. I suppose it shows that we're sorry, not *that* sorry perhaps, but at least a little.

Chapter 20
I Feel the Earth Move Under My Feet

Day 14

Today makes it a fortnight since the start of this trip. *A fortnight?* I wonder about the word. It means *two weeks*, but why? Is *fort* a contraction of fourteen, or were soldiers deployed to forts for two weeks as part of some military custom? It's a fleeting thought of no consequence, but since I'm stuck, with no place to go and nothing to do, I ponder it.

The weather is horrible. After nearly blowing the canoe away last night, the gale is now directing its fury at the tent, striking it with force as if to eject it from earth while I cower inside, hoping not to end up in Oz. Once again, I am marooned.

South of the border, my countrymen are celebrating Independence Day, but I'm stuck on a little rock in the middle of a big lake, free to go nowhere. Waves break upon the shore in endless succession and detonate in reams of white, while the treetops buck and sway like an unnerved herd about to stampede. I'm not going anywhere until things settle some.

Cooped up in the tent, I bide my time, waiting it out, trying to rest, but rest in a wind tunnel is fitful at best. For dinner, I open a can of dehydrated peas mail-ordered from some Mormon outfit in Utah. This gets me thinking about Mormonism and other isms and how humans so readily submit to ideologies and mythologies that are force-fed us in youth (some even requiring the wearing of silly hats).

As the Catholic priests used to say, "Give me a child until they are seven, and I'll have them for life."

It troubles me that my species is so easily manipulated by isms: nationalism, capitalism, theism, racism, etc. Isms make schisms. I fear this hard-wired propensity to affiliate for or against will be our undoing. By what means or when such consequence will come, I don't know, but one of these days, the nut in the foil hat sporting a sandwich board proclaiming "the end of the world" will be right.

I don't believe the end will come from divine retribution. Were we to be smote by the Almighty as punishment for our sins, it would have happened long before now. No, the end will be from something we inflict upon ourselves, an apocalypse of our own design.

Of that, I have no doubt. Hopefully I'll be gone before then. Not only have I not made any preparations for Armageddon, but at this stage of life, I'd be too old to enjoy it anyway.

The Mormons, canners of dehydrated peas, don't fool around when it comes to the End of Times. They are charged with keeping enough food stored away to see them through the Second Coming. This seems reasonable, since most grocery stores will probably close once Jesus returns.

Maybe, some Muslim-owned mini-marts will remain open, but the only foodstuffs available will be things like Slim Jims and corndogs, sure to make the apocalypse only worse.

I'm thinking this while drinking and find my thoughts growing deeper in inverse proportion to the amount of fluid remaining in the cup. It occurs to me that the Mormons might be on to something and that laying up a year's supply of essentials, especially coffee and booze, could prove a smooth move. Then you'd be set while Jesus sorts things out.

After a few more swigs of tonsil paint, I imagine a conversation with Jesus over coffee, or better yet, a highball. That would be something: the little j and big J sharing an adult beverage and shooting the shit. *What would we talk about,* I wonder? Would He be a fun drunk or a mean one? I suspect, being the Son of God, he'd be sanctimonious as hell and not have much of a sense of humor.

After a couple of my jokes fell flat, I'd probably just sit quietly, meekly nodding in agreement while he rattled off a litany of human foibles, maybe slurring his words and getting loud. One drawback to hanging out with deities is that you have to be an unmitigated kiss-ass, or else.

I add hot water to the peas. I'd been saving them to fend off scurvy and didn't plan to crack the can until my teeth wiggled, but the label, with its plump, luscious orbs agleam in butter, controls me like an ism.

After dinner, weary from too much tent time, I decide to explore the island for something to do. The whole of it is only about an acre, and even at a snail's pace, I soon reach the opposite side. Here, sheltered by forest, I am relieved to be out of the wind, but the trees above are still affected, swaying so violently I worry one might blow down and squish me. Then my eye is drawn to movement on the ground.

Wait! It's not movement on the ground but movement of the ground. *What the…?* Ground doesn't move, discounting earthquakes, and I wonder if I'm hallucinating, but then see it happen again. As I watch, a chunk of earth, the size of a prayer rug, rises right out of the ground and keeps on going until it hovers two feet above the forest floor before slowly lowering back down.

It takes me a minute to figure it out. A giant spruce, its topmost branches assailed by wind, is pushed over so that the soil-clogged roots on its upwind side are actually getting pried out the ground and lifted.

Wow! I decide to ride this heaving patch of earth and stand upon it, waiting. I sense only a little shuddering at first, but then feel myself going up, higher and higher, in spurts and starts. It's scary to be so moved, but also a thrill.

Up and down I go, surrendering to the awesome power of nature, feeling the earth move under my feet, and thinking to myself, *Now,* this *is God!*

Chapter 21
I See a Sign

Day 15

Opening my ears before my eyes this morning, I hope to hear nothing, but the incessant crashing and thrashing of wind and wave have not abated. At 5:30, I exit the tent to have a look. Sisipuk remains battered and storm-tossed, but perhaps with less intensity than yesterday. Wishful thinking? Maybe, but the whitecaps seem flatter and fewer. I think the lake has settled some. I'm pretty sure it has, but despite jonesing to leave, I mustn't allow that desire to supersede judgment. Still, I seek reasons to go, not stay. There is a tailwind, a little patch of blue poking out between the heavy clouds, and only a mile or so of open water to cross. I really want to go, but a little voice cautions: *It's too windy. Too rough! Relax and wait!* But I don't want to wait and can't relax. The thought of another day marooned here is more than I can bear.

I load the canoe to ready it in case the weather breaks, or if reason yields to impulse, which it does—the latter not the former. I get in the boat and go.

The little voice was right and delights in telling me so. Immediately after leaving the safety of shore, waves sweep the deck and water dribbles into the canoe. Again, unable to turn around for fear of flipping, my only option is onward.

Water surrounds me, frothy and peaked like the storm-tossed seas depicted in Japanese ink prints. I try not to look, instead focusing on the land ahead and making every effort to get there fast. It is amazing how powerfully one can paddle when incentivized by fear.

Once over, I beach the boat to bail. Only a few gallons got in despite the several waves that washed over. The spray deck has proven a brilliant accessory and a prime contender for the expedition's most valuable item award.

With Sisipuk Lake finally behind, the river speeds on toward Bloodstone Falls. Anything with *falls* in the name gets my attention, and that goes double for *blood*. I creep along the right bank, heading for an obvious take-out where, oddly enough, someone posted a stop sign, the genuine article, octagonal and red. It seems a superfluity since nobody in their right mind would need a sign advising them to stop here.

The river ahead is unequivocal on that point, disappearing as it does into boom and spray. But, judging from the array of tokens, trinkets, and charms lining the portage path, not all are adept at recognizing nature's signs. There must be a story to prompt the posting of this sign, most likely one without a happy ending.

Facilitated by skid rails, I am back on the river below the falls in no time. A flight of pelicans, twenty or more, glide by in tight formation, looking like birds from an Escher print. They fly effortlessly, barely off the water with nary a wing flap until, at some unseen signal, the whole flock flares, spreading their wings and deploying broad yellow feet forward in preparation of landing.

Touching down, they skim along the surface like water skiers until momentum flags, then sink and settle. It's a display of grace completely unexpected from creatures of such ungainly appearance.

Another crossing now confronts me, one I am not keen to attempt since I feel I've pushed my luck enough for one day. But, being too early to stop, and since I have to cross sometime anyway, I go. It proves a good decision as the crossing is completed without drama.

Tonight's campsite is the best yet. It reminds me of that old Hamm's beer commercial, the one on an electronic sign that scrolled around to reveal a pleasant backwoods scene with a canoe pulled up on a forested shore below a lovely waterfall, and a cozy looking tent set up by a flickering campfire. As a boy, whenever I saw that sign, I wanted to be inside the frame, and now, I am.

Tomorrow I'll make Pukatawagan. The village is but six miles from here. Alas, the party who penned my guide ended their trip there, so upon departing the town, I will no longer have any river intel. Hopefully, I'll find someone who can fill me in on what to expect of the Churchill below, but I'll worry about that tomorrow.

At present, I only want to gawk, so find a rock, lean against it, and do just that. Pleasant burbling emanates from an upstream riffle, the only perceptible sound. River, sky, and forest change in hue and texture as the sun slowly sinks to twilight. Being here, in this land of sky-blue waters, feels a great gift.

Chapter 22
On Being Fruitful

It's astounding when you think about it; God creating the entire cosmos—earth, moon, stars, galaxies, everything everywhere—in just six days, while it took humankind many thousands of years to protect just a tiny fraction of that creation though passage of the Wilderness Act.

By the time homo sapiens got around to saving some of the Lord's original handiwork, there wasn't much of it left, we having already yoked and occupied most of it.

Some see this as fulfilling God's will, for immediately upon completing creation and pronouncing it "good," the Almighty pointed down from the heavens with a long, bony finger and decreed that we be "fruitful and multiply."

And lo, it has come to pass.

In 1445 BC, when this edict was transcribed by some learned Jews into the Old Testament, there were roughly sixty-million people on earth. Now, 3,500 years later, we have increased to eight-billion. That's a lot of fruit, an amount so large as to belie understanding.

So, to lend perspective on just how big eight-billion is, consider that if we multiply this number by five feet (assuming this an average human height), humankind would, if stacked head to toe, extend for seven-and-a-half-million miles, enough to circle the globe at the equator 287 times, or span the expanse of space between the earth and moon more than thirty times.

And the begetting isn't close to being over. Each day sees a net gain (births minus deaths) of 200,000 people, which accrues to eighty million more of us annually. Eighty million little miracles added to our ranks every year, each of whom will have a carbon footprint, each of whom will contribute to habitat loss, consumption of resources, climate change, and pollution of some nasty ass shit, all of which now threatens one million of our fellow species with extinction.

We breed for a variety of reasons: to pass on our name, to have something to love, to give meaning to life, because it is expected, in the attempt to cement a relationship, for cheap labor, because everybody's doing it, to ensure a caregiver when we're old, to bolster the ranks of race and religion, because accidents happen, and because it supposedly pleases God, but mostly we do it to out of mindless imperative, no different from earthworms or fruit flies, to pass on our genes.

Reproducing is what organisms do, but surely, with our *superior* brains, humans should grasp the consequence of such unchecked population growth, not just to nature, but to ourselves. It's basic math. Infinite growth cannot be reconciled to finite resources.

Ultimately, if we continue reproducing as if there is no tomorrow, there will be no tomorrow—not one worth living in anyway. And by the way, if you think technology will save us, think again.

Howard Zahniser, the man who penned the Wilderness Act, understood this explicitly. In the genesis of his bill, he wrote:

In order to assure that an increasing population, accompanied by expanding settlement and growing mechanization, does not occupy and modify all areas within the United States and its possessions, leaving no lands protected in their natural condition, it is hereby declared to be the policy of the Congress to secure…an enduring resource of wilderness.

Zahniser also recognized that as we increased in number, the second part of God's decree from Genesis 1:28, that we subdue the earth, would be an unavoidable consequence of the first, the *be fruitful and multiply* part.

That the earth shall be wholly subdued should come as no surprise. Resources needed to power, shelter, feed, and otherwise sustain us derive from the natural world. Hence, as we increase in number, the natural world must be increasingly exploited to support us. Subdue is what we do.

It's troubling that the issue of overpopulation is seldom broached or acknowledged as the existential threat it is. No politician will touch it, and who can blame them? Any pol brave enough to take it on would be castigated on numerous fronts, labeled anti-business, anti-family, anti-God, anti-freedom, anti-American, a racist, a Commie, and never reelected.

The United States of America is not China! Will we vote for a candidate who suggests that family size be limited, that we sacrifice comfort to reduce consumption so as to live sustainably, or one who serves up pap, a panderer-in-chief promising more, better, cheaper, and faster, assuring us we can have never-ending prosperity and a clean environment, and that America's best days are still ahead?

No one wants to hear harsh reality, but it is past time we give it a listen. Some quiet night, stick your head out the window and cock an ear. What you'll hear is a soft munching, muted but constant, the sound made by eight-billion of us eating—eating things that oink and moo, cluck and quack, things that baa and bray, and even bark.

We're eating shark fins and bird nests, monkeys and bats, sea urchins and seaweed, turtles and tuna—noshing away like army ants. We've stripped the prairies, altered nearly every arable acre on earth, and are now rapidly razing the rain forests and mining the seven seas for comestibles. *Crunch!*

There goes another bite down the hatch, another morsel of wilderness, and even while chewing, we are constantly on the lookout for more.

Chapter 23
Welcome to Pukatawagan

Day 16

I make Pukatawagan by late morning after a leisurely paddle and pull in to the dock below the Northern Store. Before I can tie-off, a small launch, its engine coughing and belching smoke, limps over to the other side. There are three young Cree aboard, kind of sketchy looking.

Two are rail-thin, with bad skin, lank hair, and gaps in their grins where teeth used to be. The other is a husky fella with a buzz-cut and t-shirt that reads, 'Buy this man a beer.' It's this last one who steps onto the dock and fixes me with a hard stare.

"I'm going to need to see your permit to canoe on our land," he says with grave officiousness. For some reason, I think he's punking me.

"I don't canoe on land," I tell him, "but I'll show you mine if you show me yours."

All three break-out laughing, like this is the funniest thing they have ever heard. That's when I realize they're drunk, somewhere between tipsy and shitfaced. I introduce myself and shake hands all around, not sure if it's the custom or not. The guy I'm supposed to buy a beer for gives his name as Donovan, which strikes me as an odd handle for an Indigenous person.

His handshake is firm. The other two don't proffer names and shake hands like father's tell sons not to, with grips limp as dead fish. Donovan asks where I'm headed, and my answer elicits murmurs of surprise.

"Why the hell you want to do that?" he wants to know.

It occurs to me that wilderness may not hold the same allure for those who constantly confront it.

When I mention Stanley Mission as my starting point, a Cree village barely two-hundred miles up this same river, it doesn't ring a bell. Donovan says the farthest he's traveled is to Thompson, twice, and once to The Pas.

"I'm too busy making babies," he says through a smirk, and brags about fathering eight children with a multitude of mates. I cringe inwardly, but mask my disapproval.

Our conversation is interrupted when another boat shows up, this one brimming with teenage boys. Three girls of the same vintage walk down the ramp from the Northern Store to see what all the fuss is about down on the docks. Suddenly I'm in the midst of a dozen curious Cree. All reticence evaporates and they pepper me with questions, eager to talk. I must be the most interesting thing to have hit town in ages.

They listen politely while I describe where I'm from, what I did for a living, and wax on about Yellowstone Park, with its geysers and bison. When I finish, one wants to know if I've seen any moose along the river. I tell him no, which is true, but it's the same answer I'd have given either way. I'm not going to rat out any moose.

When I ask if anyone knows what the river is like from here to Leaf Rapids several voices chime in at once, and I can't decipher a thread of information from the tangle of talk until one very loud voice booms above the rest and quiets the crowd.

It belongs to one of Donovan's skinny pals, who stands unsteadily atop the bench seat of his boat and, sweeping an arm in a broad arc until it points more or less downstream bellows, "You go that way!"

After a bit more talk and banter, I excuse myself, explaining that I need to resupply before going *that way,* but first everyone wants to shake my hand. I am touched in more ways than one. I ask if it would be okay to take a group photo.

They readily agree and immediately assume gang poses, making Xs with crossed arms and forming fingers into symbols for something. Then I head for the store, not at all concerned about leaving my stuff unattended, feeling like I am among people who would do me no wrong.

In the parking lot of the Northern Store, a white guy, fiftyish with blond hair turning gray, leans casually against a pick-up, apparently waiting for someone in the store. We strike up an easy conversation, and I realize how relaxed I am in his presence compared to my initial reaction with the Cree at the dock.

Why is that, I wonder and conclude probably because he and I share a more similar genotype, are closer to the same tribe, and recognize it on a subliminal level. How odd! I suspect this is a natural response imbedded in our collective consciousness and no doubt honestly earned.

The man's name is Norm and he came to Pukatawagan twenty-five years ago to work a short-term job but found a girl and stayed. As we chat, a scrawny woman slithers up, eyeing me with apparent prurient interest.

"Aren't you going to introduce me to your friend, Norman?" she warbles, trying to sound sexy. I excuse myself and beat feet for the store.

The Northern Store has it all, its shelves piled high with the accoutrements of northern living: food, clothing, sporting goods, toys, traps, guns, ammo, outboards—even snowmobiles and boats. I squeeze past two strapping men in a narrow aisle of the automotive section.

Dressed in mechanic overalls, they are examining boxes of air filters but shelve the parts after taking notice of me and approach. I am taken aback, wondering what's up. Standing closer to me than is comfortable, they stare squarely into my face as if trying to intuit my soul, and then, having evidently divined a positive conclusion, shake hands warmly and say, 'Welcome to Pukatawagan'.

The words are spoken with grave solemnity and with not a hint of artifice. Little more passes between us, and they return to what they were doing before the encounter, leaving me feeling curiously honored.

After shopping, I don't linger. The emaciated coquette is still outside, lurking in wait. She opens her mouth to say something, but I just smile, wave, and hurry by. Back at the boat, I settle in and paddle away in the direction indicated by Donovan's not-so-helpful friend.

I pass a neighborhood of cheaply built pre-fabs, their gray siding faded and peeling. Above the houses, 'PUKATAWAGAN' is scrawled across a cliff face in large white letters. Glancing back minutes later, I can still make out the name, but barely. The next time I look, all evidence of the town is gone.

Six miles further on, I reach Pukatawagan Rapids. Here the river splits around an island and tumbles wildly around both sides. There is a boat skid, two-hundred yards long, that runs from the top of the island to the bottom. In places, the structure is elevated ten feet and more above rocky, water-gouged ground.

Constructed of poles and rough-cut boards, it's a rickety thing with scores of jerry-rigged repairs and doesn't feel the least bit safe as I drag the boat across. It wobbles and creaks, and I hope, with every step, that it holds.

By the time I have everything carried down, it's 6:00 p.m. and, due to the lateness of the day and some iffy water below the put-in I don't want to try when this tired, I decide to stay.

After dinner, I watch pelicans fish the tailrace below the island where the rapids encircling it come together. The boils and eddies formed in the collision of currents unnerve me. It seems I could easily catch an edge and flip.

The pelicans however don't seem bothered in the least and manage the turbulent flow just fine. I envy their whitewater skills, especially the ability to fly over anything they'd rather not float through. I wish I could do that.

After tiring of the pelicans, I switch to ants, busy in their ant ways. I've seen ants everywhere, even on tiny specks of land in the middle of enormous lakes. I wonder how they reach such remote outposts so far from mainland shores. Do they cross on ice, float on flotsam, swim, or hitchhike on birds?

Somehow, they get everywhere, and, like humans, aggressively colonize the new territory, claiming it as their own and forcing things already there to either adapt, move, or die. These ants move in constant haste, bumper-to-bumper like rush hour traffic, coming and going. Watching them makes me feel even more tired than I already am. Being an ant must be a real pain in the gaster.

Before nodding off, I reflect on the Cree I've encountered. Mostly they seem a sad lot to me, condemned to small lives in isolated hamlets with little to do but hunt, fish, get high, and procreate. I am probably being unfair and shouldn't make judgements based on fleeting first impressions. Indigenous people have been royally screwed the world over, with lands and lifestyle stolen.

If they are sad, they have good reason to be. Still, despite all thcy've endured from European interlopers, I sensed no resentment toward me, save for a smidge in Sandy Bay. Most of the people I've met seem decent and kind. Funny though—I haven't seen a single canoe among these people who practically invented them.

Chapter 24
First Arrivals

Although much of the story remains a mystery, archaeologists tell us that the first people to occupy the Americas were Paleo-Indians who arrived sometime between 45,000 to 16,000 years ago, depending who you ask.

They came on foot from Siberia to Alaska when the continents were still connected by earth and ice, following the animals they hunted, and eventually spread throughout the Americas, north and south. Because most of Canada was covered by ice until 10,000 years ago, it's a safe bet that no humans occupied the area where the Churchill River now flows until the glaciers were gone.

Artifacts discovered in the Churchill's headwaters date to 8,000 years before present. The people of the day traveled the rivers and lakes by canoe when these waterways weren't frozen and with dog sleds or snowshoes when they were. There was simply no other practical means of moving through this densely forested and swampy terrain.

Cree have occupied the Churchill River area for centuries and the many branches of this tribe still live throughout the north, from Alaska to Newfoundland in a broad arc between tundra and plain.

What is known about their traditional way of life comes from early accounts of fur traders who describe them as living in small bands of two to five families, using tepees and lean-tos for shelter, and paddling canoes made from birch bark. Because they lived generally too far north for buffalo and too far south for caribou, moose was the most important animal hunted. They also ate beaver, waterfowl, ptarmigan, and snowshoe hare, and harvested fish in stone weirs.

The other major native group here, the Dene, are not related to the Cree, except presumably through shared Paleo-Indian ancestry. Their languages are distinctly different. Cree speak an Algonquian tongue while Dene speak

Athabaskan. Interestingly, Navaho and Apache are also Athabaskan dialects, so evidently the Dene were among America's first snowbirds.

Those who didn't relocate south spread northeast from Alaska to Canada along the many Arctic rivers. Because habitat dictates survival strategies, the Dene lived very much like the Cree; small groups of nomads moving between the seasons to hunt, trap, and fish. This existence persisted for thousands of years until profoundly affected by European contact starting early in the 17th century.

The first Europeans to the Churchill were members of a Norwegian expedition under the command of a Dane named Jens Munk. Munk set out from Norway in May of 1619 in search of the Northwest Passage, but like so many others before and after, he failed to find it, so instead explored the western edge of Hudson Bay.

By fall of that year, with ice starting to clog the bay, Munk, with two ships and a crew of sixty-five, decided to winter in the estuary of a large river called the Missinipe (*big water*) by the Cree. When spring finally rolled around six months later, the entire crew was dead, save for Jens and two others. Somehow these three managed to sail one of the ships back home.

Following that fiasco, nothing much happened at the mouth of the Missinipe until the Hudson Bay Company arrived in 1688 to establish a fishery for white porpoise, as beluga whales were then called.

The locals began exchanging furs with the whalers for handy metal objects, and the rest, as they say, is history. Before long, the fur trade took over as the dominant economic activity, ushering in a cultural sea change that quickly swept across all of North America.

Fortunes could be made in furs, and because the natives excelled at catching the targeted species and wanted what Europeans would give in exchange, a natural partnership was established. Traditional subsistence, where hunters took only what was needed for survival, was replaced by a capitalistic model that operated under a philosophy of *more*, with no such thing as *enough*.

With less time to hunt and fish, First Nations people became dependent on trading posts to procure the means of survival. Flour, sugar, blankets, guns, powder, and lead were the primary staples of exchange, with liquor often used to secure favorable terms (read, *cheat*) in business dealings.

Then came smallpox and other diseases to which the first Americans had no immunity. Then came priests and missionaries to strip away the old beliefs and supplant them with Jesus, and within a mind-spinning short span of time, a way of life that had endured for centuries was traded away for one of dependence, poverty, addiction, and despair.

Chapter 25
One Little, Two Little,
Three Little Indians

Day 17

I suffer a horrible night's sleep, the worst since Wapumon Gorge. The rapids raging around the island, thundered and boomed without relent, bringing to mind Tennyson's poem, *The Charge of the Light Brigade*, another of my mother's favorites.

"Cannon to right of them / Cannon to left of them / Cannon in front of them/ Volleyed and thundered."

When I finally drifted off, my dreams were uneasy. In the boat, no paddle, spinning in whitewater from which rocks protrude like shark fins, I am swept over a falls, but find myself at its base, safe, slowly circling a pool.

Several items float nearby: a paddle, a sandal, a map, a yellow ball cap. On shore is a canoe, broken almost in two. From it, smallish footprints track up the sandy beach toward a copse of trees above. I follow.

"Hello," I call to no response. "HELLO," louder this time. Waiting. Something? Maybe. A mewing.

"Over here!" a voice cries weakly.

I hurry to the sound and find two young women, one shivering, the other still. Pressing my fingers into the hollow of the inert girl's throat, I detect a reedy pulse. Alive! They are alive. But how to warm them up?

A shout stirs me from reverie. *In the dream or real?* I wonder, not knowing. I am in the tent. *Did I hear something? An animal? A person?* Then another shout, distinct above the rapid's roar. Someone really is out there. I'd left the canoe on the ramp, blocking it, but surely no one would be using it now, in the middle of the night. I look at my watch. 1:00 a.m. *What the…?*

Dressing quickly, I hurry out into drizzle to find not one, not two, but ten young Cree, none out of their teens, standing around a small, open boat run up on shore below the ramp. They are even more surprised to see me than I them. There are five boys, three girls, and two little kids, one an infant.

As it turns out, they are returning to Pukatawagan from Leaf Rapids, having departed last evening and negotiating much of that 120-mile distance in near darkness, without map, compass, or GPS. They have no flashlights, raincoats, or life jackets and are dressed in jeans, t-shirts, and light coats. The two littlest are bundled in fleece blankets against the cool night.

The group is not lost, late, or in any distress. This is just normal getting around for them. But really, ten kids in a small motorboat, traveling 120 miles in dusk, dark, and drizzle, through uninhabited wilderness, without lights or navigational aids—how do they manage that? When I'm underway, I constantly monitor my position against both map and GPS to keep from getting lost, but not these youngsters.

They know right where they are, sure of which channel to take, what island to steer for, where the bad rocks are to avoid. They learned from their forbearers who learned from theirs and from countless generations before who plied these waters in canoes for millennia. This isn't wilderness to them. It's home.

The kids wait patiently while I drag the canoe off the ramp. Then I help them with their boat. It takes six of us to heave it out of the water and onto the ramp.

"One, two, THREE!! Pull!"

Tugging with all our might manages a slide of just a few feet each time. Only the older boys work. The others stand and watch. No one engages, either with one another or with me. The only human sound is the counting, then the 'oomph!' and scrape of the boat's bottom against wood that follows.

I ask the young man apparently in charge what the river is like from here to Leaf Rapids, and he tells me there are four portages. All, he says, have skid rails or ramps.

I ask what side of the river the portages are on, and he gestures out with his right arm and says, "All on this side."

I am relieved to get information from a credible source, from someone who knows the river well enough to navigate it at night, and from someone clearly stone-cold sober.

After we get their boat to the top of the island, they slide it back onto the river and pile in with practiced precision. The motor starts and the boat pulls away, fading into darkness, taking ten kids home, moving as if in a dream.

I go back to bed, but soon the drizzle becomes an honest downpour. Again, no fly, so out I go to attach it, and then lie back down inside listening to the rain, crash of water, and boom of approaching thunder. Lightning illuminates the tent's interior like a shorted bulb.

I launch late, sluggish after dreams real and imagined and nervous about the confused flow below, nervous enough to put on the dry suit and tie everything in. But, as it turns out, I bob through with the aplomb of a pelican. When a hard-wearing headwind makes for tough going, I embrace the challenge.

Struggling feels good. My body is holding up well, surprisingly so. There's an occasional snick in my right shoulder where something catches that's supposed to slide, but it doesn't persist or cause undue discomfort. Overall, I feel wicked strong, as if wrought of English oak.

Fourteen miles later, having reached High Rock Lake, I no longer feel the least bit oaky. Finding a campsite, I stumble around, setting up while moaning, making dinner while groaning, and finally, crawl into the tent to end this day with a great big sigh.

Chapter 26
Bio-Massive

Day 18

I exercised late into the night, tossing and turning and didn't get much sleep. By 7:00 this a.m., too tired to move, I remain abed, fuzzy brained, as if my head is stuffed with wads of Kleenex. Deep thoughts are impossible to exhume and shallow ones slow to surface. Oh well, I don't need a brain to function. I can push the boat through water on muscle memory alone—could do it in my sleep, if I could sleep.

There is nary a breath of wind when I start, but by mid-morning, a gentle puff nudges me helpfully. It doesn't last. Instead the wind strengthens and swings around to come on abeam, which I bitch about until it shifts another ninety degrees to become a truly bitch-worthy headwind. Muscle memory has to crank it up a notch.

High Rock is immense, a mostly linear lake but with huge side bays that take me a mile or more from shore to traverse. I don't care. I'm too foggy-headed to worry about such silly things as safety so just paddle, an autotron on autopilot, keeping to the most direct route.

The wind continues building until it's a gale. I can't stop, not for a second, or it will push me back at three times my forward speed. Progress is too hard won to have to gain it twice, so I bear down and inch along, making perhaps a half-mile per hour. Studying the map, clipped to the deck where I can see it while underway, I note a point of land two miles ahead and figure that once around it, the wind will be at my back. So incentivized, I struggle on.

When the point comes into view, it seems a long way off and, an hour later, hasn't gotten much closer. I gird myself and go. Two more hours of dogged work finally brings me to the point. I expect the gale to turn from foe to friend once I round it, but instead, the wind just flat out dies. I am cheated, but with no recourse other than to jab the paddle in the water and carry on.

Five o'clock is quitting time, but I can't find a place to camp. The first possibility is an island that turns out to be nothing more than a giant ant mound, every square inch of it acrawl with ants; the ground literally moving with their ambulation. Too creepy!

Presently, I come upon a second profusion, mayflies this time. They are trans-morphing from nymph to adult and emerging from the lake in astonishing numbers, leaving their discarded husks floating upon High Rock's surface like an oil slick. Scores come aboard the canoe to rest.

From a distance, they are merely bugs but close-up, become finely wrought objects d'art with crystalline wings set like leaded glass into a latticework of delicate frames. I am reminded of the beauty found in small things.

Finally, I find a place to stop. The wind really kicked my ass today and helped settle the question once and for all about which route to pursue to Hudson Bay. I've made up my mind to keep to the Churchill. There really is no other choice. Ric predicted I would make Leaf Rapids in fifteen days, but today is already day eighteen and Leaf remains eighty miles out.

It will take at least another five days just to get there, at which point I still won't be quite halfway. Then there is the mother of all portages, Jack Batstone's August 15th cutoff date, after which he won't chance Hudson Bay to pick me up at the mouth of the Seal and transport me to Churchill, and polar bears to consider. Reason dictates I keep to the river I'm on.

I spend the evening marveling at mayflies as the sun circles low, riding the horizon. The sky darkens to cobalt, infused with the peripatetic confusion of the insect orgy.

Dragonflies cross the swarm, snagging mayflies on the wing and flying on with the distinctive twin tails of the prey protruding from their maws like un-slurped spaghetti. Never have I witnessed such an abundance of life. It is bio-massive. Not even the white sox on the Thelon can match this.

It occurs to me that Lewis and Clark had a similar experience, only with buffalo instead of bugs. Not quite the same, but nothing to sneeze at.

Chapter 27
Latte, Anyone?

It's astounding when you consider the rapidity with which the West was *won*. In 1964, when the Wilderness Act was signed, only 160 years had passed since Lewis and Clark explored what would become fabled as the American frontier. Others followed hot on their heels: trappers, traders, land speculators, missionaries, miners, settlers, and soldiers.

What began as a trickle turned into a flood as people poured into the region to lay claim to its seemingly inexhaustible resources. It was a feeding frenzy, this so-called *winning*—first for furs, then soil, trees, grass, and gold; the sound of conquest a cacophony of snapping traps, beating hooves, bleating sheep, lowing cattle, blowing bugles, squeaky wheels, the scrape of steel laying open virgin earth, and shouts of 'fire in the hole' and 'timber'.

Puffs of steam exploded from machines and prairie winds keened through telegraph lines and taut barbed wire. It was a *sin-phony* conducted to the implacable beat of hammers: hammers on anvils, on rock, hammers joining one board to another, one rail to another, and all the while, the score punctuated with concussive blasts of gunfire. A *bang* and something fell, particularly things that stood in the way—like wolves, bison, bears, and Indians.

There were so many bison at the time of Lewis and Clark that their numbers beg credulity. Sixty million, by some accounts, the number of people living today in California, Oregon, Washington, Idaho, Wyoming, Utah, and Montana combined. They were shot for meat, for humps, for hides, for heads—marble eyes staring sightless from wood paneled walls.

Shot to deprive native people of sustenance; shot—barrels bristling from train cars—just to see if you could hit one; shot because they ate what cattle eat and had no respect for fences. It was easy. See them and shoot them. *Bang!* An animal down. *Bang!* Another staggered but still up and running. Dead but not knowing it. Great head falling to earth, scouring the plain, legs churning, trying to run, trying to live, and then only still. Dust billowing above the inanimate form like a headstone.

The grizzly too, shot to the brink. What good are they, anyway? Bears don't have souls. They'll eat your livestock and maybe you, too. The world is better without them. And wolves? You ever see a pack kill? They eat the guts right out of an animal. Eat them while they're still alive. Makes you sick to see it. Shoot them, and the coyotes, prairie dogs, rabbits, foxes, cougars, badgers, black bears, eagles, snakes. Kill 'em all!

As for the Indians—those not shot, shunted to reservations, moved to some shitty wind-blown weedy patch of ground no white man would want. Too bad but there's no room for the old ways. They'll be better off in the long run. Make farmers out of them. Give them rum and the comforts of Christianity. The land they occupied for millennia transferred to a new owner in the blink of an eye.

It ended fast, quicker than two shakes of a lamb's tail, fast enough to make your head spin. It ended, not in a whimper, but with a BANG! The American West, now under new management and open for business. Latte, anyone?

Chapter 28
Holy Creation

Day 19

It's 5:30 a.m. and High Rock's surface is sheened in light so bright it causes me to squint. There is no wind, not a breath, so I pack up and leave, foregoing humanizing to take advantage of the lull.

This day marks my third on this lake. It occurs to me that lakes of this enormity should have a name befitting their size, something to set them apart, the term *lake* being too generic and inadequate to describe a body of water this big.

Given that the Inuit have fifty words for snow, why then shouldn't boaters be granted a few more for lake? I try out a couple, *largormorph* and *lakestrosity,* but don't expect either to be part of the lexicon any time soon.

After lunch, the wind kicks in, but from astern, and I cruise before it, expecting to easily make Twin Falls, the first of the four portages between here and Leaf Rapids, and finally have High Rock behind me.

I am unsure as to whether these falls are identical or fraternal twins, meaning side by side (identical), perhaps separated by a mid-stream island, or sequential (fraternal), one waterfall following the other. Hopefully they are identical so a single carry will get me around both.

As it turns out, I won't find out, not today. Before reaching the falls, I chance upon a place of such preternatural beauty I am compelled to stop. It's a small cove, embraced by columns of rose-pink granite sequined in sun and lined with a crescent of soft, white sand.

Above the beach, an ancient forest rises in tiers against a flawless sky. The scene is perfectly still, as if painted, and the only sound, a faint hissing, probably High Rock draining over Twin Falls two miles away, heard only with closed-eyes concentration.

I strip and dive to an even more silent world, slipping through braids of bending light to linger weightless in cool depths, and remain so until fingers prune and goose bumps stipple my flesh and then leave the lake to rewarm, lizard-like atop a slab of rock. My mind is adrift and at ease until a sharp huffing interrupts the reverie. I can't at first pinpoint the source but then zero in on a family of otters, six of them, clustered offshore.

Their long necks crane above the surface like the multi-headed hydra of myth. Perhaps this is their beach I've commandeered. I'd be happy to share, but furbearers know better than to trust the likes of me, who peel off their skins for fashion accessories.

Fur was once a necessity of survival, but that's no longer the case. We have Smartwool, Polypro, Thinsulate, Primaloft, and fleece now, rendering fur obsolete, but need or not, humans are killers and continue to pursue animals for their hides to make a buck or two, or just to have something to do. An otter pelt can fetch about a hundred dollars, but what can you buy for a hundred dollars that is worth an otter?

What can you purchase that will match the magnificence of a living mink, beaver, wolverine, fisher, or fox? Whatever, it's a bad bargain. But, killing is hard-wired in us, and we're good at it, devising tailor-made schemes to exploit the vulnerabilities of every species. We can do it by club, hook, point, poison, bullet, net, or noose.

We have dogs to chase them up a tree, with no place to go until a bullet sends them crashing down. We have bait, fat, juicy, and trickling with temptation, to lure them to a trap that snaps with terrible suddenness, steel teeth shredding just perfect flesh to white bone. Or a wire tightens around their throat as they fight and flail until life ends in a gurgled rasp.

Later, someone comes to see what they've caught, someone with more pride than pity. If the animal is not yet mercifully dead, the trapper will bash the brain in with a club or crush the heart beneath a bootheel so as not to hole and devalue the hide, and take only it, leaving the rest for the birds and bugs.

Animals know we are killers, and so live like outlaws among us, coming out only at night or furtively keeping to cover—slinking away or bolting in full flight when discovered, surviving in a near constant state of fear. That's the way it is, the natural order.

After all, God granted humans dominion over all things—those that creepeth, crawleth, swimmeth, and flyeth upon the earth—so we can do with them pretty much as we want. It's right there in the Bible, in plain, unambiguous Aramaic, from God's mouth to our ears. According to Genesis, man and otter were made the same day, poofed into existence on Day Six of Creation.

When that day was done, the Almighty looked around happy with his handiwork and pronounced it "good," but I have my doubts. Perhaps, he was tired after five previous days of heavy lifting, or maybe he was in a rush and looking forward to the weekend, but clearly, he could have done better, made us kinder, gentler, more respectful and appreciative of his holy creation so we would value otters more as friends than fleeces.

It's hot as blue blazes. I don't have a thermometer, but it must be in the eighties. Maybe, the heat is keeping the bugs down. There aren't any, not one. I walk the beach naked, pressing a line of footprints, like Adam's, into shimmering sand. I'm a natural-born man. I am a creature of the wild. I am the only person living. I am free. I am fearsomely strong. I am near broken with fatigue. I bask in solitude, stoned by the beauty of creation.

Chapter 29
Your Other River Right

Day 20

Again, water dripping through the tent's mesh wakes me. I go out and fling on the fly with what passes for haste in my debilitated state. With all the practice, I'm getting good at fly erections, lewd as that may sound. An instant later, a squall drives hard, deflating the tent's wall as if some great beast is pushing against it. Thunder cracks and rolls across the sky.

I sit inside, warm and cozy, until concerns about the canoe prompt me out to check it. I'd left it tied high and dry, but tie it higher and dryer, not taking chances, then return to the tent, bringing the stove with me. I get it going in the vestibule and wait for the water to boil while watching the storm build through the narrow slice of view afforded between the door flaps.

When the coffee is ready, I sit back and relax. A cup of joe is a license to loaf. There isn't much one can do while drinking it since, being hot, it can't be readily moved or consumed in haste and so imposes stillness. It is somewhat sensual too—caressing the cup in one's hands, feeling warmth entering the body as steamy vapors rise from the potion like spirits; ethereal dancers, hips and bosoms full and undulant.

I lean back, seduced, as the rain beats steadily down.

The storm passes quickly and I'm packed and paddling by 9:00, heading for Twin Falls. Nearing them, my approach is tight to the right bank since the young man encountered at Pukatawagan Rapids assured me that all portages were on this side, but as I draw perilously close to where the river drops from view, right seems wrong.

There is no sign of a portage or take-out, and it occurs to me that the kid may not have been conversant in the basic boating nomenclature of *river right* and *left*. Perhaps all portages were on his right returning from Leaf Rapids, but river right and river left are determined with respect to the downstream view. Hence, river right is on one's right when looking down.

That it is on the left looking up is immaterial; it remains river right. These directions are a constant, immutable as a compass needle, and for good reason. In navigating whitewater, clarity of direction is paramount and ambiguity potentially calamitous, as it is for me now only fifty yards above a fifty-foot drop.

Realizing the error, I spin the boat and ferry to the other right with the strength of panic and make it, barely, before becoming one with the river.

The portage is a hundred yards over gentle ground and, with skid rails, about as easy as portages get. Still, two hours are needed to complete it in my enfeebled state.

Then, only two minutes after repacking and setting off below these falls, I am beached and unpacking above the next, as the twins are in fact fraternal. This portage too is on the *other* right. Because a steep hill must be surmounted before an even more precipitous descent to the put-in, this carry is considerably more difficult than the first.

With vegetation growing thick against the rails of the boat skid, I am forced to walk atop it, stepping gingerly on crossties and concentrating on balance. The difficulty negotiating this path calls for lighter loads, so instead of the five or six trips normally needed to get everything over a portage, seven are required here, but only to the top of the hill.

From there, the dry bags with unbreakables can be given the old heave-ho and entrusted to gravity. They trundle down, bouncing and crashing through and over brush before rolling to rest at the bottom. What's left goes back in the boat to be lowered down the ramp within it.

The ramp is steep, excessively so, about as steep as a black diamond ski run over a distance of two-hundred feet. I can't imagine how the young Cree managed to get their boat up it. Fortunately, I have gravity in my favor, but what can't be allowed is for the heavy craft to get away and careen, luge-like, to surely be dashed on the beach below.

To prevent such a calamity, I wrap the line from the bow twice around a crosstie and play it out slowly, using friction to control the rate of descent. After twenty feet or so, I run out of slack and must reposition the rope to a belay point further down.

This is when the canoe is most vulnerable to Murphy, so I make sure I'm well braced, with the rope held tightly in a gloved hand, and carefully move to the lowest crosstie I can reach to rewrap and lower anew. Little by little, in this manner, the boat gets safely down.

Back underway, I embark on Allen Lake, the nineteenth or twentieth lake so far. I've lost count. A muscular tailwind allows my tired body to rest, progress made essentially for free.

At day's end, I find a spectacular campsite with a spot for the tent on mossy, mattress-soft ground. The air is hot and humid and the horse and deer flies come out in force, seeking horses and deer but, finding neither, settle on me.

I am forced to the sweltering confines of the tent until the temperature drops sufficiently for them to buzz off. Once they do, I emerge and go for a swim while beans and rice simmer on the stove. I dine late under a sunset so sublime that everything feels like the right-right this time.

Chapter 30
Pooping Your Own Balloon

Day 21

Three weeks and three-hundred miles are now behind me. It seems I've been at this a lot longer than that. Time is supposed to fly when you're having fun, and although I am having fun in some perverse way, the adage hasn't held true.

If time is flying, it's more dirigible than jet, and the days used to mark it more or less indistinguishable, one from the next. Fatigue contributes to a sense that time has slowed, as I have slowed within it—as if time is tuckered too.

I want to cross what's left of Allen Lake early before the wind knows I'm on it, so forego humanizing and go. The wind isn't fooled and catches me square in the middle, but kindly this time, from behind, and scoots me with alacrity the rest of the way.

Gliding out of Allen Lake I am surprised to pass under power lines, thick insulated cables that droop pendulously beneath tall steel towers that troop down to the river from one side and away from it on the other, looking like broad-shouldered giants marching in file. It's an unwelcome sight. Even in a place as remote as this, the works of man encroach.

What purpose can this line serve? There's a hamlet, Lynn Lake, off to the northwest about fifty miles, but a line this big wouldn't be needed for a settlement that small. So, the electricity must be going the other way, from a dam in the north churning water to watts and sending it south to slake demand for computer screens, espresso machines, hot tubs, dance clubs, thermostats and laundromats.

Humans will go to the ends of the earth for energy, as this line proves. It does not bode well for the natural world.

I am approaching Devil's Rapids. The intel from the kid at Pukatawagan Falls was that this rapid had to be portaged, but I don't see why. It's nothing but water speeding through a smattering of rocks, all easily dodged. Mid-run I check the GPS to gauge my speed. *Wheee!* Eleven miles an hour it reads. That's like breaking the sound barrier in a canoe.

A portage cannot be avoided at Granville Falls which forms a sheer drop of forty-five feet. It used to be even higher until an impoundment downstream raised the lake level below. The portage is long, 300 yards. Fortunately, there is a skid so I manage the chore in just four trips. Trip one is the yellow dry bag with food (food that doesn't fit in either the food box or barrel), plus paddles, guitar and shotgun.

Trip two is the green dry bag containing sleeping bag and clothes. This is carried on my back while my hands take the tent and Imelda Marcos bag holding all the shoes I don't use. Trip three is the canoe, which I employ as a sled, sliding it over the rails with the food barrel and myriad incidentals left inside. And last is the dreaded food box.

Had I bothered to find out there were more than twenty portages to contend with, I wouldn't have brought it. The thought occurs to me to just leave it here along the portage trail, sans food of course, as a present to the Cree. I seriously consider doing so, but then dismiss the idea. Abandoning the box would violate the *leave no trace* credo I preached throughout my career and likely incur karmic consequence.

The fact that I even contemplated such a sin speaks to my level of fatigue. In penance for the impure thought, I hoist the box up on my back and struggle past the falls under its weight, like Jesus bearing His cross on the via Dolorosa.

Repacked, I start down Granville Lake and into the teeth of a sturdy blow. The wind doesn't let up, not for a second, and by late afternoon I've had it and stop. Although cloudy and cool all day, the sky now clears and sunshine beams down. To think: this heat has portaged 93,000,000 miles through space, past planets, moons, and meteors to me.

I go for a swim and then enter the tent to rest free of bugs. Laying face up, I dumbly watch shadows from dwarf willow and fireweed dance across the tent top. They look like characters in a Balinese puppet play. My limbs are leaden, my brain a blank, all of me overcome by a profound lassitude.

Where do thoughts come from? I wonder, having none other than this one. *What causes the mind to pick a thread and tug it? I dunno. Why am I even thinking this?* The puppets are fighting now, violently swinging to and fro. I'm rooting for the fireweed. A birchbark canoe drifts into consciousness, just shows up. *Wow! A boat made of bark.*

That's a stretch. I marvel that someone came up with such a brilliant invention. Boats are essential in this country and must be strong and light, but what to make one from? Bark! What else? You use what you have. Whoever lit on that idea had a brain like Einstein's.

Hopefully, it was some buck-toothed nerd who couldn't suck marrow and walk at the same time, a social misfit taunted, bullied, derided, and teased until one day he watched as a chunk of birch bark floated down the river and had an 'Ah ha'! moment.

A small spider, crawling up the tent's interior wall, distracts me. I saw several like it today—tiny ones, just hatched. They were kiting through air on filaments of gossamer that occasionally caught in sun and flashed silver. At first, I took these for random skeins of webbing until one drifted close and I saw a little arachnid attached.

Is this by design or accident? I know spiders use different silks for different applications, one for webs and others for climbing or wrapping prey, for example, but didn't realize that some can extrude specialized strands to carry them aloft. I marvel at the notion. Imagine, pooping your own balloon. I wish I could do that. It would make portaging so much easier.

I brought along a booklet of wilderness quotes and read one each night for inspiration prior to nodding off.

Tonight's is appropriate, a quote by Howard Zahniser: "To know wilderness," he said, "is to know a profound humility, to recognizes one's littleness…"

Littleness, it dawns on me, is a big reason I'm here. To feel a small part of something grand, a part not apart. Watching the little spider gets me there. We are kindred spirits, this tiny creature and I, infinitesimal beings sharing an unfathomable universe. I don't need all the answers. Sometimes, the questions are more than enough.

Chapter 31
One That Got Away

When it comes to Wilderness, size really does matter but, aside from North America's northernmost fringes, the areas we have consist mostly of fragments not big enough to adequately provide for either a fully functioning ecosystem or sense of grand immensity. How big should a wilderness be, anyway? The Wilderness Act directs they be at least 5,000 acres, but that's a postage stamp, not even eight square miles.

Aldo Leopold, a founding member of the Wilderness Society, believed that wilderness should be large enough to accommodate a two-week pack trip, but this vision could only be realized today with the pokiest of ponies.

So, although bigger is better, we have what we have, and the prospects for adding acres to already established areas aren't great, since, for the most part, adjacent lands are either private or, if public, managed for disqualifying activities such as motorized recreation or timber harvest.

Still, opportunities to enlarge and enhance existing wilderness do occasionally pop up. One did for the Lee Metcalf; a damn good one too. Alas, it was one that got away.

The Lee Metcalf was late to the wilderness system, designated in 1983. Oddly, its quarter-million acres were established not in one cohesive piece, but rather in four discontinuous units, the result of compromise between wilderness advocates, motorized groups, and the timber industry.

This was not the best outcome for wilderness, but probably the best possible, given the politics of the day. Some of the blame for the area's fragmented makeup can be laid squarely at the size-fourteen feet of none other than Abraham Lincoln, for it was he who authorized the Northern Pacific Railroad Act of 1864.

Linking the Pacific Northwest by rail to the rest of the country seemed a good idea, and because the government owned essentially all western lands, it made sense to pay for this enormously expensive project, in part, by granting the syndicate building the line some of this plentiful land. The deal was generous, with the Northern Pacific Railroad Company awarded forty square miles of land for every linear mile of track laid.

Ultimately, the company ended up with forty-six million acres, an amount of ground comparable in size to Washington State.

The grants were given out in a checkerboard pattern of alternating square-mile sections, both along the track and elsewhere, in so-called *indemnity belts*, the idea being to reserve some public ownership where it was sure to increase in value once the road became operational, which it was in 1883.

Former President Ulysses S. Grant hammered in the last spike somewhere between Helena and Missoula, Montana, on September 8th of that year.

The Madison Range, future home to the Lee Metcalf Wilderness, was within one of these indemnity belts. As such, alternating sections throughout the range belonged either to the Northern Pacific or the Federal Government. Over time, the government's portion became National Forest and the railroad's morphed into Plum Creek Timber, the corporate successor of the Northern Pacific.

The incompatibility of this arrangement, with every section essentially surrounded by land belonging to the other entity, grew especially apparent in the 1960s with logging occurring right next to lands esteemed for recreation. Management for both organizations became encumbered and complicated.

Worse, because Plum Creek's sole purpose was realized through timber harvest, while Forest Service objectives were not so clear-cut, the checkerboard pattern displayed on maps was becoming manifest on the ground.

By the late 1970s, with most of their properties either landlocked or logged, Plum Creek decided to sell their Madison holdings and went shopping for a buyer. At the same time, Montana wilderness advocates were seeking to add acres and areas to the National Wilderness Preservation System and, for them, Plum Creek's divestiture presented an opportunity to do just that.

This is where Lee Metcalf comes in. A U.S. senator from Montana, Metcalf brokered a deal whereby Plum Creek and the Forest Service traded tracts to consolidate squares across the checkerboard, lumping the whites and reds together with their own kind.

As a result, Plum Creek ended up with land around the growing resort community of Big Sky, including a drainage immediately to the west of it called Jack Creek, while the rest of the range became National Forest.

Plum Creek isn't a timber company for nothing, and soon saws were whirring and timber falling on their newly-acquired properties. But elsewhere, north and south, quiet reigned as a new Wilderness Area, named for its benefactor, came to be.

It took Plum Creek little time to high-grade the trees in and around Big Sky and Jack Creek, and land without logs is of little use to a timber company, so, by the late 1980s, they again decided to sell. This time they found an unlikely buyer in The Nature Conservancy (TNC).

Although not in the practice of acquiring clearcuts, TNC understood that this was no ordinary logged-out land. Once allowed to recover, Jack Creek especially would provide exceptional habitat for several hard-pressed species, including grizzly bears, mountain goats, elk, moose, and wolverine. Furthermore, the purchase would hem in the development frenzy occurring around Big Sky and contain it.

The asking price was $24 million for 165,000 acres, about $150 per acre, and TNC's offer came within a million of that. By all appearances, the deal was done, but one proviso had to be worked out first. Plum Creek operated a lumber mill near Bozeman and insisted it be part of the sale. They didn't want to be the bad guy in shutting it down, so put that onus on TNC instead. This left The Nature Conservancy in a quandary.

Although not in the lumber business, it wouldn't look good if the first consequence of a major conservation purchase led to the loss of several good-paying blue-collar jobs. Hence, TNC made the bold decision to keep the mill and operate it with logs sustainably harvested from Jack Creek. But how much timber was left and how much could be sustainably cut? Until these questions were answered, the deal was put on hold.

To get to those answers, TNC retained the services of a forester, one with impeccable credentials, but who, unfortunately as it turned out, was in the employ of a Plum Creek competitor. The nature of competition being what it is, some bad blood already existed between the two companies. Still, an agreement seemed imminent, until another wrench got thrown in the works.

Only days before the deal was to be consummated, Montana's two senators, Max Baucus and Conrad Burns (Lee Metcalf had since died), proposed an alternative arrangement, swapping Plum Creek lands in the Madison Range for timbered National Forest lands elsewhere. Presumably the senators had good intentions, but this stalled negotiations further as Plum Creek needed time to consider the new offer.

It was during this pondering period when things went seriously south. Plum Creek discovered that the competitor, again for whom TNC's consultant worked, considered the deal too sweet of one and had initiated a secret campaign to derail it. Infuriated, Plum Creek execs brought negotiations with TNC to an abrupt and permanent halt.

It was so close, just a whisker away, a deal that would have protected essentially every acre granted the Northern Pacific a hundred years before. Ultimately, The Nature Conservancy planned to return it to the public by selling it back to the Forest Service at cost.

Had this happened, much of this land, in all likelihood, would have eventually been added to the Lee Metcalf Wilderness, conjoining it across the range. That would have been a conservation triumph, an environmental coup, a glorious thing, especially in light of what came next.

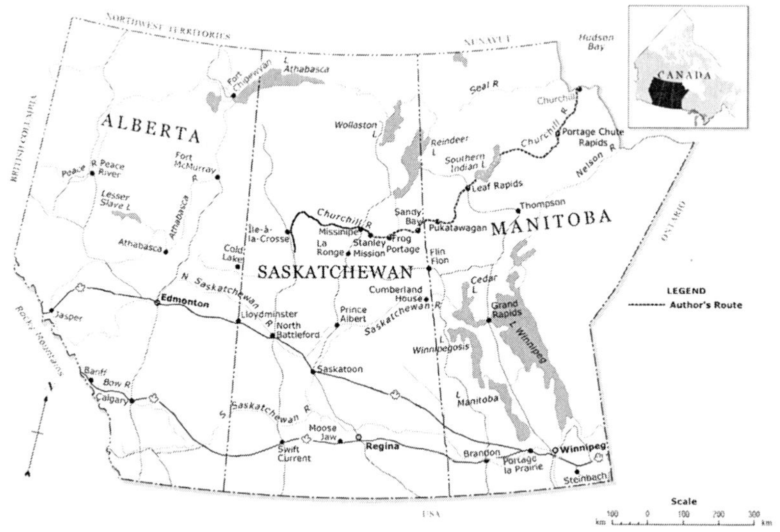

Baby mink: While scouting a rapid I encountered a family of baby mink. What a delight. Unafraid, they roughhoused and wrestled at my feet and had me laughing out loud. That humans still trap these and other animals for their skins makes me ashamed to be part of my species.

Portaging: Portaging is tough. With all the stuff I had (too much) it took five to seven trips back and forth to get everything carried around each portage. Thus, a carry of a quarter mile would entail almost three miles of brutally hard work.

Pressed into the earth by the weight of the sky. Expedition solo paddling, I was told, is like running a marathon each day. That may be an exaggeration, but if so, it's not much of one. I was worn to the bone.

In Fate's crosshairs: Southern Indian Lake is more Indian Ocean than lake. With 2300 miles of shoreline it is scary huge and crossing it in a small boat, being nearly two miles from land in any direction, is riding the edge between this world and whatever comes next.

The quintessential wilderness experience: This black bear wanted to kill and eat me and very nearly succeeded. I had to fight it with nothing more than my bare hands until effecting an improbable escape bordering on the miraculous.

Polar bear: Seeing this polar bear in Churchill, Manitoba was a thrill, but made me feel guilty too. Polar bears probably won't survive a whole lot longer in the wild because their world is melting away, and the fault that it is, is partly mine.

Chapter 32
The Boys Meet a Wood Hippie

Day 22

Only thirty miles from Leaf Rapids. I might be able to make it with a tailwind or no wind and a determined effort, but likely not in time to do errands and get to the post office where there is sure to be a letter waiting from Marianne.

Still I try, going hard until a headwind makes it clear I won't reach Leaf today. I take my foot off the gas and proceed more at ease.

Granville Lake has a pleasing diversity of scenery with a mixture of intimate passageways wending between forested islands and wide-open seascapes. It's a pleasant paddle despite the wind. I stop for lunch on a massive slab of granite canted above the river.

Spent from the morning's effort, I am content to rest, basking seal-like in sunshine, until the peace is shattered by the sounds I least care to hear: human voices. I sit up and turn to see two boats rounding a point, coming my way. Tired, grumpy, and at my misanthropic worst, I am in no mood to engage with my fellow man. I want to be left alone to rest, to think and feel, but apparently that's not going to happen.

The boaters see me and adjust course to intercept. There are three of them, two in a canoe and one in a kayak. The two in the canoe are chattering like squirrels and singing. *Maybe I can get by with just a wave*, I think hopefully, and give a halfhearted one, trying not to appear overly friendly, but it doesn't work. I'm going to be invaded. They pull up to my rock, My Rock, and spill onto it like a litter of unruly pups.

"Hey! You're the guy from Montana going to the Seal," says one with excessive enthusiasm.

They've heard about me, like I've heard about the two girls, and start tag-teaming, peppering me with questions between summersaults and cannonballs into the river.

Adam, Ryan, and Jacob are twenty-something college kids from Minnesota on an expedition they've dubbed "Rails to Whales" because it began with a train trip from Winnipeg to Jasper and will end at Churchill where belugas ply the estuary at the river's mouth.

They've been at it for two months and covered 1,500 miles thus far, including portaging the continental divide, and don't seem the least bit tired, which is irksome. Despite my initial reluctance to engage, I am soon won over by their affability and good cheer. When we depart the rock, we go together.

They must slow their pace for me keep up, but even so, I have to paddle harder than is comfortable. Adam and Ryan, in the canoe, are garrulous as crows and regale me with tales of their trip and stories about their lives in Minnesota. Adam doesn't know what he wants to do for work. He's considering teaching, but is not completely sold on the idea, hoping instead for a career in canoeing.

Back home, he has a part-time gig at a Subway sandwich shop, harvests wild rice commercially each fall, and attends classes at the local JC. Ryan goes to the same school part-time and works the other part in a restaurant. His girlfriend is employed at an art gallery in Duluth. Together they make $12,000 a year.

Ryan doesn't seem to realize that $12,000 isn't much of an income, but he's gotten used to getting by on that. Both Adam and Ryan have career paths about as clear as some of the portage trails I've traveled.

Jacob, in the kayak, is different. He's as reserved as the other two are outgoing and getting him to open up takes probing, so I probe. He attends the University of Minnesota, studying materials engineering, the kind of engineering that leads to discoveries like duct tape, Kevlar, and dental floss.

In his third year and nearing graduation, Jake has a bright future ahead, but now, since embarking on this trip, he's come to wonder whether a career in a cubicle is right for him.

Adam is the only one of the three who had ever canoed before. Ryan and Jacob are novitiates, and although a canoe journey of 1,800 miles does indeed start with the first stroke, theirs was literally that.

It would be akin to climbing up on the back of a horse for the first time and hearing someone twanging over a crackling PA, "And out of chute number two, on a pony named Bone Crusher, a cowboy out of Duluth, Minnesota…," as the gate swung open.

I warm to these lads as we paddle and get to know one another. They are my kind of kids. From long experience supervising trail crews and wilderness rangers, I can quickly recognize the type who thrive outside, who can work hard, get dirty, suffer, and like it.

I delight in their company, and the miles fly by in conversation. When talk lapses, the silence is quickly filled with song—voyageur songs that Ryan and Adam sing, full-voiced and hearty, to the rhythm of their rapidly dipping blades.

After a long afternoon, with me struggling to keep up, we reach a pleasant beach and pull out to camp. The boys are out of their boats and fishing, literally within seconds, but get no bites. Jacob goes back in his kayak and heads off to try elsewhere, while and Adam and Ryan fish out a bag of pot, fill a pipe, and offer it to me.

"What makes you think I would engage in such criminal activity?" I ask, trying to sound earnest.

"We know a wood hippie when we see one," is their vaguely accurate reply.

It seems weed has gotten a lot stronger over the last thirty years. I spend the next hour gabbing on the beach with my new young friends, alternating between silly and serious conversation, until Jacob returns with a stringer of fish—walleye and pike. Adam slathers the fillets in pig fat and fries them over a campfire.

The pig fat was gifted them seven weeks earlier by a bush dweller they encountered. I'm not too sure about eating it, but one can't be too picky under the circumstances. Adam's fish is a tour de force, a thoroughly scrumptious dish, munchies or no munchies.

Although generally quite content to be alone in the woods, I must admit to enjoying the companionship of these lively young men. It is not that I feel lonely, despite having had no human contact for the last three weeks. Rather, it is the unbridled joy these boys exhibit for their adventure, which has the effect of bolstering the delight I have in mine.

Thanks to the distraction of conversation, and working hard to keep up with the Rails to Whales crew, I made twenty-three miles today, the most in one day to date.

Chapter 33
Love It or Leaf It

Day 23

We are up against a howling headwind from the get-go, with gusts that would register on the Beaufort scale. Normally I wouldn't leave the beach in such conditions, but Leaf Rapids is only seven miles from camp and we are all anxious to get there, so we go. The brim of my Tilley hat gets pasted flat to my forehead and I batten down its chinstrap so it can't blow away.

To make progress into this much wind demands everything I have, and everything laid on non-stop. A moment's inattention or pause in paddling, no matter how brief, and the boat is turned sideways and driven back down the lake. Once broadside, it is no easy task to get it pointed back into the wind.

Doing so requires forward sweeps applied forcefully and fast, each stroke bringing the bow a few degrees up, while half that gain is lost in the intervals in-between. So, one must bear down, lean out, and speed up, until, little by little, the boat splits the wind like a weathervane.

Then you better keep it there with keen attention and constant correction, employing sweeps and J's while paddling forward with every ounce of remaining strength. Stopping for any reason, to sip water or scratch your nose, and the boat is broadside again and going the wrong way fast.

I am maxed out, battling the wind and trying to keep up with the boys. Usually, I have another gear held in reserve to call upon if necessary, but now I am using it. It is so physically taxing that I resort to stroke counting, something I almost never do.

Marianne is a stroke counter. She ticks off each stroke in her head, counting from one to a hundred, then changes sides and starts anew. It's a way for her to mark progress and avoid overworking one side of her body. But I don't like it. Counting too easily becomes an obsession that steals the focus from milieu to math.

Usually, I simply paddle on one side until that side tires and then switch, and only count when pushing the limits of endurance or when flank speed is needed to reduce exposure to risk. In such instances, counting is calming, a mantra to divert one's attention from hardship or fear, while, at the same time, serving to convince the will that these excruciations are fleeting and finite.

The objective is not, say, to get across the lake, but simply to get to one hundred. The will is a rube and easily fooled in this manner; it doesn't seem to realize that the goalpost keeps moving.

The wicked winds assail us without cease but we struggle on, eager to reach Leaf Rapids to telephone loved ones, pick up mail, eat something that isn't pike, pasta, or peanut butter, and poop in porcelain. Finally, after agonizing hours of toil, a telltale sign of civilization comes into view: a com tower atop a timbered butte. We are getting there, but still it takes two more hours of dogged work before we reach a channel leading to a boat dock a mile away.

As we approach the dock, two guys, about the age of the boys, are fishing from it. One is First Nations, and the other a ruddy blond. They pay us scant heed as we land, oblivious or disinterested. I get the impression they're stoned from the way they move, and this suspicion is all but confirmed once we get them talking. There are long pauses between our crisp questions and their halting, rambling replies.

The blond sports a garish Hawaiian shirt unbuttoned to the navel, exposing a roll of soft, white, belly fat and a pistol that looks like a luger tucked into the waistband of his shorts, its handle encased in flab. It's only a pellet gun, Jesus not having sanctified Canadians with the Second Amendment. As we chat, the guy pulls the piece out at random, gives it a few pumps, and fires it at nothing in particular.

Town is a mile away, up the Waterline Road.

The native kid suggests that one of us stay with the boats because the locals, he says, "Will probably borrow stuff," if they are left unattended.

Jake volunteers to take the first watch. One of us will return to relieve him as soon as practical.

Before starting for town, a small launch appears out in the channel, speeding toward the dock at full throttle. At the last second, after ramming seems inevitable, the craft decelerates and glides into the dock, hitting it askew with a hard bump. One of three aboard leaps out, and the boat, not wasting a second, pulls away and races back the way it came, as if trying to distance itself from something unpleasant.

The discarded passenger is a rail-thin, middle-aged Cree, bent like a question mark. He gives his name as Paul. His complexion is sallow, his hair lank, and his handshake limp. There is a bad vibe about him. Were I a dog, I'd be growling with hackles raised, so I am not pleased when he joins us for the trek to town.

The welcoming committee tags along too, so there are six of us walking up the road, clustered together like sailors on shore leave. Conversation is forced. Adam, Ryan, or I attempt small talk, asking about the weather, winter, bugs, jobs, and fishing, but receive only terse, unembellished replies. The pudgy guy with the pellet gun keeps pumping and shooting it, which seems a little weird.

When we pass a golf course, Paul allows that someone was killed there not long back, murdered, either by a golf club or screwdriver, he can't remember which. I comment that getting killed on a golf course would be a blessing for some, but no one gets the joke, or at least no one laughs. The edgy gabfest ends when we reach Highway 6, the road south. A sign points the way to Thompson, 212 kilometers away.

Another welcomes us to Leaf Rapids, 'The North's Hidden Treasure'.

Leaf Rapids was an instant town built in 1976 to accommodate an influx of miners after deposits of copper and zinc were discovered nearby. It is a model of urban planning, designed to co-exist with the surrounding wilderness, or so says the sign explaining all of this.

The *Town Centre* is indeed that—the sun around which Leaf Rapids revolves. Big enough to hold the Hindenburg, this immense building houses the schools, post office, library, grocery and liquor stores, a deli, various shops and restaurants, the recreation complex, with pool and gym, plus town and provincial government offices.

The exterior was constructed of a material designed to turn blue if exposed to air pollution, but the air has evidently remained pure since the building retains its original rusty hue.

Upon entering through big glass doors, we are immediately assaulted by a bustle of activity. People, practically all First Nations, move as people do in shopping centers, either hurrying with purpose or milling around in bored resignation. Several disreputable sorts loll on benches that line the walks and eye us with unfriendly stares. It occurs to me that we don't look very reputable either; dirty, bearded, and unkempt as we are.

The natter of commerce and conversation bounces off the concrete walls and echoes through the vast interior. It's a din, an onslaught on the senses, and an uncomfortable contrast to the quiet we're accustomed to.

We split up to take care of business, Adam to the grocery store, Ryan to call his brother, and me to the bookstore to buy maps needed for the new route down the lower Churchill.

I'm encouraged to see that the bookstore has quads, hundreds of them in labeled folders, but most are incorrectly filed, so I must search through each one, hoping to find the maps I need. After thirty minutes of this, I find none.

The clerk suggests the Department of Natural Resources upstairs, since they also have maps, so up I go. The DNR office is staffed by a lone secretary who regrets to inform me that their maps are working copies only and not for sale.

"Try the bookstore downstairs," she says.

Pinned to a wall is a gigantic map of the entire Churchill River basin, from Alberta to Hudson Bay. It's small-scale, so small that townships, areas of thirty-six square miles, are displayed in two-inch cubes. The river shows as a thin blue line snaking across the map from edge to edge.

I put on a pitiful face and ask if I might have it, even though the map would be about as useful for navigating the Churchill as a placemat depicting the Milky Way would be in setting course for Mars. Still, it's better than nothing, and nothing is all I have so far. I whine until the poor woman gives in. Once removed, a perfect square of paint, three feet on a side and shades darker than the rest of the wall, is left to mark its absence.

Departing with this near worthless prize, I head to the post office. The clerk, like most P.O. personnel, is affable and efficient. I ask if there is any mail for me sent general delivery, and she goes back to check, rummages around awhile, and returns with a letter and big box from Marianne.

We chat a bit, and I learn that Leaf Rapids was, until recently, mostly occupied by white folk, but when the mines closed three years before, the miners sold their homes for ten cents on the dollar and now ninety percent of the population is Indigenous, making it essentially a reserve town (except that this one has a liquor store).

I am impatient to read Marianne's letter, so hit the deli, order lunch, and settle in, but before I can extract the letter from its envelope, a shadow falls across my table, and I look up to see Paul, teetering above me. He cadges me out of a cup of coffee, gets more than my money's worth in added sugar, and then sits down, uninvited, across from me.

High on something stronger than caffeine, he is barely coherent, but starts pitching a business scheme, a sure-fire can't-miss deal where I would smuggle handguns from Montana to Manitoba, and he would sell them. Possessing a handgun in Canada is a serious crime, a felony in fact.

"Couldn't I get in trouble?" I ask Paul, feigning interest.

"Naw," he assures me. "Only the person selling get in trouble. Makashitloadamoney," he says.

I want him gone. I want to read my letter. I want to eat my lunch, but I'm stuck with this addled, unpleasant lunatic and don't know how to get rid of him without being rude.

In the midst of this dilemma, a very large and very drunk woman appears and sits down with us. Her head is huge and red, like an overinflated balloon about to burst. She can barely hold herself upright and lists heavily to one side of the chair.

"My wife," Paul says, by way of introduction. I ask her if she would like a cup of coffee.

She says 'cream', or something that sounds like it, and holds out her hand. I take it.

Then, with a determined effort to enunciate, she says "Creen, my name," and I get it on the third try. Her name is Corrine.

Paul ignores her and returns to rambling on about gun running, while Corrine reels in her chair, trying not to capsize, and I, finding nothing redemptive in any of this, effect an escape.

I take my napkin, scribble 'johnnysworldoguns@hotdog.com' on it, hand it to Paul, and tell him to have his people call my people, and, lying further add, "It was nice meeting you," and to Corrine, "a pleasure," then get up and go.

I want beer. I've been dreaming about beer for weeks—cold cans beaded with dew—and now this dream can come true, just two doors down at the liquor store, or so I think, but nothing is working out for me in this town. I couldn't get maps, couldn't read my letter, and now can't get cold beer. The only beer for sale is Schlitz, either regular or lite, and none of it chilled.

"We aren't allowed to sell cold beer," the clerk explains.

This is even more egregious in my view than not being able to own a handgun. What the hell is wrong with this country? I tell the clerk that selling warm Schlitz is a felony in the United States, punishable by a $5,000 fine and six months in jail. By his expression, or perhaps as a result of mine, I think he believes me.

I like beer, but do have standards, low as they may be, but not to the depths of warm Schlitz. I purchase a bottle of 151 instead and ask the clerk, while paying, if there are any other restrictions on alcohol. He says that Indigenous people are limited to one bottle per day.

"Pretty strict," I quip.

Back in the main loitering area, I run into Ryan. He looks shaken and says that a drunk tried to pick a fight with him.

He had reached his brother on the pay phone and said in greeting, "How's it going, chief?" and a passing Cree, overhearing the remark and thinking it directed at him, took offense.

The injured party raised his dukes and repeatedly drew them back as if readying to punch Ryan in the face. Despite repeated apologies for any misunderstanding, Ryan could not mollify this man, so felt it best to leave. Someone had to go back to relieve Jacob, anyway.

I have a set of maps with me, borrowed from the boys to reference the ones I tried to buy. Now, with no maps available, I enter the grocery store where 8½ x 11 copies could be had for twenty-five cents apiece. I have to be discerning about which quads to copy, having just so many quarters, so copy only the ones with rapids.

The black and white reproductions are difficult to read. I can't distinguish river from contour lines or forest from tundra, but they are better than the map I begged off the DNR. While at the store, I purchase a few items and then head back for the boats, happy to be leaving Leaf Rapids.

Walking down Waterline Road, I see two figures lurching along ahead, going my way. I am almost back to the dock when I catch up to them. *Horrors!* It's Paul and Corrine, even higher now than they were two hours ago at the deli.

Paul is literally raving, running around and yelling at retardant planes flying over enroute to a fire on the Barrington River. (I learned about this fire from the DNR secretary, and because of it, I couldn't have gotten to the Seal that way, anyway.) Paul is screaming and shaking his fists at the planes.

"Save my fucking squirrels!" he bellows, over and over, totally deranged. I hope to avoid him.

Ryan and Jacob sit in shade next to the boats chatting about the 'chief' incident when I arrive. Jacob still needs to get to town, and Ryan goes with him, leaving me alone with Paul and Corrine lurking around somewhere nearby. I take cover in the forest fringe, leaning against the road berm, trying to hide, but Corrine sniffs me out.

"May I sit down?" she asks with some formality.

"Please," I say, indicating a spot on the ground.

She explains that she and Paul are going to Paul's place on Granville Lake but haven't made any arrangements for transportation so are just waiting, hoping a boat will come by and give them a lift. We sit in silence a few moments but then hear Paul in the distance, still yelling at airplanes.

Corinne asks me for a drink, saying she could really use a 'bump'. I tell her I don't drink—that I used to but quit. Technically this is true since I hadn't had a drink for a good nineteen hours and didn't plan on starting in again for a few hours more.

A scurrying in the forest draws Corrine's attention and she leaves to investigate.

She's back in a few minutes to announce, "It was a black bear. A cub."

She tells me that black bears are dangerous and warns me to always sleep on islands. I'm thinking that these people have become completely enfeebled by civilization and lost their connection to the wilds if they are afraid of black bears. Corrine reads my disbelief.

"Be careful," she says, giving me a serious look. (It wouldn't be long until I discovered just how right she was.)

Then Corrine launches into her life story.

"I'm an alcoholic," she begins. "I started drinking when I was nine and smoking pot, too. Now I'm fifty-two."

We move into a real conversation, which gets better and better as she sobers up, and I relax in her company. Paul leaves us alone, but we can still hear him every now and again tilting at windmills.

"I'm a bush person," she says, explaining that she grew up in South Indian Lake, a small community of about 1,000 people forty miles from Leaf Rapids. She only went to school through fourth grade and didn't learn English until she was twenty. The sexual abuse started when she was eleven.

"Where were your parents?" I ask.

"Drinking," she says. Her parents essentially abandoned her and two younger sisters when Corrine was thirteen. They lived off moose and fish and caught frogs for 'frog soup'. When only twelve, Corrine, as part of some rite of passage, was put in charge of three other children, aged nine to eleven, and told to take them in a canoe to Tadoule Lake, a Dene village on the Seal River more than 200 miles away.

She had been shown the route over the divide once, a year before, but couldn't remember all the twists and turns, and the group became hopelessly lost. They had no compass, maps, tents, or sleeping bags, and little food and remained lost for three weeks.

After the first week, out of food, they lived mostly on spruce worms, dug out of bark.

"They tasted like peanut butter," she tells me. "They were good!"

At night, the kids bent willow clumps over and tied the tops to make a shelter.

"The bugs beat us up pretty good," she says.

Finally, in desperation, Corrine started a forest fire on an island and they were rescued when fire fighters came to put it out.

Corrine has several scars on her face and three long parallel ones on the inside of one arm. I ask about them. She touches a small wound near her eye and says she was stabbed there with a screwdriver. The wounds on her arm were from a hatchet. Someone attacked her with a hatchet!

Suddenly, the stream of obscenities that had been distant draws near, and Paul emerges from the trees. Except for the word 'fuck', I can barely understand him. Corrine asks him nicely to please watch his language. He responds with a string of *fuck you*'s directed at his bride; the spew accompanying these invectives bursting in sunlight like tiny fireworks.

Corrine says to Paul, "Not doing so good, eh?"

Paul replies, "No shit, Sherlock," and wanders off, much to my relief.

"Has he ever hit you?" I ask, emboldened by her openness.

She says that he used to kick the shit out of her, even when she was pregnant, but one day she picked up a barrel that weighed 150 pounds and brained him with it.

"He doesn't mess with me anymore," she says, matter of fact.

"So, you have children?" She had three, a boy and two girls, but only the girls are alive. Her son was killed—murdered at twenty-six. She doesn't say much about the daughters. One lives in Winnipeg and wants Corrine to come live with her, but Corrine doesn't think she will. The furthest she has ever traveled is to Thompson.

"I'm a bush person, but I'll never go back to South Indian Lake," she says. "Too many perverts."

Paul wanders back. He's in a little better shape and points to the channel in the river we crossed earlier.

"We almost drowned there," he says, "last fall."

They were drunk, and he was speeding. The boat struck a partially submerged log and flipped, dumping them into the chilly water. They barely made it to shore. Paul blames Manitoba Hydro for the log. He thinks Manitoba Hydro owes him a new boat and starts getting worked up about the injustice of it all.

To change the subject, I ask Paul if he's always lived on Granville Lake.

"No, not always," he says.

After his parents drowned when he was eleven, he lived in foster homes, group homes, and Indian residential schools all over Manitoba. There was one home in Winnipeg he liked.

"It had food, a nice place to sleep, and school," he tells me.

I learn that this is the first time these two have been together in seven months, having separated when Corrine walked out after some altercation. They are trying to patch things up, but from what I can tell, it's a long shot.

"Paul's family, they don't like me," Corrine says. "They say I'm fat and ugly."

Paul says, "At least they're not blind, Sherlock."

Adam, Ryan, and Jacob return at 7:00. I've been talking to Corrine for two hours and have warmed to her. She is honest, smart, and open, a good person, but our conversation leaves me low. It has not been a good life for her, or Paul either, and it doesn't appear that it's going to get better. Neither of them, it seems, ever had much of a chance.

The boys and I shove off, not wanting to delay a minute longer in this grim, unhappy place. We make camp a short distance downstream, all of us weighted with a sense of sadness from our time in Leaf Rapids.

When I finally get to read Marianne's letter, my sorrow evaporates. It's a sweet note, full of news about cats and the garden; that it has been raining and the hills are green; that she loves me like crazy.

I'm glad somebody loves me, that somebody cares, that I matter to someone. I head to bed glad, but with one regret. I wish I hadn't been so snooty about the beer. A warm Schlitz would really hit the spot about now.

Chapter 34
Behind Every Great Fortune

The Jack Creek Story Continued

Jack Creek, that plum of a drainage in the Madison Range that Plum Creek Timber corporation nearly sold to The Nature Conservancy, instead went to someone else: a real-deal wheeler-dealer named Tim Blixseth. Blixseth was a self-made timber baron from Oregon with several fortunes won and lost and a bankruptcy or two already behind him. In 1992, he bought all of the 165,000 acres Plum Creek was selling for $27.5 million.

Of those acres, Blixseth really only cared about 13,600 of them, forest and rangelands bordering Big Sky. He realized that real estate near ski resorts had tremendous development potential and lit upon the idea of building a high-end hidey-hole for the uber-rich—essentially a gated community with ski runs and golf. He called this brainchild the Yellowstone Club.

The Yellowstone Club is a resort so exclusive that only the genuinely well-heeled need apply. That's right: prospective buyers had to apply and money alone wasn't enough to swing the deal. In addition to cash, aspirants had to demonstrate to Blixseth's satisfaction that they weren't assholes. The club was an asshole-free zone. As such, Bill Gates was in, Larry Ellison was out.

Once accepted, members paid $300,000 to join, coughed up annual fees of $36,000, and were required to purchase property, which cost anywhere from $2,000,000 for a lot, up to $26,000,000 for a lot more—say a 20,000 square-foot mountain manse, replete with heated driveway and $5,000 German-made ski boot dryer.

Members have access to fifteen chair lifts, an eighteen-hole Tom Weiskopf-designed golf course, three lodges, tennis courts, spa, and swimming pool. Thrown in, at no extra charge, is easy access to the Lee Metcalf Wilderness, conveniently located right next door. How exclusive is that? But, you better act fast. Membership is capped at 864 homesites. That's the good news. It would be a shame to ruin the environment with over-development; and rest assured, none of your neighbors will be assholes.

To the west of the Yellowstone Club, over the divide on the Madison side, is Jack Creek, a drainage of 25,000 mostly clear-cut acres. Having no interest in it and needing capital for the Yellowstone Club, Blixseth sold Jack Creek to a wannabe tycoon from Ennis named Lee Poole for six million dollars, just $240 per acre.

Originally from Cleveland, Lee had come to the Madison Valley in the 1970s to work as a ranch hand for some landed gentry. He immediately fell in love with the place, as anyone who ever gazed upon it from the back of a horse would; a lush valley bounded by stunning ranges, through which a gorgeous river flowed. Having found his Shangri-La, Lee now only needed the means to enjoy it in style.

Lee was a charmer, full of bonhomie and impossible to dislike, with personality of the type you could take to a bank and use as collateral. Jack Creek was one of his favorite haunts. He hunted the drainage each fall, before Plum Creek hauled out the trees in trucks, leaving the trailhead in pre-dawn chill to pad silently through snow toward the fluty strains of bugling bulls. Lee knew Jack Creek intimately, better than most. He saw grizzlies, black bear, cougar, and coyote.

From a modest start as ranch hand, Lee began a rapid ascent through economic strata, first by opening an art gallery in Ennis and then dabbling in real estate. With some moneyed partners, he'd purchase ranches and sub-divide them, not into small lots, but into large tracts he could peddle to wealthy out-of-staters seeking to own a piece of the Big Sky.

These were not speculators planning to profit by further sub-dividing and flipping the land, but lifestyle buyers. Once they had the trophy home, guesthouse, fish pond, horse barn, tennis court, art gallery, and skeet range, they were good, and in fact willing to enter into conservation easements to limit or even forego further development.

In exchange, they could realize generous tax breaks from the government. Lee recognized that catering to this crowd could reap a windfall and, by pushing conservation easements, he could do well by doing good. 'Environmental capitalism', he called it. Lee's plan for Jack Creek, like

Blixseth's, was to develop a gated community for the well-set set. His would be called Moonlight Basin.

Because Lee had such reverence for Jack Creek, his development plans were carefully considered to be environmentally sensitive. Thus, when chainsaws began to cut and bulldozers commenced to scrape, it was to place environmentally sensitive ski runs along the slopes of Lone Peak.

Environmentally sensitive roads were constructed to environmentally sensitive home sites, to say nothing of the eighteen-hole golf course, or the Moonlight Basin Lodge—with bars, restaurants, hot tubs, and pool—all built with the good of the environment in mind.

Both Blixseth and Poole did exceedingly well in their ventures, at least initially. They made fistfuls of dough. Blixseth bought castles in Europe, a swanky resort in Mexico, and a mega-yacht. Lee considered buying an island in the Caicos. Both borrowed heavily, more than $300,000,000 each to pay for operations and infrastructure, and things were great until 2008 when it all went *kablooey* with the subprime lending fiasco.

The clover was over. Neither developer could cover the debt on all that borrowed money, and both Moonlight and the Yellowstone Club fell into receivership. As for Tim and Lee, they just faded away, having in the end, done neither particularly well nor good.

The subprime crisis is long over and Big Sky, Moonlight Basin, and the Yellowstone Club, with a new consortium of venture capitalist now running the show, are booming like never before. Mansions and condos are springing up like mushrooms after a rain. A five-star hotel is under construction in the middle of Moonlight Basin, on land nearly recovered from Plum Creek's plundering.

Habitat, once the best available in the Madison Range for wildlife, now belongs to billionaires. The area is an economic engine for southwest Montana, helping the Gallatin Valley grow and fill up with houses, and providing heaps of jobs for realtors, roofers, chefs, private pilots, plumbers, maids, masseuses, and sommeliers.

Folks are making a killing, and there's no end in sight, but it's a killing made from something already dead: wilderness. As the saying goes: behind every great fortune is a great crime.

Chapter 35
Out to Sea

Day 24

The boys and I get underway at 8:30, heading for the rapids that give Leaf Rapids its name. We are nervous since some locals told us these were dangerous and had to be portaged, but this proves untrue. We run through without even needing to get out to scout.

Now on Lake Opach, with no current to help, the boys move along faster than I can keep up. I'd kill myself trying. Besides, I like going my own pace without having to hurry or wait, which is a big reason solo travel suits me.

"You fellas go on," I tell them, yelling through cupped hands because they are already so far ahead.

They heave to and wait for me to catch up, and when I do, Adam proposes that we rendezvous in ten days, give or take, on North Indian Lake, 140 miles down. They plan to layover there for several days to fish and explore. Not far beyond North Indian we'll enter the realm of the great white bear, and Adam likes the idea of joining forces for mutual protection.

That suits me, but I'm more worried about whitewater than white bears. The rapids of the lower Churchill are reputed to be frequent and fearsome, but that's all I know, having no decent maps or reliable intel. I like the idea of running the hard sections with the boys, just in case.

So, we agree to meet sometime, somewhere, down there, if it works out, and then they paddle off, pulling away like a Maserati from a moped, Adam and Ryan singing, Jacob tagging along behind, silent and beaming. Within thirty minutes, the only sign of them is an occasional flash from a paddle blade caught in sun.

I push on, not looking forward to Southern Indian Lake and hoping to get to it and through it as quickly as possible. Ric warned me about the lake, calling it 'real bullshit' and suggesting I cross over to the Seal in large part to avoid it.

For one thing, Southern Indian is scary huge: 778 square miles with 2,300 miles of shoreline. In contrast, Yellowstone Lake in Yellowstone Park, which seems immense when on it, has only 110 miles of shoreline—a mere pond in comparison. Southern Indian Lake is more like the Indian Ocean.

Once the lake was reasonably svelte, but it grew morbidly obese in 1975 after Manitoba Hydro impounded it. Because there were no hydro plants on the lower Churchill, the company reasoned those waters were going to waste, but, if that water could be shunted south to the Nelson River, where several hydro-electric dams were extant, that waste would be converted to watts.

And so, with some impressive engineering and a lot of heavy equipment, an impoundment was constructed and a ditch dug to divert eighty percent of the Churchill to the Nelson.

The project raised Southern Indian's surface by ten feet and, as the lake came up, it spread out and over the relatively flat surrounding terrain to inundate vast areas of forest, killing hundreds of thousands of trees. The drowned trees eventually toppled over and drifted away to jam hard against every windward shore, like tetrahedrons at Omaha Beach, making landing, even in a canoe, difficult to impossible.

Then, soil from the flooded forests washed into the lake and covered its bottom in muck, suffocating aquatic vegetation and turning beaches into fetid bogs. Worse, methylmercury, released from the submerged soil, polluted the lake to such an extent that the resident fish became toxic, better suited for thermometers than fillets, and a thriving commercial fishery, which had provided good employment for the local Cree, collapsed.

No wonder Ric discouraged me from coming here. I'll have to negotiate eighty miles of this ecological catastrophe, including several perilous crossings, before I'm back on anything resembling a river. The only part of Southern Indian Lake that I am looking forward to is the getting off it part.

Twenty miles from last night's camp, I find tonight's—a flat spot under trees beyond a muddy beach girded by a gallimaufry of snags. I manage to reach shore only partially slimed.

It is not a nice camp, although the mosquitoes don't seem to mind. Ric was right. This is a bullshit place. I haven't even quite made it to Southern Indian proper but already have a sense that the big lake and I are not going to get along.

Chapter 36
Beware the Ides of July

Day 25

The first order of business today is crossing two miles of Lake Opach. I don't approach any crossing casually, having been schooled by several close calls that a miscalculation or bit of bad luck could get me killed, so I launch early, hoping to beat the wind. However, the wind is also up and at it early. This one seems an over achiever as well, another can't-stop-to-scratch-your-nose headwind.

By 1:00, after five hours of non-stop paddling with no quarter given, I reach the end of Lake Opach and pull out on a peninsula to rest. I'm surprised to find a building here, a shed constructed of steel, long abandoned by the looks of it. Tall double-doors at the entrance hang askew on their hinges.

The dingy interior is lined with metal floor-to-ceiling shelves on which nothing is stored save for a few crumpled beer cans and a rat-gnawed plastic bottle that once held two-cycle engine oil. The building had to have been skidded here in winter, pulled by a tractor over ice, and used, no doubt, in support of the now defunct fishing industry.

Hey! On a concrete apron below the doors, I find a message scrawled in charcoal. It's to me from the boys. They camped here last night, having managed nine miles more than I yesterday. Those kids can scoot. Of course, two in a canoe are more than twice as efficient as one. Naturally, there is the added horsepower, but a big advantage with two is that a canoe is much easier to steer.

For me, every stroke results in the boat veering away from the side paddled on, so J-strokes must be employed to counter that force and stay the course. Even after getting the hang of it, the J-stroke is a bit awkward, requiring technique and strength, especially against a robust headwind, and no matter how well executed, it always applies a bit of brake, slows cadence, and retards momentum. On the positive side, I'm sure to have forearms like Popeye's by the time I get to Churchill.

Over lunch, the wind intensifies. It whooshes through the trees, bending them to improbable angles and working to liberate panels of corrugated steel from the building's roof and walls. I hunker down amidst the keening and clanging, trying to rest. There is no point in paddling.

One hour turns to two and two to four and still the treetops buck and sway and sheets of steel flap and bang. By late afternoon, with no sign of let up, and having grown weary of waiting, I decide to go despite the wind.

If anything, it is stronger now than when I stopped. Into the teeth of it, even bringing the paddle forward takes effort. The GPS reads my speed at a half-mile per hour, and that's giving it pretty much all I have. I embrace the challenge and resign myself to work.

After an hour of struggle, and covering a distance I could have easily walked in ten minutes, I make Sucker Narrows, a short channel that connects Opach to Southern Indian. Hopefully *sucker* refers to a species of fish and not to boaters foolish enough to attempt the aquatic monstrosity that Opach flows into.

I remember looking at Southern Indian Lake on Google Earth prior to leaving Ennis and thinking, *Holy shit! Glad I'm not going that way.* That's when the plan was to leave the Churchill near this point and cross over to the Seal. Now, I get that *holy shit* feeling again, only this time because I am going that way. The part of the lake I drift into is enormous, and it's just a side bay.

Granted, I wanted to feel small and insignificant during this trip, but on this lake, I'll be less than that—a mote of nothingness upon a universe of water. As I paddle out onto the immensity that is Southern Indian Lake, a little voice, pitched high like a Munchkin's, cautions, *Beware the ides of July*, it warns. *Beware.*

Chapter 37
A Distant Shore

Day 26

The compass is superfluous today with the wind, again flexing its muscle, coming from the northeast, the direction I must go. To stay on course requires only that I head directly into it.

At 07:00 I set out, only instead of '0' it's more like *Ow!* 7:00. My body rebels at motion. It would prefer to laze and loll, but I urge it to action. My job is to get off this lake and to do that, I have to be on it.

I island hop, keeping to their lees to cheat the breeze, and bearing down to scurry through exposed gaps in-between. Large swells begin to oscillate, like sine waves building. As long as there are islands to hide behind, I feel safe, but when the islands abruptly end, I find myself peering across a vast expanse of water to a far distant shore.

Turning on the GPS to see just how far that distant shore is, I discover it to be 3.66 miles. That's a lot of open water. Midway, I'll be almost two miles from land in any direction; intimidating even in calm conditions. The swells are large and lazy, about two feet from crest to trough, and not breaking. The canoe can handle them without problem, but I am acutely aware how quickly conditions can change.

I've ridden that edge before and know full well the peril posed. Plenty of canoers have died in crossings like this, and I don't want to be one of them. They start out, maybe a bit hesitant, like I am now, but go for it, being impatient, like I am now.

I sit in the canoe, holding position just off shore, bobbing and rocking, trying to decide whether or not to risk it. My imagination takes off before I do, and I see myself heading out, a small boat swallowed up in this vastness of water.

It will be a bit dodgy at first, up and over the waves, and freaky to be so far from land, but the boat drives on, making good progress, until conditions change. Halfway out, the wind intensifies. I'll see it coming, fanning the surface ahead as powerful gusts touch down. Suddenly, whitecaps appear, their ragged tops popping up here and there, growing in size and number.

You're still okay, I will tell myself, the boat clearing the waves, but not by much. They are now head high to my seated position, bearing on in endless succession and coming alarmingly close to topping the rails.

Although unbelieving in a higher power, I will beseech one now. *Please, Dear God. Please see me safely to shore.* Shore? I'll catch glimpses of it atop the crests: a peaceful scene, bathed in sunshine, but a long way off. The bigger waves start to curl and break. Several smack the hull, sending spumes washing over, and liquid begins pooling at my feet.

I'll need to bail but can't because of the imperative to paddle. Keeping the boat headed up and moving is the only hope. Then, another wave hits and more water spills in. The canoe floats low in the water, lists heavily from side to side, and then the unthinkable. I capsize.

The shock of cold makes me gasp. Drifting, clinging to the boat, only the upturned tips of its bow and stern now visible above the surface. I tell myself to *KEEP CALM!* in near panic. Finding the whistle hanging from my life jacket, I will blow it, a shrill penetrating blast that can be heard for a mile or more, if anyone is near enough to hear.

I will think of Marianne. She is probably in the garden tending vegetables with her cats.

When the spare paddle floats off, I'll grab it and try to wedge it back beneath the deck, but now everything is floating loose inside and it won't stay. When the paddle comes free again, I'll just let it go.

Waves block my view of land. Some break over my head. *Think!* I can't stay here, won't be rescued, can't tow the boat. I'll have to leave it and strike out for land. It's only two miles! Heck, people swim the English Channel. *I can make two miles*, I will tell myself and then start, swimming toward an unseen shore.

These are my thoughts as I peer across Southern Indian Lake. The land over is indistinct, a blur of green. I take off, paddling hard, building momentum, each stroke terminating with the quick flick of a *J*. The GPS reads my speed at four miles an hour. That counts as moving the boat, especially against this wind.

I'm breathing hard but feeling good, strong, like I can do this as long as I need to. I can even go faster if I want, and to prove it, I do, really digging in, twisting, and straining. The land ahead gradually comes into focus, as if turning the knob on binoculars, and the green morphs to forest.

Soon, I can make out individual trees, and little black dots just off shore turn into bobbing birds.

I reach the beach and step out. My legs are wobbly from effort. Looking back, the place where I started seems a long way off, impossibly far to have crossed in such a small boat. Nearly four terrifying miles. I allow myself a howl of triumph but it's really more a roar of relief.

Chapter 38
Leave It to Beaver

Day 27

Ugh! 5:20. I crawl out of the tent, make coffee, and sit on a rock above the lake, listless. I can barely manage to lift the cup to my mouth and do so only after thinking about doing so a half-dozen times before getting it done. A young beaver appears, swimming just offshore. She (for some reason I think she's a she) is wary but apparently more curious than cautious and paddles around in tight circles directly below my perch.

Only fifteen feet separate us. She's a lovely little thing. Most of her is submerged, but I can make out her shadowy shape beneath the green water, see her tail ruddering this way and that, her feet propelling her along like a windup bathtub toy. The small, black nose is set barely above the surface and her ears are arched high and articulated toward me.

With every pass, two dark, inquisitive eyes appraise me. She doesn't slap her tail, dive, or show any sign of alarm as she repeats the circuit again and again. *The naiveté of youth*, I think. She must not have encountered a human before or she wouldn't be so trusting. Had she any inkling as to the cruel saga of our shared history, she'd be drumming the water like Ginger Baker, warning all beavers near and far to run for their lives.

It was during the mid-16th century that my kind began taking an interest in her kind. The North American Beaver (*Castor canadensis*), the genus to which my lady friend belongs, had a European cousin, *Castor fiber*—a species that was nearly extirpated by the time Europeans discovered the New World.

Unfortunately for the Castor clan, their hides are especially well suited for hats, hats of all kinds, like the gaudily plumed bicornes that topped Britannia's seamen as they ruled the waves, not to mention the chapeau of their nemesis,

Napoleon, and the pom-pommed shakos of his *La Grande Armée,* worn enroute to Waterloo.

Washington's beaver hat was a tricorne, in which he crossed the Delaware, and Honest Abe's, a stovepipe, its crown perched seven feet above the hallowed ground of Gettysburg as he delivered that famous address. For centuries, essentially every male head in Europe, from popes to crofters, as well as those in North America, were roofed in beaver, and demand for their hides was high.

Luckily for hat wearers, there were plenty of these wood-gnawing, dam-building, water rats in the New World—90,000,000 by some estimates—and fortunes could be made in catching them. Catching them wasn't even hard. The hard part was getting to where they could be caught, across untold miles of trackless wilds.

Lured by the promise of these riches, trappers pushed into the interior of North America, seeking furs. They ventured on foot, snowshoe, horse, and canoe, by whatever means possible, exploring every river, creek, rivulet, and runnel to the furthest reaches of the continent.

Beaver can be caught several ways: by shooting them (which devalues the hide), tearing apart their lodges and grabbing them when they try to flee, or, most commonly, by setting traps underwater baited with castoreum, a secretion beavers use to mark territory and a scent they are powerless to resist.

Investigating what must be an intruder, the beaver swims to the bait and triggers the trap. Once sprung, it grips them tightly around the body while a chain staked to the bottom holds them under as they thrash in panic upward for air. Within a minute or two, the struggle is over, and the animal goes still. Skeins of tiny bubbles dribble from the inert form, as if from a pin pricked innertube; rise to the top and pop.

When the trapper returns, he pulls the limp, sodden body from the water and skins it, then stretches the hide on a hoop of willow to dry. The ears, nose, and little holes where the eyes were remain, giving the thing the look of a strangely flattened form of fauna. Shrunken legs and clawed feet protrude from the edges like the limbs of thalidomide babies.

The natives were soon co-opted into the enterprise, enticed to a cash economy with *Castor canadensis,* the coin of the realm. One skin, stretched and dried, could fetch three-quarters of a pound of colored beads, or a brass kettle, or twelve dozen buttons, or a blanket, or two hatchets, or two shirts, or two pounds of sugar. For eight skins, they could get a gun, and for eleven, a three-gallon cask of rum.

Once dry, the pelts were pressed into bales, each weighing ninety pounds (sixty beavers worth, give or take), and sent downriver in canoes to deep-water ports on the St. Lawrence or Hudson Bay, where they were lowered into the dark holds of ships bound for Europe to slake demand for haute couture. Meanwhile, the fur catchers turned around and headed back to the wilderness for more.

Beaver hides provided the impetus for exploring North America, spurring development and settlement. From pelts to pavement, you might say. Although unwilling participants, this animal started it all.

So, I drink my coffee and watch this marvelous creature ply the water beneath my dangling feet. It's a flirtation, at least it is for me, but she eventually tires of my company, dives, and disappears.

I watch the concentric rings shimmer and spread from the last seen point, hoping she'll come back, but she doesn't, leaving me smitten and bereft. What a beauty! Never could she look nearly as good atop somebody's head. Not even the Pope's.

I break camp and paddle, keeping close to shore, and make good time until the wind kicks in. By early afternoon, it's too blustery to struggle on, so I stop for a temporary bivouac and lay down on a cushy patch of sphagnum to rest. After a couple of hours of waiting for the wind to wane, when it doesn't, I take off anyway.

It's hardly worth it. Paddling as hard as I can gains only a few more miles and further progress proves too expensive. I pull out onto a narrow strip of cobbled beach with barely space enough for the tent. It'll have to do.

I only managed fourteen miles today despite a Herculean effort. As tired as I am, it seems it should have been considerably more. Will this headwind never end? Hopefully, I'll do better tomorrow. I plan a jackrabbit start. I want off this lake.

Chapter 39
Any Port in a Storm

Day 28

I do better than a jackrabbit start, pushing off from my sliver of beach at 5:00 a.m. Aided by an obliging tailwind, I cover fifteen miles handily by noon—a mile more than achieved all day yesterday. Keeping to the most direct route requires three exposed crossings, each about a mile.

Even though conditions are fair, I cross as quickly as I can. There is no point lollygagging when the Fates can deal aces and eights at any time. And, as if to prove it, a big blow materializes right after lunch that takes me completely by surprise.

It arrives out of a clear sky with no sign foretelling the change. Fortunately, I am running close to the coast when it hits. Sudden gusts beset me with such force that I am obliged to desperate paddling exclusively on the offside to keep from being driven ashore. Waves, like ocean combers, advance in queue, growing bigger as they near.

I keep just beyond the break, bobbing up and over each in turn. As the waves pass under and roll on, they grow larger still, pushed up by shallows, to momentarily block all view of land, and then collapse suddenly, as if punctured, to reveal the snag-snarled shore awash in white.

I keep a sharp eye to windward, on the lookout for the proverbial *ninth wave*, the rogues of seafaring legend that are much bigger than the rest. These giants loom out of the horizon like leviathans. Because they are so much bigger, they break farther offshore, meaning I have to turn away from land and hurry out to stay on their good side.

If caught inside, they'll roll me. One nearly does. In this instance, too slow to respond, I reach the wave just as it begins to rear and curl. The canoe goes vertical up its face and I feel myself sucked back and down, about to be flipped ass over teakettle, but instead, an instant before the wave breaks, the bow splits the crest and the boat flops safely into the trough behind. A narrow escape. I reposition to deeper water.

On it goes like this, up and over, hour after hour. I grow confident in the craft's ability to handle the swells and relax, my hips loose in the seat, one with the boat.

By mid-afternoon, the sky spins with crusty, iron-colored clouds and the lake turns a dingy green, splotched with upwelling blossoms of brown. The wind has not abated, and I've spent the last three hours paddling exclusively on my left side to counter the wind that would otherwise shove me to shore. I need to rest, but there is no place to stop with the jumble of dead trees set hard against this coast.

For several miles, I've paralleled a peninsula but suddenly reach its end. To continue means a two-mile open-water crossing. I consider it briefly. The land over blinks in and out of vision through swirls of mist. Whitecaps stud the passage. Attempting a crossing now, in these conditions, seems a poor idea indeed, so I make for an island, a speck of one, a half-mile out. It is my only option for refuge.

The island's trees tousle wildly as I approach, like strands of hair in a speeding convertible, imparting a sense of chaos. I can't make it all the way in afloat because of a labyrinth of logs blocking the way, so exit the boat in waist-deep water and lead it through. It follows like a tractable hound, trusting me to find safe passage. With every step, my legs sink shin-deep into muck like quicksand.

Fanned roots and tangled trunks stop forward progress. Some trees can be moved but most are water logged, hard aground, and won't budge. These I either wade around or climb over. When as near to the island as I can get, I unpack the boat and carry everything in, load by load. Then, after the canoe is empty, I pull it across the blockade of trees and onto precious land.

The island's surface is covered in thick sphagnum and my feet sink into it almost to the depth of the offshore ooze. I tear up fistfuls of the stuff to wipe mud off my legs but end up just smearing it all over instead. This is an awful camp. There is no flat ground and barely enough room for the tent between standing and fallen trees, but at least I'm off the water and safe. The wind is a din, slashing through the boughs above, but on the ground, it is relatively calm, calm enough for bugs to come out.

They appear in force and drive me to shelter, but the tent proves unbearably hot so after only a few minutes inside I unstick myself from the floor and wade in the lake to muscle logs around, clearing a channel to facilitate escape as soon as conditions allow.

Dinnertime comes, but water dipped from the lake is so full of grit and mud that I don't care to cook with it. Instead, I dine on jerky with crackers and the last of the cheese, then lie in the tent to rest both body and mind, but the disquiet of wind and water affords rest to neither. I stare up at the tent's shuddering ceiling, hoping a tree doesn't come through it, hoping tomorrow will bring some relief.

Chapter 40
The World's Worst Buddhist

Day 29

At 3:00 a.m., I awake to the same cacophony I nodded off to: wind—an oppressive, ceaseless keening—and water, unremitting eruptions of waves pounding the shore. If anything, it has gotten worse. I lay in semi-shock, curled on my side, feeling helpless and small.

At first light, I crawl out of the tent to have a look. Dark squalls smudge the sky like dirty fingerprints, and the lake churns muddy brown. There is nothing to do but wait, so I wait. I read and wait, inventory the food box and wait, nap and wait.

Then, bored, I try for a Zen state, first lying on my back looking up to watch the treetops sway, and next rolling onto my belly to peer into the moss, following individual strands of color—orange, yellow, and brown threads woven through the matting. I stare at runes in birch bark, attempting to decipher their meaning, but find none. I am so over waiting I can't wait not to wait. No doubt I am the world's worst Buddhist.

By 4:30 in the afternoon, I've had it, no longer able to transcend or accept. The thought of spending another minute here, let alone another night, is more than I can bear, so despite the weather, which hasn't improved a whit, I load the boat and paddle onto the angry water and over to the tip of the peninsula, the jumping off point for the crossing I must make to continue.

Dangling offshore, I gaze across the treacherous miles of open water. The swells are bigger than any so far attempted. I'll probably be okay, if they don't get any bigger or start to break, but I'm hesitant, gripped by fear. *Don't go!* my head says. *Don't go!* my gut says.

Once I leave here, I'll be committed with no way to turn around or stop. So, I bob and gaze, unsettled and unsure. The elements are arrayed against me—wind, wave, fetch, and now the distant rumble of thunder. I should wait, but I don't want to. I'm not a good waiter. Clouds, both silver and dark, are sprent above, whirling in confusion. I bob and gaze some more, trying to get up the nerve to go, hoping conditions will improve.

I do this for another hour. Nothing changes. Hell, if I had taken off when I first got here, I'd be across by now. The distance over is exactly 2.05 miles, according to the GPS. Forty-five minutes of hard paddling, or maybe thirty minutes of *really* hard paddling.

I hate this indecision, but every time I resolve to go, the paddle poised to take the first stroke, my heart quickens and I chicken out. It would be stupid, indefensibly dumb, to venture out in these conditions. If Marianne were here, no way would I try. I wouldn't chance it with anyone, but with just me, I'm tempted.

Teddy Roosevelt comes to mind.

"In any moment of decision," he said, "the best thing you can do is the right thing, the next best thing is the wrong thing, and the worst thing you can do is nothing."

It's a pithy quote, but I'm not sure it makes sense. In fact, I am pretty sure it doesn't. Certainly, doing nothing has got to be better than doing the wrong thing. Still, T. R. had it going on—a man of action. I resolve to go.

"Go," I say the word aloud and dig in, jabbing the paddle into the water and pulling hard as thunder booms like a starter's gun. The canoe responds, moving away from land and out onto the storm-tossed lake.

"Go, go, go," becomes my mantra and metronome as I bring the boat to speed. The swells come in from behind, looking as if to swallow me up. I sense their approach in the motion of the boat, first a lift, then wobble and dip as they overtake, pass under, and spool away ahead like trundling barrels. Walls of water surround me. Water is all I can see. More thunder.

"Faster!" I feel I'm going as hard as I can, but go harder still, impelled by fear. Dip, pull, twist; dip, pull, twist; in furious sequence I move, a madcap machine taxed to the max, the needles on its pressure gauges red-lined and rising.

Past the mid-point, I start to feel better, like I'm going to make it. Every stroke brings me closer to land and safety. I keep at it, taking nothing for granted, not letting up.

One hundred strokes to a side, "One, go, two, go, three…ninety-nine, one hundred, SWITCH! And go!"

I complete the crossing in thirty-three minutes. Thirty-three minutes on the edge, but not over. I feel good. I feel great, like a gambler raking in a pile of chips after a high-stakes bet. Dopamine, adrenaline, whatever it is, courses through my body, giving it a sky-high buzz.

With plenty of daylight left, I keep going to make up for the late start and to take advantage of the wind that has mostly hobbled or halted my advance on this lake, but now hastens it with a push. I cruise easily in a seascape of large, lazy swells, yawing and slewing, making progress pretty much for free.

Finding a place to camp proves challenging with the infernal phalanx of snags blocking every potential landing site. After several failed attempts, I finally get ashore at the base of a moss-covered hill that rises steeply from the water's edge.

There is no beach, so all loads must be carried a hundred feet up it to a bench before I can set them down or they will roll back and land in the lake. This takes several trips to complete. Then, the boat. It doesn't need to go all the way up, so I drag it just high enough to be out of the water and secure it to a tree using a knot employed to hold stock. As with a horse, I want to find it right where I left it.

The only spot large enough for the tent is seventy yards along the bench in a small clearing. To get there requires going over, under, or through fallen logs and thickets of snowberry and stickery wild rose, so I bring only the essentials needed to camp and food for dinner, leaving everything else piled on the bench above the canoe.

I dine late, Spanish style. The sunset boasts the colors of flamenco with cotton-candy clouds lit and streaked in manifold fiery shades. I sip tea and watch the colors spread across the sky. Dragonflies prowl the air, their wings rattling like shuffled cards. The mosquitoes are no-shows, laying low, perhaps sensing danger.

I am relaxed and relieved. Although managing only seven miles today, they were a big seven because the last of the deadly crossings are now all behind me, and I am seven miles closer to the end of this never-ending lake.

Chapter 41
Animus

Day 30

Missi Falls Control, the dam that impounds Southern Indian Lake and allows only twenty percent of the Churchill to flow from it down its natural course to Hudson Bay, is in sight, or rather a com tower near it is. Although still many miles away, the spindly form stands in silhouette against the gray sky, a red light blinking from its top.

Headway has been hard won. The day began at 5:30 a.m., with strong winds lathering the lake and demanding tremendous effort for trifling progress. If I hadn't made the big crossing yesterday, I'd still be stuck on Ennui Island, hating life. As it is, I don't hate life, but have taken a serious dislike to this lake. Evidently the feeling is mutual.

Southern Indian is so persistently contrary that it seems personal, as if this lake and I have some score to settle, as if mortal enemies locked in animus. Of course, this is irrational. A body of water can't care one way or the other whether I drown in it or float easily through, but the lake's treatment of me belies that notion.

As I crawl along its eastern shore, with winds abeam and waves that troop in like a rabble, my sense is that Southern Indian is out to get me.

By late morning, I make it to Namayo Narrows, an intimate passageway between forested islands. Sheltered behind them, the wind is quelled as if someone unplugged it, and I paddle for the first time in a long time in quiet and calm.

Rounding one of the islands, I'm surprised to see structures ahead, a compound of some sort. At first glance, it looks like a going concern with several buildings clustered around two large cylindrical fuel tanks, but as I draw near, it's clear that the complex is abandoned. I disembark on a half-sunken dock and go ashore to look around.

This was, and not so long ago either, a state-of-the-art fish processing plant that now stands neglected and forlorn. There's a bunkhouse with no bunks, an office with no desks, a spacious storage shed in which nothing is stored. The largest building, constructed of steel, contains a sizable room where stainless counters and sinks line the length of two walls. The floor is concrete, sloped inward toward a grated drain at the center.

Obviously, this was the fish processing room. Posters, urging fishermen to maintain the value of their catch with proper cleaning and icing, cling tenuously to the walls, their corners curling. A rusting scale on metal castors stands near a heavy-duty sliding door, useless now with nothing to weigh.

Back outside, I approach the tanks. They lay horizontally, side by side, on a concrete slab. Each once held 20,000 gallons of fuel. I rap the nearest with a pipe. It rings hollow. The other does too. There is a rebar ladder welded to its side that I climb to gain the top.

From this vantage, twenty feet up, I surveil the site. There's a lot of stuff, most no doubt skidded over ice from a long way off. People worked here, slept, and ate. Fishermen converged in boats, sterns piled high with nets and holds brimming with fish—shock-eyed and silver-scaled white fish, lake trout, burbot and pike.

The catch was loaded onto handcarts and wheeled into the processing room where men in slick yellow pants and black rubber boots gutted and cleaned them, working quickly with razor-sharp knives, efficiency born of habit, scales glittering like tiny gems on fingers stained with nicotine. Heads, fins, and tails lopped off, bellies slit and pink entrails stripped, rendering beautiful white fillets—waxen, shiny, and bright—layered into sparkling ice.

The sounds of laughter, water spray, a generator's hum, flocks of gulls wheeling, keening, waiting for the contents of slop buckets to be cast upon the water. Chits, checks, or cash changed hands. Seaplanes touched down and took off, straining for the sky, heavy with fish.

It's a sad scene observed from atop the tank, one of failed enterprise and dashed hopes, but perhaps more such failures are needed to elevate humility over hubris in order to realize that some places are best left alone. But, I kid myself. Humans don't learn from mistakes, not for long.

Below pink tufts of insulation, snagged on stalks of fireweed, bow back and forth in wind. These are the only things moving.

Departing this 'colossal wreck', I paddle on, still in the shelter of Namayo Narrows, but only for another mile before reemerging to open water. Southern Indian's disposition has not improved, its surface assailed by gusts powerful enough to tear the tops off waves and send them flying. Down the coast, breakers explode against dark cliffs in geysers of white.

I dare not venture onto that violent space, so pull out on the sheltered side of an island to wait. Hours pass, but the wind continues without cease. I give up on further progress, unpack the boat, and set up camp. Although still early afternoon, with only eight miles to show for eight hours of industry, this day is done. Score another point for the lake.

Chapter 42
Getting to the Point

Day 31

At 2:00 a.m. I come awake, anxious about the weather, wondering if it will ever let up so I can escape this aquatic hellhole. Cocking an ear to listen, hoping to hear the soft rustling of leaves or gentle lapping of water against shore, I am instead assaulted by the sounds of pounding surf and wind beaten boughs.

Looking out, a few stars are visible, but even in the dead of night they are muted in dusky light. Out on the lake, it is still too dark to see. If I could see, and determine that conditions were propitious, I'd go, take advantage of the lull and leave, but since I can't, I go back to bed instead.

Three hours later I arise for real, load, and launch. Because camp is to the lee of the weather, I can't tell how bad it is out on the lake until paddling around the island to see. *Shit!* It's still crazy wild out there, storm-tossed and fuming. I drift for a while in dejection, feeling like a prisoner whose hoped for parole has been yet again denied.

The wind drives me before it, the wrong way, back toward Namayo Narrows, so I take out on another island to keep from losing more ground and settle in to wait.

After a couple of hours, the futility of breaking free of this lake today becomes evident, so I unpack everything I had just packed, unstuff everything just stuffed, and set up the tent. The circumstance of not being able to go when so badly wanting to seems an insufferable inconvenience.

We moderns are seldom thwarted in plans to go where and when we want, the weather having little bearing on our movements, but that's relatively new in human history. For most of our existence, we were subject to the whims of weather and moved only when it allowed. I try to accept this, but patience is not one of my virtues, so I sit and stare sullenly upon the restless water and curse it.

In mid-morning I detect a change, or think I do. Maybe it's just wishful thinking, but it seems the wind has shifted some, a few degrees from west to north. If true, the prospect for leaving here has improved since such a change should cause a commensurate shift in wave direction as well, bringing them on more toward the bow instead of abeam, thus improving the chances of going over them rather than they over me.

At 11:00, I decide to give it a try, despite the gale and unsettled sea. I am unsettled too, about paddling in such a tempest, but reasonably sure drowning won't be of issue since, for the most part, I can hug the shore.

There is no reason to be farther from it than to remain outside the break line, and if I do swamp or roll, I'll be pushed toward land and not away from it. Still, finding safe harbor amidst the tangle of snags that gird this coast would be a matter of luck.

Paddling for all I am worth barely moves the boat. The waves haven't yet realigned to the change in wind so I must deal with gusts ahead and swells abeam. Running this way is risky. The canoe wobbles atop the crests as they pass under, then drops into troughs where I can't see anything but water.

Every few minutes a big set rolls in, forcing a dash out to where I'd rather not be. Once the danger posed by big waves passes, I fall off and let the elements nudge me back in closer to shore.

In and out, up and down I go, constantly adjusting position relative to risk, far enough out so I don't get rolled, close enough in in case I do, feeling like I am continually courting disaster.

Whenever a heading can be maintained close enough to land where I feel safe, I call it *cheating*, because being broadside in these seas feels like I am getting away with something.

During these interludes, I paddle along chanting aloud, "Cheat when you can," like a mantra.

When the coastline angles a bit more northward, the wind comes directly head-on and my snail's pace slows even further. At one spot, I gauge progress against a white rock on shore. With every determined stroke, the rock's position relative to mine barely changes. It's as if I'm on a treadmill.

Maybe, I move up an inch or two per stroke, but when I skip a beat to change sides, or ease up even a little, the rock begins to catch up. I don't want to be bested by a rock, so bear down with frantic strokes laid on with all my might, until, little by little, the rock falls away behind.

I navigate point to point, picking one and making getting there my sole reason to be. I don't care if I shred every last remaining vestige of cartilage left in my shoulders, I'm in full battle mode; embracing the fight, welcoming it, attacking the water, slashing at it and torquing my body to pry the boat forward. The canoe plunges and bucks, sending sheets of spray across the bow that wash over and soak me.

Once to a point, I round it, select the next, and struggle on. I carry no momentum against the gale, feeling as if I am dragging myself across sand with arms alone. The GPS reads my speed at less than a half-mile per hour, which actually encourages me. I am moving.

Point by point, hour after hour, I creep on until rounding a point beyond which there is no other. Instead, just a mile away, light-colored rock bridges a gap between dark woods, a feature obviously manmade: the levee at the end of the lake.

The wind, now behind, pushes me rapidly before it, toward the finish line, when suddenly the surface parts directly ahead to reveal a rocky reef. The canoe slams down upon it and grinds to a halt while waves spill into the boat from astern. I spring out and push the craft across the shoal to deep water, then get back in and paddle on. This is the last mishap to befall me on Southern Indian Lake.

I'd heard that Manitoba Hydro maintains an all-terrain vehicle and trailer at the levee to assist boaters in getting over it. I find a small shed housing both ATV and trailer, but the tires are flat on the trailer and completely missing from the ATV. I wouldn't have used it anyway. Not only would that be cheating, but I hate those things.

Although at a hundred yards the portage over the levee isn't long, it still takes ninety minutes to get everything around, spent as I am. When finally finished, I lie prostrate on the ground while the insects buzz and bite. I don't put up much of a fight. It takes too much effort to swat them. Southern Indian took more out of me than they can.

Each day on that infernal lake was a struggle, but today was the worst, a totally insane effort. I managed just four miles in seven hours of absurd paddling. A bullshit lake indeed, but I won. I feel like celebrating, but that would take energy, and I'm plumb out.

Chapter 43
In Defense of Muscle Power

Traversing Southern Indian's contrarian waters was the toughest physical challenge I've ever faced, but the satisfaction derived in meeting it, commensurate to the ordeal endured—sweet victory after hard battle. Teddy Roosevelt would have approved. According to him, nothing is worth doing unless it involves 'effort, pain, [and] difficulty'.

But, T. R.'s trifecta of worthiness is not a standard shared by some large percentage of public land users today. For many of these not so rugged outdoorsmen, nothing is worth doing unless it comes easy.

Until recently, ease was not an option in moving through backcountry. Muscle power was the only means to do it and those too lazy, out of shape, or disinclined to suffer, stayed home. But that changed, thanks to a proliferation of machines. Now, one can get almost anywhere they'd care to go without breaking a sweat.

Advances in horsepower, suspension, and design have tamed terrain. Jet boats operate in mere inches of water, snowmobiles climb slopes steeper than most skiers would dare descend, motorcycles reach highway speeds on rough mountain trails, and ATVs, essentially miniature jeeps, can transport you and your crew to the way back with a six pack. These innovations have led to a machine invasion on public lands today.

I shudder to think what the wilderness system would look like now had such contraptions been around in 1964 when the Wilderness Act was passed. Suffice to say, it would be considerably smaller.

I'll admit, grudgingly, that machines have a place. They afford the opportunity for folks who can't otherwise access backcountry to do so, and, they can be fun. I understand the attraction, having utilized the gamut of all-terrain vehicles while working.

Still, for me, they never delivered any sense of accomplishment, as if I had done something worth bragging about or felt particularly proud of. Those who throttle for backcountry kicks would disagree. I've listened as motorized enthusiasts extol the virtues of the 'sport', claiming to seek an experience no different from any other backcountry user—to enjoy freedom and adventure unbound in nature, but, even if true, how can one hope to find such rewards aboard a noisy, smelly machine?

Would a spectacular view afforded by dint of effort be equal to one driven to? Could a fifty-mile ride on a motorbike prove as satisfying as a hike of five? Different strokes for different folks, sure, but I want neither a two-stroke nor four-stroke conveyance bearing me down the unbeaten path.

Crossing eighty miles of Southern Indian Lake in two hours on a jet ski might prove a cheap thrill but could never equate to paddling that daunting distance over eight days of struggle and toil.

Of course, my way is just one way and not *the* way to enjoy public lands, much as I'd like it to be otherwise, and those favoring motors to muscles won't be swayed by sanctimony. But neither should they be further accommodated or appeased because opportunities for motorized recreation already abound.

The Forest Service has 380,000 miles of roads, 60,000 miles of motorized trails, and many millions of acres open to snowmobiles, to say nothing of BLM's 90,000 miles of motorized routes or the four million more of city, county, state, and federal roads in the country. Places to ride are not in short supply. Yet, for the boom and zoom crowd, enough is never enough.

Organized, well-funded, and politically connected, advocates for motorized recreation are strident in demands for more, claiming to being unfairly treated, *locked out* of the public lands if unable to access them on a machine, and arguing that only the young, fit, and wealthy will benefit should the *right* to ride is denied.

"We only want to share the trails," is their rallying cry, which sounds reasonable, but makes no more sense than Black Sabbath sharing a stage coincident with Yo-Yo Ma or smokers inviting non-smokers to belly up beside them at the bar.

On this infernally combusted world, places for motors are not lacking, but areas free of them are. It is quiet recreation that is endangered. To protect it, land managers must say 'no' to motorized advocates seeking more. Saying 'no' is critical to good stewardship and any line officer; Forest Service District

Ranger all the way up to Chief; as well as their BLM and state land counterparts, unable to utter it should never have been put in a position of power in the first place.

Imperative too is for leaders to fully consider how decisions made today will affect resources ten, twenty or even a hundred years hence. An activity that might seem reasonable to allow now, given low and infrequent levels of use, will likely expand over time and come to dominate the scene because use intensity almost always increases.

Once the camel gets its nose under the tent, things are sure to be shattered inside. Mechanized and motorized use in the backcountry pose this threat like no other.

The wilderness champion and ecologist Aldo Leopold saw this coming a century ago, writing in 1925 that:

The day is almost upon us when a pack-train must wind its way up a gravel highway and turn out its bell mare in the pasture of a summer hotel...when canoe travel will consist of paddling up the noisy wake of a motor launch...And, thenceforth, the march of empire will be a matter of gasoline and [wheels].

And lo, it has come to pass.

Chapter 44
A Current Event

Day 32

Hallelujah! There's a real river flowing out the backside of the levee where I'm camped, neither quiescent pool nor fulminating sea, but a river, moving with purpose, carrying sediment, driftwood, and soon a canoe with me in it. So far I've come 450 miles, averaging fourteen a day.

About ninety percent of that has been on lakes with no current to help, but the 250 remaining miles will mostly be on moving water and life is bound to get a whole lot easier.

Other than the river now actually seeming like one, another notable difference here is the landscape. It has changed. From Stanley Mission through Southern Indian Lake, the countryside was typified by closed-canopy boreal forest, essentially jungle that one can't see into from without or out of from within. But now, with trees scrawnier and not so densely packed, the land has opened to reveal bare ground and vistas stretching out to distant horizons. Being able to see beyond the nearest tree gives this area a friendlier feel, and safer too. Like any prey species, which humans occasionally are, security increases with sight. An important trick to survival is seeing it before it sees you, before the last things you'll ever see are tonsils and teeth.

Also comforting is the thought that I could walk out from here if necessary. Terrestrial travel is hardly possible through the impenetrable forests and bogs above, but I could cover this terrain afoot and probably make Churchill within a couple of weeks. But there is no need for that with a perfectly good canoe and a perfectly good river to float it on.

I launch onto blessed current and drift past banks of blushing stone. I have seen this river in all its many hues—green, brown, silver, blue, and gray—but here it is all of these together, streaked in a medley of color flowing through a land that appears newly made.

Stopping for lunch on a mid-stream gravel bar, I see a moose grazing in a thicket of willows. She is the first of her species I've encountered since launching. Surprisingly, I haven't seen much wildlife thus far, save for riverine mammals, birds, and the scary marmot. I thought by now I'd have seen all kinds—wolves, bears and moose—but this primeval forest holds its secrets well.

Thanks to current, I make good time, even against a robust wind. I anticipated that wind would be today's only hindrance since no rapids appeared on the map for this reach of river, but realize the maps are wrong when hearing water crashing onto rock somewhere ahead.

The GPS knows better, showing three rapids directly below my position. What a clever little device, it even displays their names: Manitous I, II, and III, and shows each as a class III run.

Class III is generally the limit for running whitewater in a canoe, at least one with me in it, but I've learned to suspect the reliability of ratings since they are influenced by a variety of variables, primarily water level and the subjectivity of the rater. As a rule, most ratings elevate rapids to a higher degree of difficulty than they actually are.

This happens for the same reason a caught fish gets bigger each time the tale of its catching is told, to make a better story and boost the standing of the teller. There is a human tendency toward such hyperbole and understanding this, I try not to let ratings either intimidate or embolden, but rather to judge for myself, assessing a rapid and then deciding how best to get from up to down.

Manitous is an Algonquin word meaning *spirit of a thing*. Like many Indigenous peoples, the Algonquin were animists, believing that natural objects and elements: trees, animals, wind, water, and even rocks have an intrinsic spirit, or *Manitous*, a spirit that can influence the outcome of events. And, because a *Manitous* can be either good or bad, and tend toward caprice, it's best not to piss them off.

As I approach the first of the Manitous Rapids, I am hoping their spirits are the 'kind' kind, and, as it turns out, they are. All three are easily run. Still, the fact they didn't show on the map is disturbing. Now I have to worry about whether other unmapped hazards might lie in wait below.

Today's goal was Gods Rapid, the next portage, but two miles from it I come to a place too pretty to pass: a grassy flat studded with giant boulders standing on end like the great stone heads of Easter Island.

After organizing camp, I decide to see if I can catch a fish. For more than a month, I've been on these fish-infested waters and haven't yet wetted a line. In truth, I don't enjoy fishing. Seeing an animal struggle for life gives me no pleasure. It's too bad I feel this way because Ennis, MT is considered the fly-fishing capital of the world, and anglers make pilgrimages to it like Moslems to Mecca. But I don't get it.

Standing crotch-deep in cold water to catch something you don't eat seems both cruel and a waste of time, but this is clearly a minority opinion where I come from. Throughout the season the Madison River teems with drift boats afloat with Cabela-clad clients flailing at the water with high-dollar fly rods.

The guides know where the fish are, in fact, know them on a first-name basis—know their political preferences, sexual predilections, religious affiliations and medical histories that invariably involve injuries to the lips and gums.

It irks me that these catch-and-release types think themselves morally superior to bait fishermen who catch, keep, and eat. But, when you get right down to it, who is more ethical: those who kill for food or those who inflict suffering for amusement?

I select a lure that I think a fish would like. It's a small spotted frog with three nasty looking hooks attached. I scrunch down the barbs with vice grips in case I catch something I don't want to keep, and then try to secure lure to line. Unable to recall the blood knot, the first several attempts fail, but eventually I fashion a tangle that holds, then walk to the end of a point and cast.

The frog arcs through the air and hits the water with a plop. *Wham!* Instant strike. I reel in quickly, not wanting to prolong the poor creature's suffering, and pull out a long, thin, eel-like thing. It's a northern pike. Because its teeth look like they could sever a digit, I dispatch it with a rock to the head before removing the hooks.

One of the fingers I was trying to save is nearly mashed when the *coup de grace* is delivered. Next, I cut off the smashed head, tail, and little fins, then slit the belly open and strip out the guts. *Yeeech!* This part creeps me out.

The catch is cooked in a thin pan over a hot fire. With no batter or oil, the skin sticks and burns while the flesh toughens and dries, except for the innermost parts that remain pink and gelatinous.

It's a horrible meal, but I choke it down anyway, obligated to eat what I have killed. If awarded a Michelin rating, it would have to be for a tire.

Chapter 45
The Sea That Bares Her
Bosom to the Moon

Day 33

The Churchill is cloaked in brume this morning, so thick it obscures the river, leaving the canoe to seem completely out of place, as if carried to a waterless plain and abandoned. The sun shines weakly through layers of haze but turns progressively brighter as these are lifted. By the time I launch the day is brilliant with sunshine, revealing the green river gliding through a canyon of reddish rock. If beauty had mass, I would surely be crushed.

Not much is known about this reach of river, but Jacob found someone in Minnesota who had floated it some years before and interviewed the guy to learn what he could. According to Jacob, according to the guy, the portage around Gods Rapid is on river right, but on approach, with the rapid clearly visible below, I see no sign of a trail on that side and have to wonder whether Jake's source learned river direction from the Pukatawagan Cree.

I park in an eddy and scan down with binoculars, confused until seeing something red, a boxy object across the river just above the rapid. I assume it to be a fisherman's net box. Why this occurs to me, I don't know. It doesn't make sense. I don't even know if there is such a thing as a net box, but, whatever it is, I note a faint linear feature running through low vegetation behind it that continues up a steep hill to the bench above, no doubt the trail.

The box turns out to be a plastic five-gallon jerry can. Used as a chew toy by some large-toothed critter, it is perforated throughout. On the side facing the river is a message to me, written in magic marker.

"Jonathan," it reads. "Portage is on this side! It is real bullshit! Came through Thursday. Hope the river and big lake treated you as well as it did us. CU in 9 days. RAJ."

The boys were here five days ago, evidently having gotten through Southern Indian Lake without a hitch.

It turns out that the portage really is bullshit. Reaching the bench above the beach requires an ascent so steep I can reach out with a hand and touch the face of the slope without bending over to do it. Then, after gaining the top, it's a half-mile hike to the put-in below.

The work is brutishly hard under a hot sun and I reel with exhaustion even on the deadhead returns. The temptation to curl up under a tree and sleep is almost irresistible, but the bugs, for their cruelties, keep me moving.

Three hours and five miles later, I'm done, in more ways than one. When the last load, the still one-hundred-pound food box, comes off my back, I feel myself floating, as if unbound by gravity and untethered to earth.

In the river to cool off, I float for real. The water is pleasantly cool, blue, and bubbly. I let it carry me in circles around an eddy, then go limp and sink down where the only sounds are the hiss of water and beating of my heart. Then, thoroughly chilled, I crawl out and sprawl across a slab of sunbaked shield to rewarm.

It's hot as blue blazes and the light blasting down is intense in its brightness. It shimmers from every leaf and needle of every tree, shoots from the rocks in rays, and bedazzles the river with an infinity of dancing diamonds. Suddenly, I am beset by a beauty so profound, I fall helpless before it, unable to move. Grasses wave, trees sway, shadows play, the river rolls.

Everything pulses with light and life. My throat tightens, and I find myself on the verge of tears. This land is alive, and I alive with it. In this moment, I need nothing more, want nothing more, can contain nothing more.

Later, back in the boat and drifting, I am spent, physically and emotionally. I don't paddle, there is no need. Rather I lay atop the load, my feet splayed across it and my head resting on the stern rail. One hand trails the water while the other shields my eyes from the intensity of light.

Bird songs and river music fill the air. The boat spins at the whim of current, revealing clouds, then trees, then cliffs in turn, when suddenly, and from nowhere, images of a grocery store infiltrate my consciousness and lead to an epiphany.

The typical American grocery store, if you give it a moment's thought, offers abundance that beggars belief. Stroll those scrubbed and well-lit aisles and behold the cornucopia so prettily displayed, the thirty-seven varieties of hot sauce, oodles of noodles, staggering selection of breads, crackers, chips, and cheese; sausages (patties, links, and Viennese), fish in tins, jars, frozen, and fresh; lima beans, kidney beans, refried, and red; pop tarts, pot roast, pot pies, and pizza; greens—cruciferous, stalked, and leafed; fresh fruit, dried fruit, candied, and canned; yams, ham, spam, and jam; whole milk, two percent, almond, and soy; and menageries of meat shiny in cellophane.

It's an absurdity of plenty, from soup to nuts, and all of it—the epiphany here—ends up coming out your butt.

And metaphorically it's the same with most everything—cars, guitars, garden gnomes, smart phones, PCs, PJs, posters, toasters. Everything is eventually excreted and dumped. Yet the ultimate fate of stuff does not dissuade us from seeking and amassing more, more than we need or could possibly use. Why?

Are we predisposed by some biological imperative to gather and hoard, laying on fat reserves as a hedge against lean times sure to come? Maybe it's the satisfaction derived from a successful hunt, be it mammoth or merchandise dragged back to the lair. Or perhaps something more insidious is at play, a culture of consumption into which we've been inculcated, a new religion to serve the gods of mammon whose minions preach that enough is never enough and that the road to Heaven is paved with stuff.

Consumption has robbed us of true wealth, supplanting satisfaction with desire and consigning time to the acquisition of what we don't have rather than an appreciation for what we do. This quest for more is despoiling the planet as precious resources are mined and wasted on things of little consequence.

Ironically, this consumption will ultimately consume us, ensuring an impoverished existence upon a burned-out ball amidst piles of plastic prizes and mounds of moldering junk.

Again, my mother comes to mind.

"In getting and spending we lay waste our powers," she'd recite, a line from a Wordsworth poem entitled *The World Is Too Much with Us*. Anna Lou used it in a failed attempt to inspire me toward thrift, but that was not the poet's intent. He wrote it as a scold of society's fascination with materialism and estrangement from nature.

The boat bumps against something, jarring me back to the present. I sit up and take stock of my surroundings. Trees, river, rock, and sky. It's good. The wilderness abides. I gulp some water, feeling the coolness of it moving down my throat and spreading through my chest, and splash some from the river onto my face, becoming more alert. Then, I take up the paddle and carry on.

At 4:30, wrung out from all the work and coming down from the natural high, I stop. My body's done enough for one day, moving me twelve miles, seven on water and the rest on land, back and forth around Gods Rapid where I was moved in time, space, and grace.

Chapter 46
Cogito, Ergo Sum

Day 34

I'm out of it. I don't know what day it is and have to think a bit before coming up with the month. Usually at the end of each day, I make a journal entry to record anything interesting, sights and insights, but didn't get around to it yesterday, the pencil being too heavy to heft after the exertions at Gods Rapid. I try catching it up this morning but find the details of what happened only hours before hard to recall.

I know there was paddling and portaging but other than that, it's a blur. My life is a blur. I move through time as if through an impressionist painting where colors blend and edges bend, and the scene is indistinct and slightly out of focus. Reality is now a 'surreality' involving one, never-ending day.

The lack of diurnal/nocturnal division intensifies this sense of dislocation. I awake in the same yellow place and struggle through the same wild space, arriving hours later, seemingly to where it was I left. My days are spent in endless toil, with no one to help. It is all on me. The lifting and carrying, setting up, and breaking down.

I stab endlessly at water, forcing the boat through it, constantly moving, twisting, bending, pulling. Nothing comes easy. Rolling over in bed is hard. Getting dressed is hard. Sometimes, even stirring coffee is hard.

And yet—here I am, happy and enjoying myself beyond measure, totally content and imbued with purpose.

With no one to talk to, I spend a lot of time in retrospection with thoughts sometimes serious and sometimes silly. The unexamined life, so said Socrates, is not worth living. I reflect on my mother and father, trying to perceive them outside the filters of veneration through which parents are commonly viewed—to see them as people. They were great company: smart, funny, generous, and loving, although not without flaws.

Both drank too much and suffered periodic bouts of melancholia. Despite having had stellar careers, neither thought they had achieved enough. I never felt that way, as if I had anything to prove to anyone. That was one of their gifts to me.

Comparing their lives to mine, I think my choices were better, more in keeping with who I am. Perhaps that was a result of good parenting, or maybe just because I had more choices, or simply the way things turned out.

I think about the tragedy and comedy of the human condition, our venality, ignorance, and arrogance, the fervor and certitude devoted to dogma and myth, our tribal tendencies, insane fecundity and genocidal genius.

We are a cruel and selfish species and ultimately doomed, I fear, because our ability to think and reason is no match to the lizard brain with its tendency toward superstition, aggression, and self-serving stupidity. Thinking about my species embarrasses me to be a part of it.

On the lighter side, I think about Joe Montana, Rowdy Yates, Jerry Garcia, and the Three Stooges. I think about past loves and entertain delicious thoughts. I think about thirst and how good it feels to quench it. I think about how we have it made with macadam, motors, and Big Macs.

I think about beauty, Marianne and Montana, and about Flash, my cat. But mostly I think about moving the boat and how godawful tired I am.

I think therefore I am. *Cogito, ergo sum.* Cogito, ergo sum bitch, is more like it.

There were geese today, quite a few, and appropriately enough, Canada geese. I thought this breed had forsaken wilderness for soccer fields and school yards of southern climes, but evidently not all have succumbed to the trappings of civilization. These are kindred spirits and theirs is a honking I can handle.

By late afternoon, having paddled hard against wind all day, I think I've done enough. I make it barely onto Northern Indian Lake and immediately seek a place to stop. The first possibility is an island with so many dead willows set against it I cannot land. The next is a rookery where I am attacked by scores of angry gulls and terns.

I settle for a tiny speck of rock with barely enough room for the tent, but it does offer a patch of mossy soft ground on which to set it. Still, when I do fall asleep, it is not in the tent but outside, lying on rocks. I wake up, lord knows when, to find half of my dinner uneaten, on a plate atop my belly instead of in it.

I don't bother to stand, opting instead for the easier way of crawling to the tent on hands and knees. My last thought before nodding off is that tomorrow, I think I'll find the boys, if they are still around.

Chapter 47
The Voyageurs

Despite the travails I've borne, compared to the voyageurs, who plied these same waters, my excursion would seem a luxury cruise. Reflecting on what they endured makes me feel like a slacker.

The North American fur trade moved by boat, and the men who paddled them were known as *voyageurs*. Most were French Canadian. Barrel chested, squat, and sturdy, they seemed genetically engineered to propel canoes through water.

Typically, a voyageur's day would begin at 3:00 a.m. with a shout of, *"Se lever! Se lever!"* (Get up!), prompting them from blankets spread beneath an overturned canoe. They would launch immediately, without breakfast, and paddle several hours before stopping for a morning meal of pea soup gruel fortified with pork fat.

Then they would resume, going hard at it, forty to sixty strokes a minute, until midday, when lunch was served aboard, meaning they halted their paddling long enough to wolf down some pemmican and biscuits while still afloat. Brief stops were also made every hour for a smoke break when the men filled their pipes and enjoyed a few puffs before pressing on.

So important was this ritual that distances came to be measured in *pipes*, with a typical day entailing fourteen to sixteen of them. Depending on wind, current, and number of portages, these canoe men would travel thirty to ninety miles a day, at speeds averaging four to six miles per hour, employing 30,000 to 50,000 paddle strokes to do it.

Their boats were wrought of bark, like canoes the Cree used only bigger. There were two main types. The largest was the Montreal canoe, thirty-six feet from stem to stern and six feet in beam. These were the freighters, designed for the Great Lakes and primarily used to transport trade goods between

Montreal and Grand Portage (at the western end of Lake Superior) and return with furs, a roundtrip of 2,400 miles.

Usually powered by ten to twelve voyageurs, the Montreal canoe could carry 6,000 pounds of cargo plus another half-ton of food. With no time to hunt and fish, the voyageurs carried their own provisions. In total, with men and gear, this boat had a payload of 9,000 pounds.

Grand Portage was as far as a Montreal canoe could practically get because to continue further west required a nine-mile carry across difficult terrain to gain the waters accessing the interior. At six hundred pounds, not only were these boats too heavy to haul very far, but their size made them ill-suited for the smaller rivers and streams of the northwest. Here the *canot du nord,* or northern canoe, proved the better choice.

At twenty-five feet long, the *canot du nord,* paddled by four to six voyageurs, had a load capacity about half that of a Montreal canoe, and being relatively light at 300 pounds, could be portaged by two of the crew, freeing the rest to carry cargo.

Hauling loads over portages was a major part of a voyageur's job. They were essentially beasts of burden with each man expected to tote 180 pounds at a time, about as much as you'd put on a mule. But, instead of a saddle, cargo was carried using a tumpline: a strap that wrapped around the voyageur's head and supported the load against his back.

It seems superhuman; carrying 180 pounds of trade goods nine miles across Grand Portage in one direction and lugging an equal weight in furs back, all in a day, and getting up the next morning to do it again.

From Grand Portage, the voyageurs paddled, pulled, and portaged their boats north and west through smaller rivers, lakes and ponds to reach massive Lake Winnipeg, and then proceeded 200 miles along its western shore to where the Saskatchewan flows in.

Then it was up the Saskatchewan to the Sturgeon-Weir, and up some more to Frog Portage to gain the Churchill, and then up it another 250 miles to the continental divide before descending on rivers flowing north to finally reach Fort Chipewan, the fur trade's northwest terminus on Lake Athabasca.

Here the voyageurs would winter, waiting the half-year for the ice to break up so they could start back, in boats brimming with furs, for Montreal—3,000 miles and 120 portages away.

By all accounts, the voyageurs loved this life. One is quoted as follows:

I have been twenty-four years a canoe man, and forty-one years in service; no portage was ever too long for me, fifty songs could I sing. I have saved the lives of ten voyageurs, have had twelve wives and six running dogs. I spent all of my money in pleasure. Were I young again, I would spend my life the same way over. There is no life so happy as a voyageur's life!

Hmmm. Whatever floats your boat.

Chapter 48
Rendezvous

Day 35

With no reason to rush, I take a leisurely morning. If the boys are still on North Indian, they can't be far, no more than ten miles anyway, since that's as far as this lake goes. So, I enjoy a second cup of coffee, catch up on the journal, and spend a little time strumming the guitar before mustering the will to move.

Paddling away from camp, I am troubled by a niggling suspicion that I'm going the wrong way. The compass proves me right. I'm off ninety degrees from the direction I thought I was heading. East has become south, as if gremlins somehow sabotaged the Silva overnight. But, a more likely explanation is that my navigational skills are to blame.

I'm no Magellan, but generally manage a fairly accurate guesstimate of where I am, but now I'm flummoxed. The map doesn't match the coastline I see, nor does it display all the islands that litter this lake. These crappy copies are not only indecipherable but inaccurate as well. I click on the GPS for enlightenment and, when the screen pops on, so does a lightbulb above my head.

Suddenly, it dawns on me that the maps predate the impounding of Southern Indian Lake and show this reach of river as it was before eighty percent of it was diverted to the Nelson. This explains why Manitous Rapids weren't on the map. They were submerged when the maps were made, as were all the islands that surround me now. Northern Indian is lower, by a lot, than it used to be.

Duh! The reason was obvious and should have occurred to me well before now.

Cutting across the lake, I keep a sharp eye out for sign of the boys. I try glassing with the binoculars, but the water is too rough to hold them still. With bare eyes, the only potential anomaly to the landscape are two large boulders on a beach far down the lake near its outlet. In quieter water, I put the glasses on them and, as I turn the dial, the boulders turn into tents.

The camp seems deserted when I reach it but my shouted 'hello' brings Jacob, bed-headed and yawning, from one of the tents. Adam and Ryan, he says, are off hunting antlers. This is their new *raison d'être*, as evidenced by an impressive pile of sheds from the heads of moose and caribou they've found and stacked on the beach.

In late afternoon, I watch as two small figures struggle through a distant bog, sheens of water kicking up from their legs as they splash through, and their arms whipping around like whirligigs, clearly in defense of bugs. Soon Adam and Ryan stand before me, big smiles beaming from their man-boy faces. It's good to see them, these three young lads doing what all youth should do, being footloose and free upon the planet before that opportunity is lost to mundane life.

I am a bit surprised to find them, considering how long it's taken me to get here. We had separated eleven days ago with a fuzzy plan to meet somewhere around here, sometime around now, and here we are. We have rendezvoused. In the morning we'll continue on together, joining forces for mutual protection against the two white hazards below: whitewater and polar bears.

Chapter 49
An Accidental Purist

Day 36

The boys have a "No Watches!" rule. At the start of their trip, each stowed his watch away to be free of its ticking tyrannies for the duration. With no instrument to mark time, they instead rely on the cycles of the sun and dictates of the body to regulate activity; sleeping when tired, waking when rested, and eating when hungry.

I like the idea: surrendering to the rhythms of the wilds. It's what I did at that wonderful age, before idealism got corrupted by comfort, convenience, and habit. At twenty-one, I would never have deigned to defile wilderness with a watch and thought ill of the unholy hypocrites who did. But at sixty, my grip on dogma is no longer as tight.

I did consider ditching my watch for this trip but ultimately decided against it. Without a watch, how would I know if I paddled too much or too little, or whether I was adequately rested after getting up early or late and not knowing which? With no watch, I might launch when it wasn't launch time, lunch when it wasn't lunchtime, or go to bed before bedtime.

I thought about trying to divine time the old-fashioned way—using the sun—but in the far north that's a tall order. In summer the sun seldom sets, reducing the periods between day and night to a crepuscular amorphism that makes it almost impossible to gauge the hour with accuracy. And in the morning, the sun doesn't announce itself with a burst over the horizon as it does in lower latitudes.

By the time one wakes, the sun's been up for hours, an insomniac star pacing the sky. You can't tell if this is the new day dawning or the old day dying. Plus, the sun's morning position is only vaguely to the east and in evening westish at best. Mostly it idles around the southern sky, further confounding the intuiting of time.

Okay, so I'm set in my ways, calcified, a slave to routine, a wilderness phony, but the thought of not knowing the time was unnerving, and I was already unnerved enough. I left Stanley Mission with the thing snugly strapped to my wrist and glanced at it constantly to monitor, calibrate, and regulate.

But, three weeks on, I was purified when it stopped *tocking* to me and died, rendering me timeless in a timeless place, a wilderness purist redeemed, albeit by accident.

So, when the boys and I break camp this morning and paddle out of North Indian Lake, none of us knows exactly when. After what seems a few hours, we reach Wilson Rapids. Although only seven miles from where we started, the boys decide to stay because the fishing is so good.

They waste not a second in wetting a line, literally stepping from their boats with rods in hand and hauling in pike or walleye with nearly every cast.

Walleye are also called *pickerel*, which seems more apt for pike, but pike are referred to as *northerns* or *jacks*. These are the species most commonly caught. A top-tier predator, pike are voracious and super aggressive. They eat about anything: frogs, bugs, birds, and other fish, including their own kind.

Cut one open and chances are you'll find a smaller pike inside and perhaps another, smaller still, inside of that one, nested together like Russian matryoshka dolls. Pike inhabit fresh waters of the Holarctic, which includes the northern regions of North America, Europe, and Russia. Yet, despite being salt water intolerant, they've managed to disperse to far-flung habitats separated by hundreds of miles of inhospitable ocean.

How did that happen? Perhaps they co-evolved from a salt tolerant progenitor or maybe the pike diaspora occurred when seas weren't so salty? I'm clueless as to why this is and think on it while the boys fish.

The Churchill is chockfull of fish, and it's a good thing since fish fuel the ecological economy. Like a one-industry town, the entire functioning of the ecosystem here is dependent on fish. Otters gobble down fifteen percent of their body weight in fish per day. That would be like me eating twenty-seven pounds of fish and chips, only without the chips.

Pelicans consume four pounds each day; bald eagles, a pound. Add in frogs, foxes, mink, osprey, bears, terns, loons, and raccoons, and clearly it takes a superabundance of fish to support this community of life.

Fortunately, fish are prolific. A single pike lays about 50,000 eggs—a walleye as many as 400,000. Happily, the females don't have to sit on their eggs to hatch them. They just lay them and leave. The sticky ovules sink to the bottom and cling to gravels and weeds.

Eventually, the males swim over to sprinkle on the secret sauce. Within a couple of weeks, larvae begin to emerge, and although most end up pushing up daisies before ever getting to smell the roses, millions make it to fry, grow to fingerlings, and with luck, reach adulthood.

Several of these *lucky* ones find their way onto Jacob, Ryan, and Adam's hooks at the base of Wilson Rapids. The boys catch a score or more in mere minutes and keep several for our dinner.

Adam grills them to perfection over a campfire. He cuts out the cheek meat on the walleye and offers these to me. The cheek meats are the choicest cuts, equivalent to the back straps of an elk, and delicious! Little wonder so many of the animal kingdom are partial to fish.

After dinner, we decide to get the boats below the rapid so as not to have to deal with it in the morning. The boys carry theirs around, but I opt to run Wilson in an empty canoe with Adam in the bow. There is no line on our side of the river, it being shallow and stair-stepped with rocky ledges, so we ferry over to the opposite shore, hoping to find one there.

The only choice is a narrow slot, not much wider than the canoe, sluicing along the bank. After a steep descent, this fast water collides with slow, causing the flow to compress into a succession of large standing waves which tail out onto a pile of rocks.

To miss the rocks, we'll have to make a mid-stream eddy where we can stop and change direction. Eddies are extremely useful in maneuvering whitewater, but getting into them isn't always easy, and missing this one will mean a swim for sure and maybe a broken boat.

As we start down, the canoe surges forward with each of Adam's powerful strokes. Speed is not critical here, so I keep my paddle in the water, using it to brake and steer while Adam provides the propulsion. When ready for the eddy, I turn the boat toward it, aiming to hit it high, just below the large boulder that forms it.

As the bow crosses the eddyline, where the opposing currents meet, Adam flings his paddle across the hull from left to right and plants it in the water to execute a perfect bow draw, while I sweep on the opposite side. The boat spins around with astonishing speed, like a fishtailing sportscar.

Never did I imagine a canoe could turn like that, at least not on purpose. Now, parked and pointed upstream, we exit the eddy on an upstream ferry and paddle with determined, matched strokes, moving slowly but surely against strong current, and gain shore just below camp.

For the rest of the evening, we loll or rather I do, while the boys fish. The river flows, looking like molten metal in the low light. Terns, in defiance of gravity, hover over small pools and dive for minnows that twist and flash like slips of silver when caught and carried off. These birds are ineffably elegant, like animated origami and I watch them until time for bed, whatever time that is.

Chapter 50
Fluffy, Fluffy, Fluffy

The boys' obsession for fishing brings to mind one of my failed crusades while working: an attempt to restrict the practice of fish stocking within the Lee Metcalf Wilderness. Most high mountain lakes, those in the Lee Metcalf being no exception, were historically fishless, a waste of water to fishermen. Adding fish, so they could be caught, seemed a universal good.

However, in Wilderness, managed to protect and preserve natural processes, it isn't. Introducing something to an ecosystem that was never there and doesn't belong is a recipe for ecological catastrophe. Think rabbits in Australia, mongooses in Hawaii, tree snakes in Guam, lake trout in Yellowstone, or cows and humans pretty much everywhere.

In the case of fishless lakes, the sudden appearance of a top-tier predator dooms native populations of amphibians and invertebrates. They are quickly eaten out of house and home, or just plain eaten.

Aside from these biological impacts, the very idea of relegating sacred wilderness waters to put-and-take fisheries is anathema; a perversion of the principles for which wilderness was established. It troubled me, so, as manager of the Lee Metcalf, I decided to try and reel the practice in a bit.

Complicating this attempt is the fact that the Forest Service, despite having management responsibility for Wilderness, has no say in whether or not the lakes within them are stocked. This authority is reserved to the states. The Wilderness Act is clear in this, giving primacy to states with respect to the management of fish and wildlife within their borders.

In Montana, this power rests with the Department of Fish, Wildlife, and Parks (FWP). FWP decides which lakes to stock and what species to stock them with and can proceed without the need to consult or cooperate with the federal agency managing the land.

From FWP's point of view, fish stocking is a win/win. It enhances use and enjoyment of public lands, garners support for the agency, and generates revenue from the increased number of fishing licenses sold. As such, FWP stocks practically every lake, pool, puddle, and pond they can. In the Lee Metcalf, there are thirty-seven lakes and the state has seen fit to stock them all, employing helicopters intruding upon wild space to do it. Then, because most high mountain lakes cannot sustain a fishery for more than a few years (these waters were fishless for a reason), the helicopters must periodically return to maintain populations of precious piscines.

An unforeseen consequence of this practice is that once fish are present in a lake, they create an artificial attractant, luring people to places they would not otherwise go and causing impacts that would not otherwise occur. Trampling, overgrazing, and an accretion of fire scars, social trails and litter result as people are drawn to stocked lakes, not necessarily to experience wilderness, but to fish.

Additionally, opportunities for solitude are diminished and wildlife displaced. Clearly, fish stocking degrades wilderness in myriad ways, and now, because of the blogosphere, these impacts are exacerbated when someone lands a lunker, brags about it online, and lets the secret out of the creel. Suddenly, Lonesome Lake isn't lonesome anymore.

Admittedly, fish stocking satisfies a public desire. There are plenty like the boys who can think of nothing better than casting into the clear waters of a high mountain lake. As such, I begrudgingly concede that some level of fish stocking be tolerated, but not to the extent of putting fish into every wilderness lake.

After pondering the problem, I came up with a modest proposal to marginally restrict fish stocking within the Lee Metcalf and arranged a meeting with FWP to discuss it and hopefully gain their consent. The suggestion was to remove seven of the thirty-seven lakes within the wilderness from the stocking program.

These seven were the most pristine and least visited, with no permitted outfitter use or trails accessing them. As such, they were the least likely to generate controversy. I figured FWP would readily agree to this request from a sister agency, modest as it was, but that isn't how it turned out.

Instead, they freaked. The regional manager expressed concern that going along could create a precedent that might ultimately usurp the agency's authority to manage fish and wildlife on National Forest lands (hardly likely since that authority is clearly delineated in the Wilderness Act), but at least he was polite about it. It was their fisheries biologist who was downright hostile.

This individual listened with unconcealed contempt, and then asked, with arms crossed indignation, "What are you going to do at a lake with no fish in it? Read a book?" FWP's answer was an unqualified no.

After the meeting, I was cautioned to go slow in pressing the matter further, but I had a burr up my ass. The state's adamancy made me mad, so I hit the gas instead, preparing a PowerPoint about the negative impacts of fish stocking in wilderness, entitled "Something Smells Fishy Around Here" and took it on the road to proselytize against the practice to any audience that would have me.

At one of these presentations, I ended up getting in trouble. The Montana Chapter of Backcountry Horsemen had invited me to address their annual convention in Butte. Three hundred people were in attendance when I mounted a soap box to deliver my anti-fish stocking diatribe and, unbeknownst to me, one of them was an upper-echelon manager with FWP who had recently co-authored an agreement with the Forest Service for the management of fish and wildlife within National Forest Wilderness.

I knew about the document, had even read it, but was not overly impressed. Like many white papers, this one was full of platitudes about the importance of cooperation and communication between agencies, but offered little else. I mentioned the document in passing, went off script a bit, and referred to it as 'fluffy'.

Within a week, I got a copy of a letter written to the Regional Forester from the FWP official who attended my talk. He was grievously offended by the characterization of his document as "fluffy," claimed I had poisoned the relationship between FWP and Forest Service, and demanded that something be done to admonish me for these transgressions.

In response, the Regional Forester called the Forest Supervisor who called the District Ranger, my boss, to discuss an appropriate punishment. After some back and forth, it was decided that I would be reproved with a *letter of counsel*, a formal document used to deal with lesser disciplinary matters.

The letter would detail the specifics of my offense, counsel a change in behavior, and be placed in my personnel file as a permanent black mark. When she finished the letter, the ranger handed it to me and left with a wink. What the letter counseled was that henceforth I was to cease and desist from using the word 'fluffy', unless referring to a cat.

In the end, it didn't turn out badly, either for me or the lakes in the Lee Metcalf. To my knowledge, FWP imposed an informal moratorium on restocking the seven lakes I had proposed be dropped from the stocking program, and I'm back to saying 'fluffy' whenever I damn well feel like it.

Chapter 51
An Artist's Eye

Day 37

Were it not for coffee and a bladder that is no longer cast iron, I'd stay in the sack, but because of the bladder I have to get up, and because of the coffee, I want to. There is no sign of the boys, and I'm glad. I like mornings to myself, sipping joe in silent repose and taking in the scene.

I often use these quiet times to look for the overlooked, the little things and hidden treasures not normally noticed, seeing as I imagine an artist would. I know a few artists and most have an uncanny ability to discover beauty in places others would never think to seek it.

Daniel, an artist friend from Great Falls, for example, was walking home one night when he chanced upon a discarded juice can in an alley behind a fast-food joint. The can had been stepped on and crushed, and Daniel marveled at how neon, reflected from the restaurant's signs, sprang from its squished concentricities.

Besotted, took the can home and used it to inspire a work entitled simply 'Can'. The finished product looked nothing like a cast-off container. It was a mesmerizing abstract of stacked rings, oscillating in 3-D and aswirl in light; rubbish rendered to beauty.

What a gift to see like that. Anyone can find beauty when it clobbers—as in a field of flowers or glorious sunset—but to discover it in less obvious haunts, say the convolutions of wood grain in driftwood or dewdrops glistening from a spider's web, requires an artist's eye. I don't claim to have one, but when I think about it, I try.

I get two hours to myself before Adam emerges from his tent and starts a smoky fire. He is sleepy, silent, and slow. There is no sign of the other two. This is a rest day for them, having decided to spend another day at Wilson to fish, but I'm heading out. Adam and I confer and come up with a plan to meet at Billiard Lake, fifty miles down, in two or three days. As I push off, Adam is squatted beside his fire, blowing on it, urging it to life, a still figure enveloped in smoke.

Auspicious conditions carry me easily to Fidler Lake. A trip tip passed on by the boys mentions a large sandbar here that, at low water, requires a lengthy detour to circumvent. When the bar comes into view, it does appear to block a direct route across the lake. Going around will add extra miles best to avoid, so before committing to the detour, I haul out on an island to make sure there is no other way.

The island is occupied by hundreds of roosting gulls and terns who make it clear I am *persona non grata*. They circle above in an agitated mass, squawking and swooping, even striking my head in the attempt to haze me away.

Naturally, Hitchcock's *The Birds* comes to mind, and I flash on a vision of my pecked and rent corpse staring vacantly from eyeless sockets.

From the island's highpoint, I get a clear view of the bar below and see that a channel does cut through, so hurry back to the boat, harried by angry birds the whole way.

The channel isn't much of one. In places the boat scrapes to a stop on sand and I must push it through, using the paddle to pole, furrowing the bottom as I go.

Back on moving to water, I make only a few miles more before deciding to stop. There are several good campsites, and I pick one by an eddy that seems a good place to swim. However, wading into it requires stepping on rocks encrusted with yellow slime. I've encountered this stuff before and it is undoubtedly one of the more slippery substances on earth.

Although fully aware of just how slick it is, and taking great care in placing my feet, I lose my footing anyway and go down hard. My left hand catches on a rock, breaking my fall, but maybe the thumb too. The joint is dislocated, but pops back into place when I pull on it. After a while I test it, rotating it around. It hurts, but apparently isn't broken.

Foregoing the swim, I lean against a tree at the water's edge and soak the injured appendage in a bucket of tepid water. Good grief, a simple misstep here can lead to dire consequence. I wash down a few pain killers with rum and spend the evening watching the thumb as a purple bruise spreads across it, trying to see it as an artist would.

Chapter 52
Down with the Ship

Day 38

Morning arrives. My injured hand is puffy, discolored, and sore. Its throbbing forestalled sleep, so now I am in no mood to hurry. Hurrying is not my thing anyway. It was all I seemingly did during my working years, always rushing, trying to catch up. Since retiring, I've become philosophically opposed to haste.

To wake and rush is not the way to start a day. It inhibits relaxation, inspiration, contemplation, creativity, and self-realization. One can't be in the moment when hurrying through it. Luckily for me, I couldn't hurry now if my pants caught fire. In this chronic state of enervation, haste is an impossibility. I am fagged, wrung out, whipped, wiped, and spent. Every cell has had it. Every molecule and atom. All movement is in slo-mo, as if underwater or on the moon. Thinking has slowed too, with thoughts dribbling in piecemeal and not congealing to meaning for several moments, if at all. For some reason, the melody *I'm Bringing Home a Baby Bumblebee* plays on a continuous loop, *basso* and *adagio*, echoing through the hollows of my head.

Last night, I awoke to thunder and rain. Muted flashes of lightning lit up the tent's interior unspectacularly, like a fluorescent bulb blinking out, as if the lightning too was afflicted with lethargy. Now, past the time to rise and shine, I remain in the tent, cocooned and listless, listening to the baby bumblebee song until, over it, I force myself up.

Once I start, a benevolent current conveys me at three miles an hour with no help needed, so I just go with the flow until reaching the day's first rapid. According to the map, there are nine to deal with today. I suspect that any rapid that makes the map has earned its notoriety and merits caution, but the first features only a solitary hydraulic that is easily passed. *Maybe this will be an easy day,* I hope, until coming to the second rapid and finding it un-runnable.

The river tumbles over a series of steep ledges, leaving no option but to portage. With no trail, everything must be carried around on ground strewn with boulders the size of kitchen appliances. Once repacked and about to get back on the water, I look up by chance to see Jacob, his mop-top popping up behind a refrigerator-sized rock. The boys have caught up already.

Together, we scout the third rapid from a mid-stream gravel bar. This is my kind of rapid, intimidating to look at, but easily run, thanks to a neat sneak. I point it out and encourage the boys to try it, but they aren't convinced.

Often when sizing up a rapid, there is a tendency to focus on the perils and not see the prospects. I assure them that the sneak's a cinch, but they want to watch me run through first.

After demonstrating that the sneak is a snap, Adam and Ryan settle into their boat, game-faced and silent, then, after giving the rapid a thorough looking over for a minute or two, Adam shouts, "Let's do it!" and off they blast, literally flinging paddles at the water as if in a race.

A common mistake in running whitewater is the assumption that there is a need for speed. Sometimes this is true, but speed is not always a friend. It allows less time to maneuver, obstacles close fast, and if you do hit something, you are likely to hit it hard. Often it is best to work slowly through a rapid, dissecting it to use currents and features to advantage.

Backpaddling may even be called for, but Adam and Ryan rip down at Mach III, blow past the optimum stopping place and only avert disaster by running aground. Then the pair leap from their boat, whooping and high-fiving in triumph, leaving no doubt that running whitewater is fun—most of the time.

The next rapid, an enormous river-wide hole into which the entire river pours, is not runnable. No way would we make it through upright, but the portage around looks nearly as bad, requiring a carry of three-hundred yards across a stupid-steep side slope studded with brush. It would take me hellish hours to complete, and I can't imagine doing it, so look for another way.

The only option I see is across the river where a small eddy swirls against the bank. If we can catch that eddy and get out of the boats onto the steep rocks that front it, a short carry will bring us to back the river below the hole. But, it's a big *IF*.

The eddy is small with room for only one boat at a time, and I'm not sure there is enough upstream flow to keep a boat from drifting out the bottom and into the hole directly below. Miss the eddy and a swim is certain. Still, I want try and suggest we do, but level-headed Adam nixes the idea at a glance.

"Too risky," he says, and looking again, there's no question that he's right.

Ryan and Adam, resolved to the portage, start humping gear up the hill.

Jake and I don't follow, still holding out for an easier way. Directly below us a cliff rises from the water's edge, thwarting any chance of lining the boats further down, but we can reach the top of the cliff by scrambling up its flank, and so do, for a last-ditch look, before surrendering to the portage.

Aha! From the vantage forty feet up, we discover that the hole doesn't extend quite all the way across the river as we assumed. A slot of fast water, four feet wide, sluices between the base of the cliff and the hole, and beyond that, the cliff indents into a small bight of calm water, a little harbor just big enough for our two boats.

If we can somehow maneuver them past the hole and into the bight, we'll be able to sneak the rest of the rapid by hugging the right bank. Jake and I put our heads together and hatch a plan.

Needing plenty of rope for the plan to work, we combine all our spare cord and add it to the bow and stern lines of Jake's boat. Then, while I secure the kayak, Jake scrambles back to the top of the cliff with the extra-long line attached to the bow.

We can't see each other, but at his shouted signal, indicating he's in position, I start playing out line while he hauls in. My job is the easy one, standing in one place, but Jake has to hop from rock to rock along the precarious clifftop to maintain an angle of pull that will keep the boat out of the hole as we finesse it through the slot.

It works. With the kayak safely secured, it's the canoe's turn. This will be trickier since the canoe could flip if it gets even slightly sideways, and, with no one to play out line from behind, I'll have to go down with the ship, hanging from the stern to steer and stabilize.

I strip, jump in, grab the canoe and shout "Ready!" as loud as I can above the rapid's roar and immediately feel a sharp tug as Jake starts pulling me down.

Swinging my legs to fend off the cliff in one direction and kicking away from the hole in the other keeps the boat centered in the slot, and whenever it starts to wobble or tip, I hoist myself up to act as a counterbalance.

Passing within spitting distance of the hole, I get a good look into its agitated innards, but Jake has me on a tight leash and yanks me safely through.

We end up waiting for the other two a good thirty minutes before they show with their last load, bug bitten and sweaty. Jake and I feel pretty smug about getting by the hole without having to portage, but try not to show it.

Thankfully, the remaining rapids are all easily run and after the ninth, we make camp, figuring the time equal to the number of rapids run. I want to sit and savor the day's adventures, but can't get that bumblebee song out of my head.

Chapter 53
Pressed into the Earth by the Weight of the Sky

Day 39

"God never made an ugly landscape, so long as it is wild." So said John Muir. Except for the God part, I couldn't agree more. Up early and waiting for the boys, I see beauty in every view. It abounds in the sun-spangled greenery, the bejeweled blue of dragonflies resting on reeds, the wavy tresses of aquatic weeds asway in current, and in the smooth sheens of water purling endlessly over rock. I sit quietly, watching, trying to take it all in.

The boys usually don't emerge from their tents until 8:00 or so, and since one of them showed me that my GPS has a clock, I turn it on to see what time it is. Six, it says. I can relax a bit more, but not much.

Once the boys are up, they go from zero to sixty in seconds, bustling with an energy that is tiring to behold. They can be fed, packed, and ready in the time it takes me to track down a missing sock. But not today! With the big head start, I am ready when they are.

We make it only a mile before a rapid forces a carry over an island. Two bald eagles, perched side by side high in the branches of a raggedy snag, watch warily as we pass by beneath. Adam and Ryan manage their gear, canoe and all, in one trip, and then come back to help me.

Meanwhile, Jake is crouched beside his kayak, yanking stuff out of it. His camera is missing. As the principal photographer for the Rails to Whales crew, its loss would be a calamity. After going through everything, Jake concludes he must have left it at last night's camp and decides to go back to find it.

Adam and Ryan will wait for him here, but I'll press on, being slower anyway. We'll reconvene this evening on Billiard Lake, at a site shown on the map as an outfitter camp.

Within a mile of parting, the river spreads out over shallows and strains through a section crammed with boulders. It's more of a pinball run than rapid, but with all the potential wrap-rocks, deserving of a look. I angle toward shore but run aground before reaching it, so leave the canoe hauled out on shoals and wade in the last thirty-feet.

The beach is a narrow strip of cobble and sand below a bench of dark woods. As I make my way along, a loud crashing emanates from the forest directly above and, looking up, I see something big and hairy flitting through the trees, getting close. It's a moose I think, a moose I hope, but the head that emerges from the boreal fringe to peer down at me from just twenty feet away belongs to a big black bear.

I yell at it, tell it to get its hairy ass back in the woods, and it does, spinning in haste and dashing back into them, but the sounds of retreat soon taper to silence, prompting me to curtail scouting and withdraw to the canoe. Every few steps, as I hurry along, I shoot a glance over my shoulder, checking my backtrack, and sure enough, on glance three, the bear emerges from the trees, drops to the beach, and starts to follow.

This is not typical black bear behavior in my experience. All bears of this breed I've encountered before, and there have been several, invariably flee once they realize what I am, but not this one. It comes on, getting closer, head down and eyes fixed on me and nothing else.

Clearly, I am being stalked. Too bad for the bear, but I reach the boat and shove off before it gets within twenty yards. As I drift by, the animal is perched at the water's edge, its head swiveling like a magnet to metal, watching me pass with sad, sad eyes.

With scouting interrupted, the rock garden must now be run cold. I maneuver amidst the many boulders, mostly back paddling to slow the rate of descent and pull away from obstacles in my path, managing to miss every one. I almost give in to gloating until remembering how such conceit invites consequence.

The rest of the day is uneventful, up to Billiard Rapids. These form where the river constricts and drops before flowing into Billiard Lake. The rapids are a quarter-mile long and busy with holes and rocks, not an easy run but preferable to portaging. In the event of a flip, I reason, the lake will provide a good recovery area.

Aptly, I feel like a pool ball careening down Billiard's turbulent flow but reach the lake still sunny-side up and cross to the rendezvous point. It's an abandoned moose hunting camp. The place is an eyesore, strewn with all sorts of discarded junk.

There are rusting cans, corrugated sheets of tin, and several sections of stovepipe squished flat. It seems a perfect testament to the outdoor ethics (or lack thereof) of the far north; if you don't need it, leave it.

After setting up, I lay in tall grass, supine in sunshine. I don't move, feeling like I can't, as if pressed into earth by the weight of the sky. I remain so, totally inert for an hour, maybe two, long enough that the boys should have been here by now.

I begin to grow concerned that the bear might be the reason for the delay until a paddle flash across the lake relieves me of worry.

When they beach, Adam steps ashore and asks coyly, "Guess what Jake got?"

"His camera?" is the obvious answer.

He had in fact retrieved the camera, but in the process saw a molting goose, ran it down and killed it. Jacob holds the dead bird up by its long, broken neck, the big body swinging like the pendulum of a great clock. It would never have occurred to me to catch a goose, with my bare hands or otherwise. A city kid sees a bird in distress and calls the SPCA. A country boy catches it and has fresh meat for dinner.

Jake squats by the lake, yanking out fistfuls of feathers that catch in breeze and swirl away across the water. Once the bird is plucked and dressed, he cuts it into small chunks and fries them over a fire in the last of the pig lard. They look like golden meatballs.

Again, I'm not too keen about ingesting pig lard that hasn't seen the inside of a refrigerator in more than eight weeks, but we are all meat-starved and the smell makes resistance futile. We devour the goose greedily, smacking it down like wolves, our lips and fingers slick and shiny with grease.

After dinner, I hit the hay, goosed and gassed. All is right with the world, but if it wasn't, I'd be too tired to know the difference.

Chapter 54
Rapid Transit

Day 40

I awake like the Tin Man, badly needing oil. Between stiff, sore, and tired, it's a challenge to get dressed, especially putting on socks. I dare not try while standing for fear of falling, or breaking a toe while hopping around for balance, so do it while seated on the ground, first fishing the sock's open end over the toes and then rolling to one side and reaching back to yank them around the heel and up. Thankfully, the boys aren't out to witness this pathetic spectacle, but it's still a humiliation, even unto myself.

Jacob, Adam, and Ryan, once up, bustle about preparing to leave. I don't share their enthusiasm for an early start, so when they are ready, bid them, "Go." They paddle away, all perky, while I return to unlimbered lumbering, happy to not have to hurry.

Tonight, the boys plan to camp above Mountain Rapids, twenty-five miles down. I hope to join them so we can run Mountain and the fearsome stretch that supposedly follows it together. But that is tomorrow's concern. There are at least six rapids to contend with today. I have no idea what to expect. They could be anything from rock gardens to waterfalls.

By the time I launch, the wind is brisk from the west, which is fine since today's course is easterly, but with the wind comes a squall and by noon it's raining. I put to shore and don the dry suit.

Raindrops stipple the river's surface, animating it with a mesmeric display of expanding and colliding rings as I drift along through clumps of willow, like baby Moses in his basket amidst the reeds. This is handsome country with the river bordered by banks of gray granite streaked in black, and the land beyond glowing green. Atop distant ridges, tall trees stand in silhouette against the angry sky.

Something downstream catches my eye: a white speck loping through brush. *A wolf!* She looks so much like Otter, my long-gone husky. Upon seeing me, she stops, flattens, and stares with keen and curious interest as I pass, then turns and vanishes into forest with a spring, leaving me feeling wistful for my dog.

I reach the first rapid in late afternoon, a single wave with ample room to pass on either side—it's nothing. So too, it seems, is the next, where the river splits around a gravel bar and I must choose which side to take. The left channel is higher than the right, meaning it will drop to equilibrium somewhere below, a drop either gradual or abrupt, but I can't see far enough down to tell. My gut tells me to go right, but I dawdle, unsure, until the river pushes me left and makes the decision for me. Rounding the head of the bar, the current accelerates, flowing smoothly in what seems an unbroken plane. But something more sensed than seen causes me to be uneasy.

Is that a slight break in the surface ahead? Maybe, but there is nothing to indicate such, no splashing or other signs of turbulence. Still, alarm bells start going off, and trusting them, I spin the boat left and go hard for shore and in so doing, barely avoid being swept into a very nasty hole, a keeper, so-called because things that go in don't always come out.

Although violent, the hole is eerily silent, owing to the low angle of entry as the river slides into it. I escape disaster by the skin of my teeth.

Now, I am completely unnerved; that hidden hazards like this could be lying in wait below has me gripped in fear. Intrepid resolve turns to trepidation as I continue on down this dangerous river, nervous and cowed.

The next rapid is a mess of rocks and waves. Most of the flow sheers right and right into a deep hole backed by an eight-foot breaking wave. Can't go that way. The other side is fast current over shallow water, so I beach the boat on river left and start down to scout, hoping to piece together a run so I don't have to portage.

What I find isn't promising. The channel is chockful of rocks, holes, and shoals. I study the rapid a long time, trying to tease out its moods and predilections, throwing sticks in the water to see where the current takes them, and conclude I can probably run through, providing I make an eddy partway down to avoid consequential hazards immediately below it.

Then, past those, the river slams up against a cliff at a bend and to keep the canoe from getting slammed into it too, I'll have to execute a quick spin and paddle like a nut to pull clear. The run is complex, with lots of moving parts. The crux is making the eddy.

To mark it, so I don't miss it, I wade into the water and pile rocks into a cairn so I know exactly where I need to turn. Then, fearful but resigned, I start back for the boat.

I only go a few steps before a small animal pops in and out of some rocks at eye level beside me. I don't get a good look at first. It was weaselly shaped. *Probably a muskrat,* I think until it pops out again and I see that it's a baby mink. From only six feet away, the baby clambers deftly down a sheer rock face and joins four others just like it at the bottom.

One has a minnow in its mouth and, apparently in no mood to share, squeezes through a narrow crevice and disappears. The others poke their heads in and out of crannies and holes, vanishing and reappearing like whack-a-moles. They are so delightfully cute that I forget all about the rapid.

After determining me harmless, the babies wriggle out of their hiding places to roughhouse and wrestle at my feet. I crouch down with the camera, trying for a group shot, but they approach so close I have to continually back up in the attempt to get them in focus.

Finally, I give up on a family photo and settle for a close-up of the boldest. Then, the fun over, reality reasserts itself, and I return to the boat to do what must be done.

The run does not go well. By the time I spot the cairn, I'm past it, and the eddy too. The current is faster than anticipated. Plan B is to keep the boat bow down through the rocks so if I do hit one, the canoe won't wrap, end up bent like a horseshoe around it, but I get turned sideways anyway, smack a barely submerged boulder, and splash into the hole below.

The boat goes hard over and I'm positive it's going to flip, but somehow it doesn't, instead remaining in limbo on its side between up and down. I do nothing, not knowing what to do, when, after an interminable few moments, the canoe lurches upright, impelled by some unseen force, and floats free.

I don't have any idea how that happened and don't have time to dwell on it. The bend where the river collides with the cliff is coming up fast and I'm facing the wrong way with no time to execute a turn. Instead, back paddling for all I'm worth, I try to stay clear, but smack the wall anyway and ricochet back into current.

Catching an upstream edge, the boat almost flips again, but doesn't again, and I float onto untroubled waters. *Jesus! What a shit-show.* I was bullied from the get-go and couldn't do anything right. Although I made it through, I don't feel good about it and realize it was only dumb luck that saved my ass from a wicked swim.

What was left of my confidence is now completely gone and the river remains steep, fast and pushy. This is no fun at all. I begin to feel irritated at the boys for abandoning me. Running this stretch would have been so much better together, but I have no cause to hold it against them; I told them to go.

They would have waited had I asked, but I don't like asking anyone for anything. Besides, I chose to make this trip alone as a test of mettle, to see whether I was brave or chicken-shit. Turns out, I'm a bit of both.

I run the last rapid, paddling hard, kneeling for stability. I know it's the last rapid because a canoe and a kayak are pulled up on the beach below it. There's a fire going. I step out of the boat cold, tired, and shaky. Rain is still falling. All I want is to get out of my wet clothes and crawl into bed.

Later, warming in my bag, I think about the little mink. The thought of these amusing creatures makes me smile. Then I think about today's rapids and the harder ones to deal with tomorrow, and that thought provides no pleasure at all.

Chapter 55
More River Than I Want

Day 41

Rain pinging off the tent fly wakes me. Amplified from within, it sounds like a hard rain, however, once I'm out, I find that it's little more than a drizzle; but now I have that song, *A Hard Rain's Gonna Fall*, stuck in my head. I know Dylan wasn't singing about rain. Rain is a metaphor for comeuppance, but I don't want to face either today, not with the hardest part of the river beginning immediately below.

It's cold, high thirties, with strong gusts sending dark clouds scudding low. I can see my breath. The drizzle is just a few degrees from sleet, and everything a shade of gray: earth, sky, and water. The darkest gray is to the north, the way I'm going.

Peering down through occlusions of mist, I can just barely make out a bend in the river, beyond which everything blends to murk. Below that bend lies a reputed six miles of fearsome whitewater. This is the day I've been dreading ever since opting to forego the Seal and keep to the Churchill. Now, I want to get it over with, so I can stop worrying, or worry about something else for a change. I wish the weather was better. The world is friendlier in sunshine, rivers especially, but the Churchill doesn't appear friendly in the least, more ill-tempered and testy, as if it got up on the wrong side of its riverbed.

Still, I'm going. Intrepid explorers, lunatics, and fools, share this: they sally forth in fair weather or foul. And certainly, I fit into one of those phyla, somewhere along that taxonomic spectrum, probably more toward the fool's end.

The kids are smarter. Hunkered down, they're waiting out the weather, playing hearts in the big tent, leaving me to face this day alone. I sort of wish they'd go with me, for safety's sake, but the bigger part, slightly bigger anyway, is content to confront this on my own.

At least, I won't be cheating. I chose to go solo as a test of courage and skill, and today, it seems, is the final exam. I'm nervous, almost as nervous as the day I left Stanley Mission six weeks ago. I fold and roll the soggy tent and pack everything into the boat. It goes fast now after forty-one days of practice.

Because of the weather and good chance for a swim, I layer up in Polypro and put on the dry suit. Usually I only keep the ditch kit close enough to grab if I have to abandon the boat, but today I'm wearing it, fastened to a strap slung over my shoulder in case the boat abandons me. If I do dump, it will likely be in fast water where the canoe could be swept away or broken.

Before putting on, I stand in the rain and talk to the boys through their zipped-up tent, saying goodbye. I might not see them again, for a variety of reasons. Three voices wish me luck. It seems perfunctory, spoken above the *thip-thip* of shuffled cards, like telling someone about to climb Everest, "Have a nice hike," without looking up from a magazine. They don't come out to see me push off into all that gray.

The current, fast and strong, and wind, blowing with force upstream, makes it hard to control the canoe. The sound of water crashing on rock dominates all senses. I can't see very far down because the river drops so steeply—that and the mist.

"This is more river than I want," I whimper aloud.

Below, a jagged line of what looks like flame, only white, flickers bank to bank, revealing a ledge hole. The only way to miss it is to run aground on shallows, which I do, bumping and scrapping and leaving several rocks splotched with purple. It is boat abuse, pure and simple, but Kevlar is tough stuff. *Tough enough,* I hope.

The river is a minefield of black rock protruding from whitewater. I work the paddle constantly—stroking forward and back, drawing, prying, and bracing, to get the boat where it needs to be.

"This is more river than I want!" I'm puling now.

Honestly, had I known the river was going to be like this, I'd have quit at Pukatawagan and jumped on a train. I'd be home by now, all safe and sound. Instead, I'm here in the howling wind, assailed by rain and rapids, freaking out and whimpering.

I talk to myself out loud—directing, encouraging, and admonishing. "Watch that rock!" I shout, "DON'T get turned!! Shit! PADDLE! Good! Whew!"

The rapids follow in quick succession. Where one ends, another begins with almost no break in-between. When I can't see well enough from the river, I get out to scout from shore.

Walking on the wet granite is almost as treacherous as running the rapids, and I move deliberately, taking small steps and testing each before committing to it, moving with the caution of an old man on ice. Whenever I reach a vantage and can see, the river below is white: white, white, and more white receding into mist.

More river than I want.

I enter a section where the Churchill narrows and speeds through a canyon with steep walls facing both sides and worry about the sudden appearance of a rapid here with no way to stop or get out. It almost happens.

After slinging around an S-turn, I see the river ahead pouring into an enormous fulminating hole backed by a towering wave rearing up and continually crashing in on itself. It looks like a giant mouth tearing at the water and gulping it down.

I ram onto the right shore to stop and get out to scout. There is no way around, not on water. The entire river funnels directly into the hole. Clearly, I have to portage, but the side I'm on is essentially a cliff and I don't think I can manage a carry across it.

The other side is where I need to be, but an awful lot of current sluices between me and it, all of it rushing hell-bent for the hole. Crossing is a long shot, but I have to try.

I paddle, pole, and drag the boat upstream as far as I can to gain as much distance as possible between me the hole. Then, when ready, I angle the canoe for an upstream ferry, pick a rock on the opposite side to aim for, and strike out, flailing at the water for all I am worth.

It doesn't work. Not for a second. Not for a stroke. The instant the boat contacts the current, it is flung around and down. The canoe almost flips, forcing me to forego paddling momentarily and hang onto the gunwales while the craft rocks and spins out of control.

Then, it smacks a wave sideways and takes on several gallons of water, becoming unbalanced and slow to respond. Paddling doesn't accomplish much but, thanks to providence, the canoe swings into an upstream attitude. Now at least I can paddle against the current to lessen the rate of descent. To my left, just thirty feet above the hole, a small eddy swirls against the right bank. It offers the only hope of getting out of the river before ending up in it.

I claw toward the eddy with desperate strokes. The hole roars directly behind, groping for me with frothy tentacles. When alongside the eddy, I crank the bow toward it and drive in, but it won't hold the boat. The eddy is shorter than the canoe is long, so even with most of the boat in and the bow nudging shore, the stern remains canted in current, getting tugged on. If I stop paddling, the river will drag me out and suck me down.

The good news is I can maintain this position as long as I keep up the maniacal paddling. The bad news is, I'm tiring. I have to either find a way to get out or give up. The bank is slab rock, wet and slick. It rises from the river at a pitch that looks too steep to stand on. *What is my angle of repose,* I wonder?

If I try to step onto it, I'm pretty sure I'll slip and slide into the river. Maybe there's an underwater ledge I can use. I probe down quickly with the paddle, hoping to hit something solid, but find only water. The lapse in cadence causes the boat to drift halfway out of the eddy, and I employ several frenzied strokes to pull back in. Now what?

There's a vertical crack in the rock, about three inches wide, just above the waterline abreast of me. I can't reach it because of the boat's canted angle away from shore, at least not with my hand, so I try a foot.

With no break in stroke rate, I extend my left leg toward the crack and hook it with my heel. By bending the leg, I am able to draw the canoe in a bit. I try another quick probe and this time hit something. There's a narrow shelf two feet down.

"Don't slip," I caution, quickly moving my left foot from crack to shelf and left hand from paddle to crack while keeping hold of the boat with my right leg.

Then I snatch up the bow line and scramble up the bank on hands and knees to a boulder around which to wrap the rope. I try pulling the canoe out of the river, but heavy with water, it comes up only a few feet. In this attitude, bridging land and river, the hull slams onto rocks with every rise and fall.

I slide back down the rope and frantically unload what I can reach with one hand while hanging onto the rope with the other and make several trips up to rocks and little ridges I can use as chocks to keep gear from rolling back into the water.

The awful banging, as the canoe is constantly bashed, never stops. Then, with the boat finally emptied enough, I heave it from the river and tie it fast. Only now can I take a break to catch my breath and rest.

The portage is a horror. First everything must be carried fifty feet up to a narrow ledge, ascending a slope I wouldn't care to climb even without a canoe and a couple hundred pounds of gear. A slip will only be arrested by water. Once everything is to the ledge, it has to be hauled across a hundred yards of treacherous side slope, again with nothing to stop a fall but the raging Churchill below.

I step gingerly, using cracks and carbuncles in the rock for purchase. Once across, it's a steep descent to a stone slab canted above the river where I can lower the boat back onto it. To reach the slab, I slide down to it on my butt with hands and feet deployed as friction brakes against the slippery rock.

In all it takes five trips, back and forth, up and down, across this hazardous ground to complete the portage. From the mid-point, there is a good view downstream, but I don't like looking at it. The river winks white into the distance as far as I can see.

When again underway, I deal with it, one rapid after another, hoping each will be the last. I run what I can, portage or line what I must, doing whatever it takes to keep moving down.

Around each bend I hope to find calm water, indicating the end of this ordeal, but encounter only another rapid instead. One is a twelve-foot waterfall that takes some time to clear. I have to unpack everything and lower it down on a rope past a jumble of rocks to get to the base of the falls.

Once done, I am stumbling with exhaustion. Before continuing, I break for lunch. Turning on the GPS to check progress, I'm appalled to discover that I've come only four miles and it is already five o'clock. I've been at this for nine hours and managed just four miles!

Setting off below the falls, I float into a huge pool, big enough for a float plane to land. I enter the coordinates into the GPS in case I might need to summon a plane to rescue me. I label the location 'Emergency Landing Site'. (Actually, I label it 'Emergency Lanbing Site', but I know what I mean.)

The sound of rushing water remains a constant and I expect the next rapid at every next bend. Supposedly there are two more miles of whitewater and I'm determined to have them behind me before stopping, but as I proceed, the water becomes calmer, and soon the flow turns tranquil and smooth. I glide along on glassy current, shadowing a black bear walking along the left shore. I wonder what it's eating; looks like slim pickings to me.

With this in mind, I decide to camp on river right and take out on a sandy beach. I am shivering and so tired I can barely stand. My hands have no strength and hardly work, but I struggle out of the dry suit into dry clothes, then build a fire.

I have a bite to eat, and further revive with hot chocolate generously laced with rum. Then I start to feel better. Then I start to feel good. Then great!

This day that began in dread, ominous and gray, ends in quiet beauty. There isn't a breath of wind, and the clouds have mostly disappeared. I sit by the fire, warm and dry, and watch the sunset.

The sky is smeared in color: oranges, reds, and yellows, stretching out across it in every direction. The colors deepen moment by moment, become fiery against darkening space. It's magnificent and just keeps getting prettier and prettier and prettier.

Chapter 56
The Ritz

Day 42

Whoa! July is done for and so too almost six hundred miles of the Churchill. I'm done for too. Those miles have taken a toll. Clearly, I am no spring chicken, or if I am, that spring has sprung. A systemic enervation is now the norm.

I awake in a fog of fatigue, cocooned in my yellow womb, unwilling to move, resisting being born unto a new day. Most of the time, I feel drugged, light headed, and heavy limbed. Good grief, I am hagged beyond belief!

Aside from exhaustion, I'm holding up pretty well. My hands are swollen, fingers like parboiled wieners, my wedding band cinched into puffy flesh. Painful splits on my fingertips and lizard skin on hands and feet attest to the aridity of this environment, despite all the water.

My right shoulder catches occasionally when paddling and aches a bit when I sleep on that side, and there's a bunched-up knot on the little finger of my left hand where some connective tissue popped loose and rolled up inside like a retracted window shade. My knees click and clack, along with my back, with every step and bend, but other than that, I have no complaints.

I lie in the sleeping bag, thinking about getting up, but thinking about how tired I am too. Thought directs energy, and I get even more tired thinking about how tired I am. I need to overcome some serious inertia this morning just to roll over and unzip the bag, exit the tent, and start the day.

"Up on three," I tell myself and count it off, but nothing happens. "One. Two. THREE. UP!" Again nothing. So, this is what delirium feels like, a malarial stupor, an opium overdose. I try in German—they're a disciplined people.

"*Eins. Zwei. DRIE. AUF!*" Still no action.

I have no idea what time it is other than time for caffeine. Coffee becomes my focus, like water for a man lost amidst Saharan sands. All I really care about now is coffee. Coffee in the morning and rum in the evening and whatever happens in-between no longer seems to matter much. I roll over, the first step to getting up. My sleeping bag is zipped all the way to the top and I can't get out without zipping it partway down.

I grope for the zipper pull, find it, and tug, but the slider jams on a fold of fabric. I'm trapped. Houdini would have a hard time getting out of this bag. It occurs to me to panic, but I don't have the energy, so take a deep breath and trace along the zipper with my cracked, swollen fingers, find the jam, pull it free, and open the bag just enough to slither out.

After two cups of coffee, I'm able to function, sort of. I hang my boating clothes—still wet from yesterday's rain and splash—to dry in wind and start packing mindlessly, from muscle memory alone. Stuffing the sleeping bag does not go well. Physicists claim that the universe, all those zillions of stars and planets, were once compressed into a sphere the size of a golf ball. I look down at the wads of material refusing to stuff and think, *Those guys are full of shit.*

Once ready, I turn on the GPS to see what time it is. Eleven-eighteen, it says. Late! But, it's only 10:18 in Montana, so let's call it 10:00. That's not bad. I hope to make twenty miles today, which shouldn't be a problem with the river discernably downhill and moving, barring any long portages or difficult rapids.

The first rapids I reach are called The Fours. Not knowing what to expect, I assume these could be four rapids or two or more Class IVs. I'm still spooked from yesterday's fear-filled float and don't desire more whitewater anytime soon. Happily, The Fours, and The Twos that follow, are mere riffles and present no threat to mind, body, or progress.

It's another gray day with the river in pewter flowing past columns of rock that rise from its surface, shiny and black. Sandy bluffs, eroded into spindly spires topped with scraggly clumps of stunted spruce, like something sprung from the mind of Dr. Seuss, line the shores. The landscape is moving from boreal forest to taiga, mile by mile.

A cow moose grazes in willows two hundred yards away. I drift quietly, not paddling and keeping still so as to pass without scaring her. I try to avoid causing animals to change behavior, to stop whatever they are doing and run—

they have it hard enough—but despite my good intentions, the moose sees me, stares hard a moment, then takes off in a rush, high stepping over willows with long, gangly strides.

Sorry, moose.

I make good time, moving at three to five miles an hour all day, and reach the confluence of the Churchill and Little Churchill Rivers by 6:00. Just downstream a cabin stands atop a bench on the opposite bank so I proceed to a landing spot below it where four small skiffs lie bottom up in tall grass.

It seems I've stumbled upon a moose hunting camp. Several piles of antlers that once graced the heads of this species are scattered around the grounds and a huge rack is affixed to the lintel above the cabin door. No wonder the moose I saw took off when she saw me.

With no one around and no sign of recent occupancy, I decide to stay. The cabin is unlocked, so I go in. It's pretty rough—windows speckled with fly shit, an uneven, delaminating plywood floor, a chair with springs poking up through its stuffing, and everywhere evidence of rodent tenancy. There are two bedrooms, each lined with bunks.

All the magazines are about hunting or fishing. I was hoping for something more stimulating. The place is dingy and dirty and gives me the creeps and, with as many mosquitoes inside as out, I decide out is better than in so set up the tent in the yard.

A half-sheet of plywood nailed to spruce poles serves as a table and a folding metal chair, borrowed from the cabin, are luxuries beyond imagining. I build a fire and, while dinner simmers, enjoy cocktail hour warm and relaxed.

After all these weeks of sitting on the ground, the chair seems a sinful pleasure. I've got it made: a fire, a table, a chair, and best of all, an outhouse. Were it not for all the mosquitoes, this could be the Ritz.

Chapter 57
Wildeor

Scaring the moose en route to the Ritz got me thinking about wildeor. Wildeor is the root word for wilderness. It's Old English for *place of wild beasts*. Sadly, there aren't many such places left, we humans having appropriated the lion's share, the moose's share, and most every other critter's share for ourselves, and this appropriation continues non-stop. Tomorrow there will be less wildeor than there is today.

According to the World Wildlife Fund, populations of mammals, birds, fish, amphibians, and reptiles have declined an average of sixty-eight percent since 1970, mostly due to habitat loss as humans convert wildlife habitat into our own, seeking more corn, cows, and condos. Scientists refer to this die-off as the *sixth extinction*, and unlike the previous five, this one's entirely on us.

All land was once wildeor. In 1609, when Henry Hudson discovered the island now known as Manhattan, porpoises plied the surrounding rivers, wolves howled from what became Washington Heights, and black bears roamed blueberry bogs in today's Central Park.

If you live in California, chances are good that little more than a century ago grizzlies roamed your neighborhood. There were ten thousand of these bears in the Golden State prior to the Gold Rush.

They ate acorns under oak trees and caught salmon in clear streams that now trickle to the sea in pipes. There are no more California grizzlies. The last of the breed was shot in 1923 while trying to kill a horse, for want of anything else to eat.

Lands west of the Mississippi and east of the Rockies were once part of the richest ecosystem on earth, an American Serengeti of unbelievable variety and abundance. Meriwether Lewis was lucky enough to see it. On September 17, 1804, while camped along the Missouri in what is today South Dakota, he got up early and climbed the bluffs above the river to explore. Gaining the top as the sun crested the horizon, Lewis looked down onto a 'forest of plumb trees loaded with fruit'. The ground all around was completely occupied by what he called 'barking squirrels', prairie dogs, "an animal that appears here in infinite numbers." He also saw wolves, hawks, and polecats (black-footed ferrets) in great number, and 'immense herds of Buffaloe deer Elk and Antelopes' feeding on the hills in every direction.

"I do not think I exaggerate," he observed, "when I estimate the number of Buffaloe which could be compreed at one view to amount to 3,000."

Lewis' 'plumb forest' now lies a hundred feet beneath the surface of Francis Case Reservoir, a 'peaceful paradise for outdoor enthusiasts', according to the South Dakota Bureau of Tourism. The buffalo, elk, barking squirrels, and polecats don't live there anymore. They were pushed aside for humans and the Great Plains haven't been that great since.

Less than ninety years after Lewis and Clark showed the way west, the immense herds of bison they marveled at were gone, reduced from countless millions to fewer than a thousand in that eyeblink of time. It was unimaginable, unfathomable slaughter. In 1882, for example, a professional buffalo hunter named 'Yellowstone' Vic Smith, realizing his occupation would soon end for lack of buffalo to slay, set out to set the record for the most bison killed by one person from a single stand within an hour's time.

Locating a sizable herd, one of the last remaining, near present-day Glendive, Montana, Vic started the clock and went at it. Understanding that bison are matriarchal, he first shot several cows in the hips so they couldn't run and would just stand, hunkered in pain. Without the cows to lead them, the rest of the herd milled around while Vic methodically gunned them down, one by one.

He stopped only briefly to change rifles once the barrel of the one being fired got too hot. When the hour was up, 107 dark forms lay still upon the plain. Vic had set the record. He is also credited with killing another 5,000 bison over the course of that year.

As an old man, Vic came to regret this wanton slaughter, realizing he had hastened the demise of something truly magnificent, but there can be no forgiveness for that.

Professional hunters still operate in the American West. Employed by a government agency called Wildlife Services, an Orwellian appellation if ever there was one. Wildlife Services serves wildlife with snares, traps, cyanide, and lead, mostly to protect subsidized livestock grazing on public land. In 2014, they killed 580 black bears, 2,780 foxes, 305 mountain lions, 322 wolves, and over 61,000 coyotes, according to agency records.

These animals weren't targeted because they were necessarily in the act of attacking and killing livestock, but because they might. Innocent or guilty, it makes no difference to Wildlife Services, for whom, still entrenched in the 19th century, a good predator is a dead predator.

In the Gravelly Range near Ennis, agency hunters *pre-treat* the grazing allotments each spring before the sheep and cattle go on, flying grids in helicopters and fixed-wing aircraft to systematically gun down every coyote they see.

It's a fact that livestock and predators don't mix, but because sheep or cattle graze essentially every acre of public land outside of national parks, with little habitat set aside exclusively for wildlife, conflict is baked into the system, and wildlife, not ranchers, bear the cost. In 2018, livestock producers were charged $1.41 a month for the privilege of grazing one cow, plus her nearly full-grown calf, on public grass. Hell, it costs six times that to feed a pet hamster for a month. For taxpayers, it's a rip-off. For wildlife, it's just R.I.P.

Then there's trophy hunting, where wildlife is valued chiefly as something to bag. Portrayed as a noble endeavor pitting dangerous prey against daring hunter, it amounts to little more than a hand job for the ego. Make your list of things to slay, and all you have to do is pay: $1,350 for a wildebeest, $3,000 for a giraffe, $35,000 for a lion.

Most species are for sale—zebra, leopard, elephant, rhino, and croc. Or, if North American game is more your style, you can bag a grizzly for $19,000, or plug a polar bear for about twice that. Write a check and pull the trigger.

Cross each species off the list as they crumple and fall and be sure to take a picture with the slain, looking every bit the mighty hunter: dominant, delighted, and proud. Make a lamp from a leg, a rug of the hide. Mount the heads upon your wall, snouts formed in a fearful snarl, and sit among these trophies to conceit, puffed up in a wildeor of your own exquisite dead.

Wilderness remains the place of wild beasts, and for many species, their only place. Once I understood the importance of wilderness as wildeor, it changed my perspective on how these areas should be managed. I came around to thinking that wildlife, not people, should be the priority, meaning that management, rather than encouraging human use within wilderness, should act to limit it. But, restricting people from wilderness is tricky.

For one thing, how do you go about it? With few exceptions, it can't be achieved with turnstiles and permits, given budgetary and political realities. But, it can be, to some extent, through infrastructure, or more precisely, the lack thereof.

When young and still nonsensically pure, I considered even trails to be rude incursions into the realm of the wild, but that changed after once backpacking cross-country through blowdown so dense it took six exhausting hours to manage just three miles. Never would I go to that lake again, not without a trail.

The experience taught me a lesson. Not only are trails necessary for people to access wilderness, but their absence limits where people go and thus protects pockets of security for wildlife. Toward the end of my career, I determined that no new trails should be constructed within the Lee Metcalf Wilderness.

Shortly after making this resolution, the boss walked into my office one day excited about what he said was good news. A local landowner was willing to grant an easement to allow public access across his land to a seldom visited drainage within the Wilderness that was otherwise difficult to get to. To my ears, this was not good news, anything but, and I argued strenuously against it.

"Why," asked the boss, "should a wealthy landowner be able to enjoy the public's land with a stroll from his backyard when it takes Joe Public three hours to get there on a fast horse?"

It's a fair question, but often there are unseen consequences to land management decisions intended to enhance public use and enjoyment. Sometimes, these lead to abuse and despoilment instead.

For wilderness especially, keeping hard to get to places hard to get to is vital, both for those seeking a purer form of wilderness, doing what it takes to get away from the rest, but more importantly for wildlife. If we start punching trails up every drainage, where are animals supposed to go? Every time they see a human they have to stop what they're doing and run.

I tried explaining all of this to the boss, but as usual, my arguments held no sway. He wanted the trail and insisted that I go with him to locate a route and flag it in. As we walked from the private land onto National Forest, two grizzlies, a sow and her cub, stood up from the sage fifty yards away, looked at us a few beats, then bolted.

“Do you know what those were?” I asked.

“Yeah,” said the ranger. “Two grizzlies.”

“Nope,” I said. “Those were two good reasons not to build this trail.”

Thanks to those bears, who proved more persuasive than I, that trail was never built.

Chapter 58
Bring It On!

Day 43

Good grief, it's windy! Often, listening to wind from within the tent is pleasantly lulling, but not what's blowing out there now. It's a scary, raging tempest tearing at the tent as if to rip it from earth. Sleep is impossible. I try to remember the layout of the Ritz, if I set up near enough any trees that might blow down and hit me, but think not, or care not enough to do anything about it.

Instead, I remain inside, curled up in my bag, feeling vulnerable and small. Is it midnight or morning? I don't have a clue so turn on the GPS to see. Five a.m. it says. Time to get up. I sit by the cold fire on the cold metal chair, cloaked in my bag, sipping coffee, and girding for what I hope will be another twenty-mile day.

Out on the river, sheets of water are peeled from its surface and sent flying. They look like souls of the damned being herded to Hell. Paddling into this wind won't be easy, but I don't care. I didn't come for easy, and dealing with adversity is part of the charm, so bring it on! I can deal with whatever the elements dish out. Churchill is only a hundred miles away. I can cover that, hard or easy.

Wow! Only a hundred miles left. That's hard to wrap my head around. This trip is nearing its end and the realization that it is puts me in a pensive mood. Staring into the ash of last night's fire, I muse on the reasons I'm here and why I like this so. All alone, worn to the bone, far from anywhere, getting blasted by a relentless wind, and loving it. How did that come to be?

Certainly, it wasn't an inherited trait. For my father, outdoor adventure was dining *al fresco*. For my mother, it was a picnic in the park or hitting golf balls down a fairway. Perhaps it's one of those traits that skips a generation. My maternal grandparents did meet on a Sierra Club outing to the Berkeley Hills in 1915 when those hills still had stands of old-growth redwood. Thus, I can rightly claim to owe my very existence to John Muir, the greatest wilderness champion of all.

One of Muir's favorite haunts was Yosemite. He called it "the grandest of all the special temples of nature." My mother was keen on it too, having visited with her parents, the Sierra Clubbers, when she was ten. That was in 1929.

My grandparents found the park so crowded with cars and people they vowed to never go back, but Anna Lou retained pleasant memories of that trip and wanted that experience for me. So, when I was nine, she took me to Yosemite. We stayed at Camp Curry in what was called a *housekeeping tent*, a canvass wall tent with wood floor, sheeted bunks, and a lightbulb that hung down from the ridge pole by its wire. That passed for roughing it.

What my mother wanted most for me to see was the Firefall. The Firefall was a Yosemite tradition. Every night, a huge bonfire was set ablaze atop Glacier Point and park visitors would gather in the valley below, awaiting darkness and anticipating the big event.

At the command, "Let the fire fall!" the entire burning mass was cast off to tumble 3,000 feet down in a cascade of flame and ember.

The first Firefall was in 1872 and the spectacle lasted for almost a century until the Park Service ordered it stopped due to the environmental damage it caused. Although a colossal perversion of nature, the Firefall was magnificent and my mother loved it! To her, it was the great outdoors at its greatest.

A more memorable experience for me on that trip was touching a bear. We were driving through the Yosemite Valley, Anna Lou at the helm of the Studebaker and me in the backseat. Traffic was at a near standstill and we crept along, wondering if there was an accident ahead. It turned out that a black bear sow and her cubs were the cause.

They were standing by the road on hind legs, looking cute and begging food from passing cars. Traffic barely crawled as people took pictures and threw potato chips and sandwich bits from their cars to the bears.

Anna Lou didn't realize that I had rolled down my window. Nor did she see one of the cubs come up to it and stick its head inside the car. I petted it between the ears for several seconds before my mother glanced in the rearview mirror and saw what I was up to.

She absolutely lost it, shrieking at the top of her voice, which of course scared away my little pal, "NEVER, NEVER, NEVER touch a wild animal!" she scolded. "They are unpredictable and dangerous!"

It was good advice, and I heeded it for half a century until forced to do otherwise as a matter of survival.

By the time I leave the Ritz, the wind hasn't let up a bit and dogged effort is demanded for every inch of headway. I go into battle mode, embracing the struggle, enjoying it.

"Is this all you've got, wind?" I yell. "Hell, I couldn't fly a kite in this little breeze. C'mon, bring it on!"

The river is full of boulders, big ones scattered haphazardly like cars and trucks randomly parked and abandoned after some disaster. The sun offers only a hint of its existence. Pale and puny behind high clouds, it provides little heat, and I would be cold, save for the exertions of paddling.

After making twenty miles, I find a particularly lovely spot on an island and stop. It has good everything—mooring, tent space, firewood, and view. Large logs, weathered silver and polished smooth by wind and water, rise from the river's surface like sculpture.

I think up some art-speak names for them—*Temerity, River Wrought, Plutonic Moon, Thor's Forge*—while sitting around a driftwood fire. The wood is dry, burns hot, and snaps, sending chains of sparks spiraling up through billowing smoke.

The embers turn orange, yellow, red, and black, morphing constantly from hue to hue. I poke at them with a stick until its tip ignites; then draw runes in air while waving it out.

Dinner is broccoli and beef, freeze-dried fare, and hot cocoa, for dessert, fortified with rum. I am relaxed to the melting point. There is no place I'd rather be, by my fire, on this river, with its glorious sculptures rising in supplication to their creator. This is bliss, this is nature's temple, a moment of perfection. How could anything be better?

I suppose the wind could stop. I hope it does. I'm tired of the constant din. But if it doesn't, I can deal with it. I can deal with whatever I have to deal with. I know I can. I'm certain of it. I won't give up or give in. In fact, the struggle only makes me stronger. To struggle is why I am here.

Without struggle, what's the point. *Bring it on!* I say. Tomorrow, I'll face Portage Chute, the last rapid of consequence. *Bring it on!*

Chapter 59
Be Careful What You Wish For

Day 44

Today I had to fight; a real, no bullshit fight. It was either fight or die or fight and die, but either way, I had to fight.

I reach Portage Chute after a pleasant morning of easy paddling with good current to speed me through a particularly lovely stretch of river where enormous boulders rise from its surface like Doric pillars.

Maneuvering amidst these monoliths, I played and dodged around them, showing off to myself, seeing how close I could come without hitting one, pretending to have nitroglycerin on board that would detonate with the barest scrape. I was relaxed and having fun, with nothing to fear, other than being blown to imaginary bits.

The GPS didn't think I was quite to Portage Chute, telling me the rapid was still a mile away, but I knew better. I could see the river below narrow and drop into a commotion of sound and spray. This was Portage Chute beyond all doubt!

I paddle out of the main current and into a small bight on river left, beach the boat, and start down to scout. Giant boulders, like those in the river, are everywhere, scattered like a toddler's toys after a tantrum. Getting the boat and equipment past them will take more doing than I care to do.

This has me seriously considering running the rapid, even before seeing it, but then, two hundred yards further on, I come to an obstacle even more daunting, a scarp, eight feet high and sheer.

Gaining the top of this mini-cliff, I emerge onto a broad bench blanketed with low shrubs and wispy slips of cottonwood. Some of the shrubs I recognize as buffalo berry, adorned with clusters of small, red fruit.

Across the bench, fifty yards away, the Churchill pounds through the last major rapid I will face. I head over to check it out, hoping it isn't as bad as it sounds. A rim of pale rock, twenty feet above the river, lines it up and down, affording a clear view of the turbulent flow below. It is as bad as it sounds.

Holes, rocks, and waves are stationed inconveniently throughout, providing no clear way through. Wrapping or flipping are real possibilities. I don't want to run it, but neither can I commit to the portage, hellish as it is. After some deliberation, I resign myself to the run, decide on a line, fix it in my mind, and start back for the boat.

Nearing the scarp, movement catches in my periphery and I turn to see what it is. *Holy Shit!* A large black bear, only forty feet away, is coming directly at me. Its head is low, its mouth agape, and its eyes are locked on me in an unholy stare. I have no delusions. This animal is coming to eat me.

The bear spray is in the canoe, two hundred yards away; the shotgun too. They may as well be on the moon for all the good they'll do me. I am going to have to fight this animal with nothing more than my fists and feet.

I am not afraid, only because there is no time for fear. The bear is closing fast. In seconds, we will be engaged. Some long-dormant survival instinct, one I didn't even know I possessed, assumes control and transforms me from mild-mannered nature boy to Conan the Barbarian in a nanosecond.

A klaxon blares and every cell of my being scrambles to battle stations while anything extraneous to combat goes off-line. I am no longer aware of wind or cold. The crash of water through the rapid goes unheard. All of me is focused on the animal focused on me.

The bear comes on in measured deliberation, neither fast nor slow, never taking its eyes off me.

It carries an expression of dispassionate malevolence, as if to say, "Hey, this isn't personal, just business," the business of the wild, open 24-7-365.

Meat things are attacked, killed, and consumed by meat-eating things. Meat is what makes the world go around. If you thought it was money or love, you were misinformed.

I know what to do. In the Forest Service, I taught the summer crews how to respond in a bear encounter. I was the expert. Rule number one: don't run! If you do, you will trigger a chase response in the animal and end up bear fare within a few very unpleasant minutes. Rule number two: always keep the bear spray handy. Rule number three: your response depends on the species of bear (and really only matters if you've ignored rule number two).

With grizzly bears, most attacks result from surprise encounters where the animal feels threatened by the proximity of a species they know to be dangerous. In this instance, it is best to reduce the sense of threat you pose. Be meek, avoid eye contact, fawn, scrape, beg forgiveness for the rude intrusion, promise never to do it again, and back away, slow and contrite.

If that doesn't work and you are approached (and can't get up a tree), play dead. Usually, this gambit will keep you from becoming truly dead. A grizzly may rough you up some, claw and bite, but if you don't fight back, it will usually withdraw, leaving you alive, and perhaps without serious injury. But with a black bear, it's different. If they don't immediately run off, which they do ninety-nine percent of the time, you've got a problem because that animal sees you as food.

Your best bet now is to be aggressive, to make the bear think you're a psycho in search of a rug. Predators don't always win. Sometimes the prey gets away. Sometimes they fight back. We quarry are not totally helpless. We can kick, maybe break a jaw, butt, gouge, bite, and even inflict mortal wounds. So, the prudent predator will approach with caution, particularly with unfamiliar, larger prey, assessing, in their way, the risks and rewards before deciding to press an attack or withdraw.

That's what my bear is doing: moving on me but alert to potential danger to itself, taking my measure, probing for weakness, wanting to kill but unsure the cost.

I doubt this animal has ever seen a human before. We are in the most remote part of the river. With all the rocks and shallows, this reach is inaccessible to motorboats and float planes. There are no roads or villages anywhere near; no trails, fish camps, or cabins either. This bear can't know exactly what I am, or just how dangerous I might be.

My only hope lies in exploiting this uncertainty. If I don't pull it off, he'll swat me to the ground, rake and bite while I scream, shake me like a rag doll while I whimper, and begin tearing off chunks of flesh while the truth dawns on me that I will soon be dead.

"Get away, mother fucker!" I scream this at the bear from thirty feet away.

There is no discernible reaction. Nothing. Not so much as a whisker twitch. On it comes, walking, watching, not making a sound. At twenty feet, I charge it, running with arms upraised to make myself look bigger, and snarling invective through barred teeth.

"COCKSUCKER!" I yell, and "MOTHER FUCKER!" once more, still to no effect.

All I manage in charging the beast is to close the distance between us to nothing. The bear is literally beside me now, within arm's reach. I know it's within arm's reach because I'm reaching it, punching it in the head and face.

Good God! I think, *I'm fighting a bear. Is this really happening?*

As I punch, the predator starts to circle, moving from my right to left. I turn with it to keep to its front, constantly swinging. My left jabs are weak, ineffectual, glancing blows, but my rights land with force against the side of its enormous head and cause a brief halt to the circling before it resumes.

Near the end of its circumnavigation, I haul off and kick it in the ribs just behind the left foreleg. My shoes are little more than slippers, soft, neoprene boating booties, but I kick as hard as I can. This seems to cause surprise, and the bear stops circling and rises up on its hind legs to tower above me with paws held high.

I expect to be cuffed at any moment, but nothing happens. The bear holds this pose as if just uncrated from the taxidermist and we face each other, awkwardly, unsure, like dancers in a ballroom waiting for the music to start.

Then it dawns on me. *I have a knife!* It hangs inverted from a sheath clipped to my life jacket. I'd forgotten all about it. Short, blunt, and hardly formidable, the only thing ever cut with it was cheese, but I draw it forth with a flourish and brandish it at the bear.

"I have a knife!" I bellow in bravado (false) and surprise (real).

The tables have turned, whatever that means. Still, the thought of stabbing this creature with cold steel is cold comfort. I don't want to hurt it, or aggravate it, and fear that once the stabbing starts, this fight could get ugly for real.

So, there we stand, two statues cast in enmity, knife out, claws up, a Mexican standoff if ever there was one. I end it, taking several quick steps back to the lip of the scarp, then whirl and bound down, like a mountain goat but without the agility. Halfway, I slip and tumble to the basin below.

Landing hard, I try to catch myself with lunging steps, but fall, splayed out on hands and knees. My right hand, still clutching the knife, lands beside a rock, a round hunk of granite about the size of my fist. A gift.

I transfer the knife to my left hand, snatch up the rock with my right, and struggle to my feet in what passes for haste in my debilitated state, then turn to see if the animal has given chase or given up. *Fuck!* There it is, just ten feet away. The bear is still after me.

This is a bad moment, and something in the bear's demeanor feels different now, as if it has made up its mind. Its eyes are still locked on me, but not directly this time, more askance and with a look of pure menace. I face it, edgewise, like a fencer, knife extended and rock locked and loaded behind.

"Look bear," I implore, "I don't want to stab you with this knife or hit you with this rock, but you have to leave right now." The words barely leave my lips when the animal charges. I throw the rock, heaving it with all my might.

Funny. Ever since dislocating my right shoulder in a kayaking mishap twenty years before, I haven't been able to put any *umph* into an overhand throw. Prior to the injury, I could throw hard, with mustard on it, baseball, football, or rock, but since, I've thrown like a girl, or at least how most girls threw when I was a kid, all arm and no shoulder, but not this time.

Adrenaline works wonders, and with a glut of it coursing my system, the rock is a missile unloosed, a Nolan Ryan fastball that hits the bear square on its head right between the ears. I hear a crunch, the sound of stone on bone, normally cringeworthy, but sweet music under the circumstances.

Steee-rike! The bear vanishes in a brown blur. It is plain *poof* gone, and I'm a blur too, hotfooting it in the other direction.

Reaching the canoe, I tear into it for the shotgun and bear spray.

"HEY, ASSHOLE!" I bellow, now truly armed and dangerous, "You want a piece of me? Well, come and get it!"

I hear nothing but the hiss of wind and water, and sound of blood pounding in my ears. Then I start to laugh, uncontrollably, like a lunatic.

It takes a while before I'm restored to a semblance of normal. Talk about a narrow escape. By all rights, the bear should have had me, enjoying my adrenaline-soaked corpse at this very moment instead of nursing a splitting headache. I decide not to tempt the fates further by running the rapid.

For one thing, I'd forgotten the line, but what if I dump and end up on the left side of the river—the bear's side? I have no desire for round two with the bruin so push off and claw my way upstream to the opposite side. There is no channel here, just jumbles of rock through which the river strains. I drag the canoe over these obstacles, abusing it in myriad ways, but little by little, work my way down.

Then it occurs to me: I am morally bound to leave a note to the boys, warning them about the bear. I liberate a red strap from the load, zip the note into a Ziploc, then wade, swim, and rock-hop back up to where the boys might see it. I find a ten-foot driftwood pole, affix the note to it with duct tape, flag the top with the strap, and wedge the base tightly into a crevice between rocks. It's the best I can do.

Back at the canoe, I eat lunch: turkey jerky with crackers and peanut butter, my favorite. As I smack down these delectables, I see a hairy hump moving across the river, near where I scouted Portage Chute a lifetime ago.

"Hey, bear!" I shout and the hump stops, turns, and the whole animal emerges onto the rim above the river.

It peers at me with a puzzled expression, as if trying to focus, its tongue lolling from one side of its mouth. Then it turns and waddles off. I call after it, wishing it good luck and meaning it.

Later at camp, I pour myself a drink, a double, and sip it thoughtfully. I'm in a contemplative mood, totally drained and numb, but euphoric. I marvel at the day's events, that I actually fought a bear, and won. No way should I have survived, but I did, thanks to luck. I have always been lucky, led a charmed life.

I've learned to trust in luck, but this was more luck than anyone deserved. I was lucky the bear wasn't bigger, lucky he wasn't more confident or experienced, lucky he didn't swat or bite me. I got away without a scratch, save for a small scrape on my knee sustained when I fell from the scarp. But that was lucky too because, had I not fallen, I would not have found the rock. It was the rock that saved me.

Without it, the bear would have had me for sure, would have bowled me over and commenced ripping me apart. Strange, but there are almost no loose rocks along this stretch of river. It's all embedded slab, shield not yet broken or weathered to a throwable size, but I found the perfect rock just when I needed it.

I wasn't even looking for a rock, it just materialized, found me. And it was luck that guided the throw. A shot to the shoulder wouldn't have done it. Had I missed the head, I'd be dead.

And it was luck that the bear didn't just shrug it off, think, "Ouch, my head hurts, but fuck it, I'm going to eat him anyway."

After another slug of rum, it dawns on me that this incident with the bear was Mother Nature's way of giving me exactly what I asked for, that which brought me to this far-flung reach of river in the first place, a real wilderness experience, for what could be more real or wild than fighting for your life against some fearsome beast determined to eat you? Be careful what you wish for!

Chapter 60
Under a Sky-Blue Sky

Day 45

I awake to the sound of chattering birds, watching light play across the tent top, rapturous to be alive. I plan to make every effort to stay that way, avoid all near-death experiences for the duration of this trip, if not longer. My ultimate demise, as certain as sunrise, is no longer of immediate concern but relegated to the fuzzy future where it belongs.

So, pushing thoughts of death aside with the tent flaps, I crawl out to greet the first day of the rest of my life, but not before giving the perimeter a full three-sixty to make sure the coast is clear. Only then do I fully emerge, with bear spray in hand. I plan to keep the little can handy from now on.

During humanizing hour, I sit and sip as usual, but crane my head around every few slurps to see if anything might be sneaking up from behind. I can't quite believe that I actually fought a bear. It seems a dream, but I'm glad for the experience, considering how it turned out.

It was exhilarating, and I am pleased with how I handled myself. I didn't freeze, panic, or pee my pants. Everyone does wonder how they will respond in a life-and-death emergency. Okay, that I wasn't killed was a bit of a fluke, but still, I kept my cool. I kind of feel like a badass.

It's a lovely day for the first day of the rest of my life. An immense dome of blue arcs across the sky from horizon to horizon, but what kind of blue, I wonder? I stare at it, trying to tease out its salience, distinguish this blue from others—*Nordic eyes, ancient ice, topaz, cerulean?*

I want to really see it, like an artist, but more, to feel it. How would this blue feel against my skin? Perhaps a tad cool, cooler than other blues. It's a lean shade, stone-washed, a bone blue. *How would it taste,* I wonder? A hint of mint perhaps, pure and silky, like spring water.

I inhale, breathing in all the sky I can, filling my lungs to capacity and holding it in, and then exhale, slowly, expecting to see wispy tendrils of blue coiling up like smoke, but it doesn't happen. It's just another breath, on what would normally be just another day. But this is not just another day. This one is special because I am alive to see it.

I listen to the birds some more. There are many different calls, sweet melodies wafting. If you didn't take time to listen, you would never know they were there, all these birds hidden but for song in forest. I know I don't listen enough, always with something pressing to do, bills, lawn, laundry, a book, the game, too busy for birds usually, but not today.

I close my eyes to hear. They sound happy, but I'm probably projecting. Can anything be that happy all the time? I don't know what kind of birds they are. Vireos, nuthatches, kinglet, or thrush?

I want to know but have never applied myself to the tedious task of learning. I can't tell a warbler from a wren. That takes work, and I'm a dilettante with birds, with plants, with most things.

I watch the shadow of a fireweed dance in light breeze against the surface of a rock. The shadow morphs into a figure, a hooded sage perhaps, a Druid priest whispering incantations, revealing ancient secrets, meaning, and magic. But then it occurs to me that this dance is magic already.

Where did this plant, this delicate dancer, crimson-petalled and slender-stalked, come from? And the rock—formed from fire in the depths of earth and brought to this spot by flood and ice. And before that, from where? And the sun casting shadows on this galactic ballroom, calling the tune and setting the rhythm of this forever dance—how, why, how?

And what about me, a tiny mote of nothingness under the immensity of blue, graced to see it all? To hell with why. To hell with how. *Wow!*

I go back to the sky, back to the color. What kind of blue? Sky-blue I suppose, lame as it sounds. But, that's what it is, a pale blue, receding to infinity, where everything becomes nothing, eventually, but not today.

I hold out my hands, look at them, calloused, splotched, and brown. They do most of the work on the river and in camp. I waggle my fingers, rotate the thumbs, and marvel at the articulation. I spread fingers wide, then clench to fist. These hands can grip, grasp, touch, and throw. They can fight! I look at them in admiration. They remind me of my father's. I am thankful.

There is an auspicious wind blowing, going my way. I know I should hop to, take advantage of it, but I don't want to. I don't want to hurry off for the next thing. I want to stay in this moment, listen to birds, describe the sky, waggle my fingers, and linger, but there is only so much of that I am capable of, so after a time, I get on with it, the rolling and stuffing and stowing.

Then I shove off and float away upon this sacred river, beneath a sky-blue sky.

Chapter 61
'Ello, Governor

Day 46

The sky has not a hint of blue in it today. Instead, it's a monochromatic gray with rain streaking down from dark, tubby clouds almost too heavy to float. They scud along, bouncing off the ground like enormous beach balls. I watch them from the vestibule, sitting cross-legged, wrapped in my bag, caffeinating.

The occasional gust shivers the tent and drives rain hard against it. The storm sounds fierce, amplified from within, but it's really rather sweet-tempered as storms go, and I intend to head out as soon as I feel like it.

The Churchill moves in silver shadow, in no apparent hurry, like me. Governor's Island, tonight's intended camp, is only thirteen miles away, a chip shot with present conditions of current and wind. There are no more portages. No more scouting. The rapids are all upstream.

Today's goal is not just to reach Governor's Island, but to rest enroute to conserve energy for tomorrow's final push: thirty-five miles to Hudson Bay, and Marianne, who is probably in Churchill by now awaiting my arrival.

I have grave doubts about making thirty-five miles in a day, but will have to try. Camping beyond Governor's Island is ill-advised because of polar bears. The chance of encountering them increases in proximity to the bay, so camping as far from its shores as possible is best. Churchill isn't called The Polar Bear Capital of the World for nothing.

Adam, Ryan, and Jacob are much more concerned about polar bears than I. Their plan for their last night is to camp fifty miles above the bay and even then, post an armed sentry as an added precaution. Neither can I post a guard nor make fifty miles in a day, so it's Governor's Island for me.

I push off at noon, while a lightning storm looms from the south. Bolts of electricity rent the air, and thunder booms like distant cannon. I have no worries. Sealed in my dry suit, the storm is my friend and I sail before it, moving without effort, sitting back and watching the wild shores pass, working at the important job of resting.

While drifting, I entertain this question: what kind of bear; black, white, or grizzled, would I rather be eaten by, were I compelled to choose? With little need for rumination, I settle on the white. Not only would the hard part, the getting dead part, be handled more expeditiously with this breed, but I'd die knowing I helped an endangered species.

There's nobility in that. Polar bears are facing a grim future. They need ice to catch seals, essentially the only egg in their basket, and with ice forming later and melting sooner, to eventually disappear altogether, their fate is sealed—no pun intended. Scientists believe that unless humans stop emitting greenhouse gasses, polar bears will be gone from the wilds within a hundred years.

So sadly, there is little hope for their continued existence. We won't give up the good life for polar bears. Hell, we won't give it up for our children or grandchildren. *Ursus maritimus* will no longer roam free but carry on with a captive few, existing in refrigerated cages at big city zoos. Our fate may take longer to play out, but won't, in the end, be much different from that.

I get a hint that I'm closing in on the coast when a seal pops up next to the canoe. It didn't realize I was there and we scared one another, each probably thinking the other was a polar bear. It splashes down in a flurry of flippers and resurfaces a safe distance away, watching me with the doleful eyes of a Labrador Retriever.

I reach Governor's Island in four hours, hardly dipping a blade to do it. The island rises precipitously from the river, not quite cliff but more than hill, leaving little beach and few suitable spots on which to camp. Anything approaching flat ground is chucked with cobbles, so I keep drifting until reaching the island's northern terminus, which tapers to a mudflat before ceding back to river.

Just above the mud there's a narrow bench that will serve in a pinch for a campsite, but before committing to it, I crisscross the flat, looking for tracks. Particularly, I'm looking for tracks the size of dinner plates with claws fringing one edge, but find none. There are only bird tracks, pressed into the mud like so many peace signs.

Relieved to see no evidence of polar bears, I decide to dispense with the electric fence that encircles the tent with a deterrent of current to foil nocturnal incursions. I'd rather not expend the energy, having very little left. It's all I can do to fix dinner and a drink, and not necessarily in that order. This will be the last of the booze.

If I don't make it out soon, pink elephants will be keeping the white bears company, but I plan to make it. Tomorrow is the day. With Marianne dangling in Churchill like a carrot on a stick, I'll make it. Marianne, a hot shower, cold beer, and clean sheets—really the only offerings of civilization worth a damn—and all of it just thirty-five miles away. That's incentive. I'll make it.

Chapter 62
Didn't Make It

Day 47

The wind wakes me so early that it is still dark outside. Darkness is a rarity at fifty-eight degrees north latitude this time of year, but clearly the days are getting shorter. Summer is ceding to fall. A chilly wind presages the change.

Not only is the wind cold, it's blowing a gale; the tent simulating a grand mal seizure. Worried things could blow away, I go out to ensure all is secure: the stove, pots, paddles, and canoe. I drag the boat well up the beach and tie it to a clump of scraggly willows, then weight everything else down with rocks as rain starts to fall.

An hour later, I'm out again, scanning the skies for hopeful signs. There are none. I turn on the GPS to see the time. Five-thirty. I should be leaving now to have any chance of making Churchill, but there is no way. Maybe things will improve. I drink coffee and wait. The rain pelts, coming down sideways.

I don't mind paddling in rain, in fact I like it, but the wind has me to ground. It's coming out of the north at twenty knots or better, probably gusting to thirty. I could travel upstream easier than down. By 8:00, with no change in conditions, the only thing clear is I'm stuck here for at least another day.

With nothing else to do, I decide to set up the electric fence. A friend made it for me, and I've felt a little guilty not using it. I brought it mostly for the Seal River portion of the trip, where polar bear encounters are a given, but the Churchill doesn't support as many bears, and since I've seen no sign, I haven't felt the need for the fence.

It's a compact system comprised of six fiberglass poles, 200-feet of ribbon wire, a handful of tent stakes, and a charger. The charger is powered by two D batteries. That may not seem like much, but it's enough to send 6,000 volts of electricity up the schnozz of any bear rash enough to test it. I once watched a video, taken by remote camera, of a fence like this in action.

A dead horse, bloated and rotted to perfection, is enclosed within it when a grizzly appears and cautiously approaches. The bear circles the barrier a couple of times, and then tentatively touches its nose to a wire. *ZAP!* It's like a disappearing bear act—now you see it, now you don't. If an electric fence can prevent a grizzly from getting a dead horse, it will certainly keep a polar bear from getting me, considering I can't be half the attractant.

While putting up the fence, I hear strange noises. At first, I assume it's the wind whistling through the wires I'm stringing, but it's not. It's coming from somewhere farther off. It almost sounds like a pack of yowling coyotes, but coyotes aren't found this far north. Perhaps geese, or swans, or wolves? I don't know, but whatever, it keeps getting closer.

Looking upriver, I see the boys rounding a bend. We'd separated a week ago, and I wasn't sure if I would ever see them again. They are singing one of their voyageur songs and paddling like mad but barely moving. Even these strong lads are no match for this wind.

They pull in, cheerful as ever, and explain that they'd camped five miles up, having sensibly decided that the fifty-mile plan was too ambitious. Now, because of the wind, they must forego the forty-mile plan as well.

They see the fence and want their tents within it too, so I erect it to its maximum size, but even so, only two tents can fit inside. Jacob and Adam will sleep in one and Ryan will bunk with me. We pass the day reading, dozing, playing cards, singing, looking for interesting rocks, and chatting about what men generally chat about—beer and women—but also, more seriously, about how it feels for this adventure to end.

This stellar troupe set out eighty-five days ago and paddled 1,850 miles since. For me, it's been forty-seven days and close to 700 miles. We all feel pretty good about what we've accomplished, like we've done something worth doing. But tomorrow it all ends. Then what?

On the river, Adam, Jake, and Ryan know what they are about. They have a mission, a purpose, a sense of belonging to water, wilderness, and each other, but after Churchill that gives way to a less certain and simple reality, one constrained by clocks and bells, the need to pick a future path, and the imperative to earn. Peter Pan must reattach his shadow. Huckleberry Finn has run out of river.

There is a new reality in store for me too: retirement. I've had a job since fourteen, but now have no need for one. I'm not the type to stay at home swatting pickleballs and mowing the lawn. I'll have to reinvent and rediscover myself too, but haven't a clue what that will mean or how to go about it.

We turn in early, save for Jake who will take the first watch as sentry, shotgun at the ready, on the lookout for bears. Adam will relieve him at some point during the night.

I'm not taking a turn, not in the least worried about bears. My concern is getting enough rest, but that could be a problem, sharing a tent with Ryan. He talks, unburdening himself. He talks about his father, his mother, his brothers, his girlfriend. He wonders if he loves her, being unsure what love is supposed to feel like.

"You'll know when it's real," I tell him, pleased to offer some avuncular advice, no matter how trite. Ryan is still talking when I drift off.

The night passes. Jacob, then Adam, standing guard throughout, looking for bears, hoping for the aurora, but seeing neither.

Chapter 63
Churchill

Day 48

The sun isn't close to up when the boys start racketing around. It's just a pale glow, a vague orange smudge hinting at day beyond distant hills across the river. I look at my watch, forgetting I don't have one. "What time is it?" I ask.

"Four," a passing shadow says.

There is no wind. Silhouettes dart back and forth, bending, lifting, carrying. Tent stakes chime, tent poles clack, and sleeping pads hiss while being squeezed and rolled.

At a quarter to five, the boys push off.

"See you in Churchill," they say through inky darkness.

"See you in Churchill," I say back.

Their shapes fade and disappear. For a minute, I hear the rhythmic splash of paddles, and Ryan talking, but those sounds soon dwindle to silence, leaving me, once again, alone with the river. I pack quickly and launch the second I can see. I am daunted by the prospect of paddling thirty-five miles.

If I manage even three miles an hour, it will take eleven hours plus to reach Churchill. I don't know if I have it in me. Conditions aren't bad. There is no wind, but not much current either, since the gradient is almost flat. The river becomes wider and shallower with every mile, and I must seek out the deeper channels to keep off the bottom.

I see a black bear lumbering along on shore, flitting in and out of vision between trees, then a moose munching willows. A lean and leggy wolf trots upstream, pauses briefly to watch me pass, and then resumes an easy lope. Tundra swans honk and wheeze from a marsh off river.

Suddenly, I am buzzed by an arctic tern, screeching in high dudgeon, a minnow in its bill and a parasitic jaeger hot on its tail. The birds streak across the sky like errant missiles, inches apart, in synchronized flight that belies belief. Finally, the jaeger miscalculates, zigging after the tern zags, loses ground, and gives up. The tern jets on, yammering non-stop as if still pursued.

Except for this interlude, I keep at it, paddling hard without pausing to rest. I want to make as much progress as possible before the wind comes up, which I expect it to do by early afternoon.

I steal bites of energy bar between strokes and pee in the bailing bucket when there's peeing to be done, and paddle—paddle like I was born to paddle, as if I've always paddled, will forever paddle, as if paddling is the only thing I have ever done or will ever do. It becomes automatic, reflexive, hypnotic, stroke after stroke. There is no then or when, only a constant immutable now.

After several hours, I register a faint rumbling and stop to listen. It must be the weir. There are no more rapids. I turn on the GPS to check time and position. Two o'clock, it shows, and the weir is near. I am only six miles from Churchill. Six miles! From 700 down to six. I've managed twenty-nine miles in slightly more than eight hours.

Good lord, that's good time! I'm beat. The rumble turns to roar, becomes scary loud. I see white splashing across the river in a line. Orange signs, affixed to buoys, are picketed above it in several places. I read one through binoculars. "Keep Away," it says. "Danger!"

The weir was constructed to mitigate adverse effects caused by diverting most of the Churchill to the Nelson. Before the weir, this section of river was substantially dewatered and rendered non-navigable, even for small boats. Wetlands for wildlife dried up. The weir was constructed to raise the water level above it and remedy that.

As I approach it, the crash of water grows louder still and unnerves me. The structure is essentially a low-head dam, and low-head dams, often referred to as drowning machines, are dangerous. I'm unsure what to do, how to proceed. To the right I see a tower, like a watchtower, with stairs to a viewing platform.

If I climb it, maybe I'll see a way past the weir, so I head that way and enter a narrow channel that leads to a small marina. The marina has docks but no boats, a parking lot but no cars, and a building, equally empty. The place is deserted. I get out of the boat and sit on the dock, spent and numb, too tired for thought or action, too tired to stand.

When I finally coax my body to move, it's to dig out the satellite phone to call Marianne. She made it to Churchill and answers on the first ring. "Where are you?" she anxiously asks.

"Hey, Sweetie. I'm six miles upriver, by the weir, but I don't know how to get around it. See if you can find out." She asks if I want her to try to find someone to pick me up. I tell her that I'd prefer to make it the whole way, but to please check about the weir and I'll call back.

Hanging up, I climb to the top of the tower. On the landings, where the stairs turn, there are interpretive signs explaining about the various fish found in the river, but I don't take time to read them. I'm looking at the weir and can see it clearly. It doesn't seem to present much of an obstacle, just a bunch of rocks that the river barely flows over.

I think I can simply paddle up to it, unload the boat, and haul it over. But the wind is starting to freshen, a headwind of course. The Maple Leaf flying above the lonely marina begins to snap, and the hooks on its halyard clang loudly against the metal pole.

I decide to get going and call Marianne to tell her the plan. When she answers, she says she's already enroute, having wheedled a ride from a young man employed by Manitoba Hydro. She explains that they're coming in a pick-up with racks perfect for hauling the canoe.

"We're almost there."

I look out over the taiga and see dust billowing behind a white vehicle speeding my way. I am a bit disappointed to be picked up six miles short of my goal, but also relieved that my struggles are over.

As the vehicle gets closer, I can tell it's a pick-up, then make out *Manitoba Hydro* emblazoned on the side. There are two people inside, and when the truck stops, one of them gets out. Marianne. I haven't seen her for forty-eight days, not since Stanley Mission, a half-million or so paddle strokes ago. She folds into my arms, her head pressing against my chest.

"You made it," she says, holding on to me like she'll never let go.

Chapter 64
Between Adam and the Eve of Destruction

That first night in a bed, I hardly sleep. Too tired and wound up, the unfamiliarity of walls, hum of fans and traffic. Leaving the room in the wee hours, I walk to the hotel lobby to make a pot of coffee. While thumbing through a magazine with pictures of polar bears, waiting for Mr. Coffee to beep, someone starts pounding on the glass front door. It's not even 5:00 a.m.

The pounder is a slim young woman with short dark hair. She isn't wearing pants, save for skimpy black undies mostly covered by the tails of her shirt. I recognize her from a flyer posted at the pub advertising a blues band that performed there last night. She's the singer.

Marianne and I were going to go, but I couldn't muster the energy. She motions for me to let her in, so I get up from the couch and go open the door.

Stepping in, she looks up at me and says, "Fuckin' drummer," by way of explanation, then weaves her way down the hall and disappears around a corner. *Ah.* Back among the civilized.

After breakfast, Marianne and I go looking for polar bears. Although still too early in the year for the big gathering, we see two. One, a smallish bear is walking the shore near town. It doesn't seem to have much fat.

The other is swimming far out in the bay, maybe returning to land after abandoning a thawing floe many miles out. What a thrill it is to see them, but the sight also makes me sad. Their world is melting and the fault that it is, is partly mine.

That night we dine at the pub. Being in a town and among people again feels very strange, a bit of sensory overload. Really, the only thing I did not have to adjust to upon reentry was Marianne. Marianne is easy to be with. She lets me be me with no pretense required. We'd been married twenty-five years, so being back together takes no getting used to. She says I've lost weight.

She says she was worried. I share some stories about the trip, how the bear almost made her a widow, the natives I met and birds I saw. Marianne loves birds. Then the bartender comes over. He's heard I had just come down the Churchill and informs me that two girls completed the same journey a couple of weeks before.

"What did they look like?" I ask.

"Quite strong," he says, and I wisely leave it at that.

After a second night when I didn't sleep much better than the first, Marianne and I carry the canoe along Churchill's dirt streets, over the railroad tracks and through a neighborhood of squatter shacks to the river. It's a calm day and sunny. Beluga whales ply the estuary, the so-called white porpoise that first brought the Hudson Bay Company here in 1688.

The whales come by the hundreds to calve in the river's relatively warm waters and they dot the crossing like whitecaps. As we paddle, several travel with us, tracking pale green beneath the surface, and close in, nearly nudging the canoe. I worry we could be upset, but they are only curious, if not friendly, and exhibit the kind of benign behavior I wish humans displayed to our fellow species.

Marianne is all business when she paddles. She never stops and every stroke is strongly applied. The boat, without cargo, and with both of us digging in, moves quickly toward our destination, Fort Prince of Wales, located across the river on a point above its confluence with the bay. The fort is a formidable structure, constructed in the shape of a star with massive stone walls thirty feet thick at the base and twenty feet high.

HBC built it to fend off the French. The first stone was placed in 1731 and forty years passed before the last was laid. Still, when the French finally did show up, in 1782, they captured the stronghold without firing a shot.

After touring the fort, we paddle back upriver to Sloop Cove. This is where Jens Munk spent the winter of 1619/20 watching his men die. Here also, expertly chiseled in stone, we find an inscription: *S L Hearne, July 1767*. Samuel Hearne, the same Samuel Hearne who, in 1774, established Cumberland House on the Saskatchewan not far from Frog Portage.

Hearne was posted to Fort Prince of Wales during his long tenure with HBC, and used it as his base for explorations into the interior. One of those trips started out on a bitterly cold December day in 1770. With a party of Dene to guide him, Hearne would walk to the Coppermine River and down its course to the Arctic Ocean seeking copper and the Northwest Passage.

Unsuccessful on both counts, he turned around and walked back. In all, he was gone a year and a half and covered 5,000 miles on foot—a wilderness adventure almost beyond reckoning.

The next morning is our last in Churchill. We are heading home on the weekly train to Winnipeg. Marianne and I carry the canoe to the train station two blocks away while the owner of the motel kindly conveys the rest of our stuff by car. The boys are also at the station, arranging transport for their boats and gear.

The posted rate for shipping cargo is expensive, about $200 per boat plus extra for freight in excess of fifty pounds, but the baggageman, probably noting that the boys don't seem to have much money, charges them just $50 for everything, and charges me the same. I must look destitute too.

While I assist with the baggage, Marianne chats with the boys. They charm her with their effusive good cheer as quickly as they did me. Then a whistle blows and we climb aboard.

It's a thousand-mile trip that takes two full days. The train can only average twenty miles an hour because the permafrost, upon which the line is laid, isn't perma anymore due to climate change and the softening ground has caused the tracks to warp and bow.

Marianne and I have a sleeper, in which I really don't sleep. I spend most of the time looking out the window as the train limps along, staring into the forest that hems in the line. I never tire of looking at trees and pondering the mysteries they conceal. This is my reality now. This wilderness. Everything else, save of course for Marianne, seems either alien or trivial.

The trees flash hypnotically by as I contemplate what I've done, paddling 700 miles, at sixty years of age, and going it alone. I was almost killed, more than once, and certainly would have been were it not for a rock, the miracle rock that saved me.

I accomplished what I set out to do, faced fear, struggle, hardship, and risk, and not only survived, but thrived, meeting each day not knowing what it would bring and surrendering to powers over which I had no control.

And, I found the wilderness I was seeking. Granted, it wasn't a wilderness equal to what Samuel Hearne or Lewis and Clark explored, but it was pretty good considering what I had to work with. Those guys lived in a time when wilderness was abundant, but that world is gone.

Today, wilderness resides mostly in our imaginings.

Consider my trip. As isolated and largely unpopulated as the country I passed through was, it still had three villages, a dam, levy, and weir, not to mention the power lines and railroad bridge I passed under, or the planes and motorboats occasionally seen or heard.

In truth, the planet is pretty much yoked and the lands that aren't yoked yet are sure to fall, bit by bit, as the desperate poor struggle to survive and the filthy rich seek more. The wilds that remain are being burned and turned into palm oil plantations and feed lots, plowed up for soybeans, and flooded to exchange one type of current for another.

It is happening now, in real time; bulldozers cleaving roads, chainsaws felling trees, augers probing deeply into earth to seek out and suck up every last drop of anything that will burn or turn a turbine. To find wilderness today, you have to go to places considered useless for anything else. Useless for logging, farming, fishing, grazing, or mining, and hard enough to get to so it won't be exploited for its nothingness, trivialized with eco-lodges, Princess cruises, and other virtual realities.

Thomas Malthus, born about the time Samuel Hearne carved his name in stone at Sloop Cove, had it right when he said, "The power of population is so superior to the power of the Earth to produce subsistence for man, that premature death must in some shape or other visit the human race."

There is an unassailable inevitability to Malthus' prediction that humanity has refused to accept or address. Eighty million more of us added to the sphere each year, an insanity of growth that cannot be supported or sustained. Certainly, premature death will be a consequence, for wilderness, for wildlife, and ultimately, for us.

How many can this earth support anyway? Certainly, there are limits. Anyone can understand that. Finite resources cannot be reconciled to infinite growth. According to renowned Harvard biologist Edward O. Wilson (who, coincidentally or not, was an expert on ants), "The constraints of the biosphere are fixed."

He pegs the limit of human population at ten billion, but stresses that the earth can support only that many at maximum efficiency—meaning we eat grains instead of meat. Ten billion vegetarians, give or take, is our uppermost limit, but because most of us, and increasingly more of us, are pigging out on animal protein, the planet's carrying capacity will be some number less than that.

If something really good doesn't happen or something really bad doesn't happen pretty quick, we are slated to reach ten billion before the turn of the century. People alive today will be part of that populace.

I read Jared Diamond's book *Collapse* in which he examines a variety of reasons why past societies did just that. Societal collapse was brought on by climate change, environmental destruction, too much reliance on a single resource, overpopulation, and poor political choices. Sound familiar? The book is a warning, a morality play, that past is prologue to the future.

At the end of his book, Diamond, so as not to appear hopelessly glum, tries to find reasons for optimism, but clearly struggles with the effort. The straws he grasps are short and brittle. That's how I feel as well: that we are much, much closer to the eve of destruction than to Adam and Eve's Eden.

I don't see us pulling out of this. It isn't in our DNA. We aren't genetically predisposed for static sustainability, but rather to breed, alter, grow, and conquer, and in those traits we excel, but they no longer serve us well. Our only hope is to change. At the very least, we must try to change. No matter how poor the prospects, no matter how insuperable the odds, we must hope against hope and try.

I stare out the window as the train rolls slowly on toward home. The *clickity-clack* rhythm of the wheels lulls me. I can see my reflection against the glass, super-imposed upon the sea of trees beyond. It looks like I have wilderness in my soul. I think I do.

Postscript

At the end, or near it, maybe you get lucky. Maybe she wheels you out on a clear day and parks you, sets the brake, and lets you be. The sun is warm upon your face, despite the sharp breeze tugging at the few leaves still clinging to the trees.

You pry off one slipper with the toe of the other and brush the bare foot across the grass, the earth, cool and solid beneath it. Then, gazing up, you are reminded of another time, another place, with a sky like this, a sky-blue sky. It wasn't very long ago. Not really.

A gust rattles the aspen and leaves fall, spinning like doubloons. When she comes to take you back inside, she sees the slipper on the ground, bends, lifts the foot, and puts it on.

"You lost your shoe again," she yells into your good ear, but you don't really hear. You're somewhere else, if you're lucky.

Photo credit: Chris Vaughan

Jonathan Klein was not born in the right place. Raised in San Francisco by a single mother determined to mold her only child into a sophisticated urbanite, he instead surrendered to an innate ferality. Moving to Montana as a young man, Jonathan found work as a ranch hand and later discovered his true calling as a wilderness manager for the USDA Forest Service. His adventurous spirit has led to a slew of dubious exploits including hopping freight trains, a very short stint as a rodeo rider, bull fighting in Portugal, and several expeditions by canoe and kayak to the far north. Jonathan lives in Montana with his wife, Marianne, and a couple of cats.